RELATIONAL COMMUNICATION

D1527941

RELATIONAL COMMUNICATION

William W. Wilmot
University of Montana

McGraw-HILL, INC.

New York   St. Louis   San Francisco   Auckland   Bogotá
Caracas   Lisbon   London   Madrid   Mexico City   Milan
Montreal   New Delhi   San Juan   Singapore   Sydney   Tokyo   Toronto

This book was set in Times Roman by ComCom, Inc.
The editors were Hilary Jackson and John M. Morriss;
the production supervisor was Kathryn Porzio.
The cover was designed by Delgado Design.
Project supervision was done by Tage Publishing Service, Inc.
R. R. Donnelley & Sons Company was printer and binder.

RELATIONAL COMMUNICATION

 This book is printed on recycled, acid-free paper containing 10%
postconsumer waste.

1 2 3 4 5 6 7 8 9 0   DOC   DOC   9 0 9 8 7 6 5 4

ISBN 0-07-070740-5

Library of Congress Cataloging-in-Publication Data

Wilmot, William W.
    Relational communication / William W. Wilmot.—1st ed.
      p.   cm.
    Includes bibliographical references and index.
    ISBN 0-07-070740-5
    1. Interpersonal communication.   2. Interpersonal relations.
  I. Title.
  BF637.C45W55   1995
  158' .2—dc20   94-32256

ABOUT
THE AUTHOR

WILLIAM W. WILMOT is a professor of communication studies at the University of Montana in Missoula where he teaches about personal relationships, conflict management and mediation. He is author and co-author of publications such as *Interpersonal Conflict* (4th edition) and *Mediation at Work* as well as three earlier books. In addition, he has a private practice in conflict management and mediation where he helps organizations get past disputes and struggles and into collaborative modes of operating. As part of his consulting work, he is a Senior Associate of the Yarbrough Group headquartered in Boulder, Colorado.

To Roy Andes
for being there

CONTENTS

ACKNOWLEDGMENTS

No book is produced in isolation, especially one about the relational nature of communication! My gratitude goes out to family members, colleagues, and friends who have supported me both personally and professionally.

First and foremost, this book commemorates the memory of my father and the commitment of my mother. Some years after his death, she got remarried, at age 73—showing how relationships can successfully emerge after deep life crises. Also, Mom, thanks for not ever giving up on your weird son.

My children Jason and Carina continue to be sources of joy and connection. And I do apologize for the ear-splitting Bruckner symphonies in the summer of 1993 that almost blew out the walls and your ear drums. My sister, Joyce Mangus, still is my "Big Shisty" with all the affection that entails. And Tom and Janice, while officially now my "out-laws," have been supportive and made helpful comments on the early outlines. Finally, while not officially "family," Elaine Yarbrough and Mike Burr remain like family—close, nurturing, and important.

And to Mada, who after 30 years came back into my life—who would ever think I would date an English major? She gave me much needed help during my freak-out at the copy editing stage of the project. She is an exemplar of all the principles in this book.

Many professional colleagues had a hand in this book. John Hammerback said to me in 1992, during a time of difficulty for me, "This is important stuff you have to say; maybe you can say it to the profession." That thought lodged in my mind until January of 1993 when, on a 10-below-zero, sparkling day, two spike bull elk walked out on Mt. Jumbo, and as I looked at them from my study, I thought, "I can now write this book." Some years ago, Jim Neulip of St. Norbert College suggested the book title to me—he probably doesn't even remember the conversation, but it set an early tone for what I was to do. Steve Coffman of Eastern Montana College suggested some reading to me on the deconstruction of the self—and that really churned the mental wheels. Melanie Thost of Arizona State University and Wes Shellen of the University of Montana supplied helpful critiques of two chapters. Many other colleagues, too numerous to mention all by name, engaged in discussions with me over the years that were always helpful.

Other friends were crucial to my progress along a path that was sometimes rocky. Michael Marks deserves kudos for his early insight, and the members of "the group"— Stan, Greg, Cliff, and Mike—who provided a safe container for my exploration while insisting on constant reality checks. Roy Andes, co-owner of the "Shabin," was a person who never did answer when I kept asking "what should I do?" Thanks Roy for being a faithful, nonimposing friend, who allowed me to develop my own grasp of reality

My own spiritual development has been part of this process. The people of Nepal, Tibet and Roy Oswald and Carole Raush, had a hand in a journey that became much larger than the initial 1991 trip to Nepal. In the midst of squalor, there was an exultation of the human spirit that touched me deeply. When it was time to leave, I was overwhelmed with what the Nepali people "had"—and I have been fortunate to find parts of what struck me so profoundly.

Many folks helped with the actual project. Mark Bergstrom and Kirk Lacy did library work for me, gathering up the mounds of stuff I wanted to explore, and helped motivate me to read—because more would arrive each day. Thanks, fellows! All the students in the COMM 510 Class offered insightful critiques and perspectives. Betty Jo Maughan gave special help in the ending stages of Chapter 1.

My reviewers, Peter Andersen, San Diego State University; Robert Brady, University of Arkansas, Fayetteville; Cynthia Burggraf, University of Delaware; Nancy Dimeo, Rutgers University; Kathryn Dindia, University of Wisconsin, Milwaukee; David Droge, University of Puget Sound; William Eadie, Speech Communication Association; Kenneth Frandsen, University of New Mexico; Lawrence Nadler, Miami University of Ohio; Malcolm Parks, University of Washington; Brant Short, Idaho State University; Laura Stafford, Ohio State University; and Ralph Webb, Purdue University, provided a nice blend of hard-hitting content criticism with a friendly tone Their reactions improved this book immensely. Thanks to you all for your time and scholarship, and you will notice that I actually utilized most of your suggestions!

Hilary Jackson, the McGraw-Hill editor, who received weekly faxes on my progress (once I got rolling, that is), was just great. In spite of having to continue changing the "deadline" and having serious doubts if I would ever finish, she stayed connected, supportive, and available to hear the tales of woe about how much time it really takes to do a book. Her constant affirmation and good will helped me to 'stay at it.' Thanks, Hilary; I would like to keep in touch, but do I have to write another book?

My many friends at Osel Shen Phen Ling, Open Way, and FWBO know the challenges in store for us all, and I have kept my sights on concentration, generosity, joy, morality, patience, and wisdom. I appreciate your understanding each time I said "I've been out of town. . . ." Special thanks to Kopan Monastery and all associated with FPMT, with immense gratitude to Ven. Rabini Courtin and Ven. Thubten Chodron, who are wonderful teachers and models. Chodron's skillful intervention paved the way for me to continue the path at a new level.

To those of highbrow taste who were appalled that I once wrote to the sounds of Kitaro, you will be pleased to know that I upgraded to classical music—even mountain men can appreciate a fine symphony. Maybe after another book, I'll try opera.

Bill Wilmot

RELATIONAL
COMMUNICATION

THE RELATIONAL
PERSPECTIVE

Relationships are like a dance. The two partners dance close some times, far apart at others. When they are doing the same dance (like cowboy swing) it works fine. And, similarly to a dance, each relationship has its own form, flow, challenges, disruptions, and recoveries. With relationship partners in synchrony, the flow and synergistic energy elevates both. The dance becomes a thing of beauty to watch, and it looks easy. Often, however, one partner wants to do cowboy swing while the other insists on the foxtrot. And if both insist on doing their own dance, they will struggle, flounder, and fall.

For most of us, our personal relationships with family, friends, work colleagues, and romantic partners sometimes flow and sometimes trip us up—they are among the most fulfilling and frustrating events of our lives. This is reflected by college students, for example, in that the most frequent topic of conversation is romantic relationships (Haas & Sherman, 1982). Our personal relationships ebb and flow throughout our entire life span, yet our knowledge about them is often not equal to the challenges they bring us.

ASSUMPTIONS ABOUT RELATIONSHIPS

Relational Communication will unfold relationships and the role communication plays in them. The focus will be on communication in context, illustrating some of the complexities of communication in relationships as they progress over time. Rather than the simplistic "just communicate clearly, and your relationship will work" view, this book will try to broaden your view of communication in personal relationships by discussing communication and relationships within broader contexts—our cultural assumptions, our constellations of relationships, and over-time views of particular relationships.

Relationships are not some "knowable" fixed entity; rather, they change and are continually reexamined and reinterpreted by both relationship insiders and outsiders. They are, therefore, one of the most elusive and yet fascinating aspects of our lives.

Any discussion of relationships and communication rests on some fundamental assumptions. This book is based on the following set of assumptions, which will be explored in detail in the individual chapters.

I Relationships and communication are inextricably tied. Our relationships are created primarily through communication, and our communication is interpreted differently in each relationship context.

II Relationships are brought into being by our minds, and we give "voice" to them through narratives. Participants construct "schemas" (mental pictures) about their relationships, and also develop "narratives" or stories about their relationships, telling self and others about them.

III To understand fully the role that communication plays in relationships, each relationship must be examined within (1) its cultural context and (2) the overall patterns of other relationships ("relationship constellations").

IV "Self" is best understood as embedded within the webs of relationships, and participants' views of the connection between self, other, and relationship have an impact on the communicative choices they make.

V Relationship dynamics, spanning from initiation to exiting, are best understood from a dialectical perspective, sensitizing us to the contradictory pulls that exist in relationships.

VI Relationships are in a continual state of emergence, whether growing, changing, atrophying, or re-emerging. Relationships are never static; they unfold as we live them.

As part of these assumptions, this first chapter will focus on what *is* a relationship, the narratives (stories) people tell about their relationships, the different perceptions that make up a relationship, the "mental maps" we have for our relationships, and the interconnection of communication and relationships. It ends with a Model of Embedded Communication specifying how relationships and communication reflect and create the cultural and network assumptions.

WHAT *IS* A RELATIONSHIP?

In the 1800s, not much time was spent by people discussing the "state of our relationship," whereas these days relationships are discussed over coffee and lunch, in college courses, and in the mass media. Just scan the magazines in the grocery store and you'll see articles on "how to make love last," "moving from lovers to friends," and "getting your family to talk to you." Whether people openly discuss relationships or not, participants are in a relationship when they have a "sense of being in a relationship" (Duck, 1988, p. 2). The crucial difference isn't whether some outside social scientist thinks you are in a relationship by some academic criteria (Hinde, 1979), but *a relationship exists when the participants construct a mental view of it.* Those mental images of the relationship occur on many levels.

At the most basic level, Level I, a relationship occurs when there is *mutual recog-*

nition of being perceived. Whether it is someone across the aisle in a theater, or having coffee with a best friend, we become aware of being in relationship when communication processing is reciprocal. At this first level, a "relationship" is formed when:

1 You and another are behaving;
2 You are aware of his/her behavior, and at the same time
3 The other is aware of your behavior;
4 As a result,
    a you are aware that the other is aware of you
    b the other is aware that you are aware of him/her.

People are in a relationship when each *has the perception of being perceived*—when both persons can say "I see you seeing me."[1]

At the more complex level, Level II, relationship awareness occurs over and above the specific cues being sent and received—you treat the relationship as having a *past, present, and future.* As Leatham and Duck (1990) say, "You have a relationship when the partners believe in the *future* of it." A relationship emerges from its history and continually reemerges and transforms over time—continually changing. Thus, you may not be sending messages to your parents, nor they to you, but you would say that you are "in a relationship" with them. You name the relationship by things such as "I am her son" or some other relationship marker to signify its existence. Level II awareness arises from cumulative interactions with a particular person so that you "name" the relationship—it becomes a reality that transcends the particular communication messages being sent. At Level II, people speak of relationships "declining," "improving," and "being flat"—clearly relationships are conceptual realities.

Understanding a relationship is much like reading a short story or novel. As we move through time, new information is integrated into our interpretation of the events of the past and makes a difference in the present and our projections about the future. Relationship processing, however, is much more complex, because our interpretations of ongoing events affect how we respond and how others respond to us. As Fletcher and Fincham (1991a) say, "Thus, participants' interpretations of events are part of the changing flux of events as individuals mutually influence each other" (p. 79).

When we enter into a relational world, it is no longer exclusively our own—the other person is considered in the acts we do; there is no such thing as individual behavior not influenced by the relational context from which it springs. Each person's perceptions influence the relationship, because each participant affects and is affected by the other. At Level II, we integrate previous communication exchanges by constructing a view of them and projecting into the future. Thus, while relationships are derived from previous communicative exchanges, it is our mental images of them that creates their reality for us. One young man who lives alone has a girlfriend in a small town out of state. She is an incredibly good shopper who can find bargains. When he goes to the local discount store to buy food, as he cruises the aisles looking for bargains and comes upon an item, he can imagine her saying, "Now, *that* is a good value." He brings his

---

[1]This is meant metaphorically. In more general terms it would be "I process you processing me," because it can be done through sight, sound, smell, or any of the senses.

past experiences of shopping with her and pushes them forward in time to the current shopping trip. An example of this sort of "carrying the relationship with you" occurs when you imagine the reaction of parents or friends to something you have done. Whenever you think about someone's reaction, you are drawing upon past experience and pulling it forward in time.

RELATIONSHIPS AS MINICULTURES

Relationships are "private minicultures" where participant perceptions of the relationship are its reality (Fitzpatrick & Indvik, 1982). The perceived reality of relationships builds over time for the participants. And, further, as we move to new relationships, different aspects of ourselves are activated. In a true sense, each relationship is unique, calling forth diverse elements from each participant.

Relationship participants need to "make sense" of their relationships, because relationships are more than the sum of the individual parts. When two people have a relationship, there is a "third party"—the relationship itself—which has a life of its own. This synergistic creation is built by the participants yet goes beyond them. As Humphreys says, "There is no such thing as two, for no two things can be conceived without their relationship, and this makes three" (Humphreys, 1951).

Each relationship is a "miniculture," with its own norms and rules (Morton & Douglas, 1981). In all pairings, such as teacher–student, mother–son, friend–friend, or doctor–patient, the participants have their own conception of the relationship, their own "relational miniculture" that encompasses what they do and who they are to one another. These created "relational minicultures" are particular to the relationship and are more rich and complex than the general labels we all learn (such as "friends," "romantic partner," "family member"). The relationship partners develop a label, or metaphor, for their relationship, replete with its own system of obligations and rights (Hinde, 1979). There are times, of course, when one partner sees the relationship one way and the other another way—and these contrasting or *asymmetric* definitions also comprise the miniculture (Neimeyer & Neimeyer, 1985). Sometimes, a continual disagreement about the nature of a relationship (I want to be friends/I want to be lovers) may be a central feature of the relationship.

Metaphors for Relationships

People's metaphors about relationships supply meaning for those relationships. We use metaphors when we compare one thing to something else. For example, if you are in a "stormy" romantic relationship, you are comparing the relationship to the weather, emphasizing the bad weather at times. Describing a work relationship or marriage as a "battleground" conveys a different image than the metaphor "game" or "partnership."

When an ongoing relationship does *not* have an agreed-upon definition, it brings conflict and discord. Jackson says that "in a pathologic relationship we see . . . a constant sabotaging or refusing of the other's attempts to define the relationship" (Jackson, 1959). And Weick notes the same effect in organizations: "One of the major causes of failure in organizations is a shortage of images concerning what they are up to, a shortage of time devoted to producing these images, and a shortage of diverse actions to deal with changed circumstance" (Weick, 1979). Some overlap in the definitions is necessary so the participants can have coordinated action, a sense of common purpose, and agreement about "who they are."

The choice of metaphor or image for a relationship evokes a feel for the dynamics of a relationship. If a man describes his marriage as an "endangered species," it conveys the fragile, close-to-extinction nature of the relationship. Themes that emerge in ongoing relationships have been explored by Owen. He notes that thematic interpretations become a way to understand "relational life." For instance, "A male and female meet as 'friends,' become daters,' then 'lovers,' perhaps finally becoming a 'married couple' making transitions to the different relationship states or definitions primarily through communication." In his study composed of married couples, romantic dating partners, sets of relatives, sets of live-in friends, and groups of friends not living together, Owen identified some central determinants that participants use to make interpretative sense of relationships (Owen, 1984a). The participants saw their relationships illustrating the following:

1 Commitment—dedication to this particular relationship in spite of difficult times.

2 Involvement—some relationships, such as marriage and family relationships, demand more involvement than others.

3 Work—relationships require "work" to keep them functioning in a healthy manner.

4 Unique Special—this bolsters the belief that the participants have "beat the odds" and survived a "breakup."

5 Fragile—for dating couples, the fragile nature of the relationship is paramount, whereas for married couples it helps them feel they have "held it together."

6 Consideration–Respect—married couples primarily saw respect as an important gauge of the relationship, whereas others did not.

7 Manipulation—women who were dating especially noted that the person might be "playing games" or "using others" in dates (Own, 1984a).

Owen notes that relationships vary according to these themes—they are the dimensions the participants use to make "sense" out of the relational experience. And it has been suggested by Wilmot and Hocker (1993) that actively working to alter couples' metaphors can help bring change into a married relationship.

One other piece of work on metaphors for relationships has been offered by Baxter (1992b). She classified people's descriptions of heterosexual couples into four root metaphors. People saw their relationships as (1) work–exchange, (2) journey–organism, (3) force–danger, and (4) game. If you characterize your cross-sex romance as work–exchange, it connotes a process of effort and coordination, whereas seeing it as journey–organism suggests an ever-changing process of growth. Characterizing a relationship in terms of force–danger implies that it is a risky undertaking where you can be hurt and have limited control, whereas seeing it as a game suggests that romance is a set of scripts where you can win or lose (Baxter, 1992).

The parties to a relationship also reflect their "miniculture" by manifesting (1) narratives, (2) relationship idioms, and (3) symbols of relationship identity.

Relationship Narratives

People share narratives or stories about their relationships. Whether a fellow is complaining about his boss, celebrating his newfound love, or wanting to be closer to his brother, he talks about relationships in many ways. When you say, "Gee, she sure isn't the friend I thought she was. When she left me downtown, I had to walk home," you are providing a story or narrative about a relationship.

What is a narrative? It is a story, telling about a unique event or series of events (Van Kijk, 1985). Narratives organize and synthesize a jumbled set of events into an understandable sequence and come in many forms. Narrative texts are such things as short stories, diaries, and even novels or biographies. For our purposes here, however, we will focus on oral narratives—when you talk about a relationship to someone else. The relationship narratives we share with others usually are conversational stories about important events (Polanyi, 1985)—the struggle with your sister, the special time with your parents, the exhilaration of a new love relation, the fun times you had with your friends over spring break, or the breakup of a love affair. I would guess (since there is scant research on it right now) that most narratives are about turmoil and trouble—how to deal with the difficult boss, how to get freedom from your parents (or children), what to do when you fall out of love, or how to cope when someone you love suddenly stops seeing you without any explanation.

Surprisingly, people also tell narratives about *others'* relationships. Two friends sit over tea and discuss Sally and Stan and what kind of relationship they seem to have. Children will discuss their parent's marriage, especially if there is a new marriage bringing a stepfather or-mother into the picture. People will even tell narratives to you in health spas! One day I had the pleasure of listening to Martha Jane tell me about her uncle and his wife and how the uncle cared for his wife for 15 years while she had Alzheimer's disease. For Martha Jane, he "did it right" and showed her a model of commitment in long-term relationships.

Narratives not only reflect your reaction to a relationship, they also impact the future course of it. When you say, "It was a fine vacation—we love going to the North Fork," it tends to reinforce the positive features of the relationship. Similarly, if one spends a great deal of time criticizing a love relationship partner, that tends to further solidify your negative view of it. In the most dramatic cases, when an ex-spouse says, "My ex-husband and I are enemies since the divorce," it not only reflects the current reality but reinforces this view each time she complains about him.

Not only do our experiences of the relationship change, our accounts and representations of it also change. Relationships tend to flow like the wind—ever changing. To bring some order to the ever-fluctuating reality, people activate "memory structures" about their relationships. They can generate and write down typical communication events and order their relationship across time (Honeycutt, Cantril, & Greene, 1989).

Further, the narratives about the relationship change across time. The person who has fallen wildly in love gives you a far different picture of the relationship today than he or she does a year following the breakup. We reformulate our memories about our relationships quite dramatically (Duck, 1988). In the Duck and Miell (1986) studies comparing contemporary accounts of first meetings with subsequent retrospective accounts, they found people giving different accounts of where they first met. And as Duck (1988, p. 112) says, "Surra reports that about 30 percent of one of her samples of married couples were in disagreement with their own partner by more than one year about when they first had sexual intercourse together!" And, of course, when a breakup occurs people tend to alter their representation of the entire history of the relationship.

What makes for a good narrative? Polanyi (1985) suggests you need to (1) tell a topically coherent story, (2) tell one worth hearing about, and (3) introduce the story so the connection to the previous talk is clear; (4) structure the story appropriately and (5) tell a story that begins at the beginning; and (6) make it possible for the listener to know the "core" of the story—what point is being made. Fisher (1987) suggests that we are *homo narrans*—story telling animals whose narratives follow a unique set of logical rules. And we humans naturally respond to a well-structured narrative—that is, we have a "narrative rationality." We judge narratives of others based on (1) narrative probability (the coherence of the story, how well does it hang together?) and (2) narrative fidelity (how does this story fit with my own experience?). The first criteria is violated by people who tell disjointed stories, jumping from their friendship difficulties to problems with training their dog. The second criteria would be in use if Neil tells you a story about his continuing fights with his ex-lover of 10 years ago. You would use the benchmark of whether you would stay involved with an ex-lover for so long.

Narratives, being so commonplace, obviously serve important functions for the participants. First, they serve functions *for the storyteller*. By "telling our story" we come to understand our own confusing experiences (Surra, 1987; Veroff, 1993). In fact, some people state, "I don't know what I feel until I talk about it!" In a sense, *all* stories can be seen as "narratives of the self." Telling a story (1) reinforces your view of yourself, (2) contrasts you to others ("he is such a scumbag; I can't believe he stole money from his mother"), and (3) allows you to transform yourself by talk. It is well known that people in crisis "need to talk"—they have to tell their story, to "let it out" and start the process of adjustment to the changes. One poignant example of such effects was detailed by the research of Hollihan and Riley (1987). They studied a "Toughlove" group of parents, a support group for parents who had a delinquent child. The researchers concluded that the "Toughlove narrative was appealing to the participants because it confirmed their self-perceptions and absolved them of their failures" (p. 19). The parents would tell their stories with the support of others in similar circumstances. As a result:

> The Toughlove narrative proved to be comforting, engaging, predictable, and persuasive. Parents joined the group during times of crisis, many feeling as if they had failed because they had been unable to instill socially appropriate values and attitudes in their children. Shamed by the reactions of friends, realities, and child care experts, and resentful of a system that could not help and only blamed them for allowing such a disgrace-

ful state of affairs to exist, they readily embraced the Toughlove narrative as an alternative for their problems. (Hollihan & Riley, 1987, p. 23)

Second, in addition to "saving face" for the storyteller, narratives create *"acceptable
public and private accounts"* of the events. In the case of romantic breakups, Duck
(1982) argues that verbal accounts serve as "grave dressing." When the relationship is
over, one of the last stages you go through is "telling a story," a narrative, about the
relationship. You do that to both save face and bring further changes for yourself, *and*
to create public versions of the relationship for the consumption of others.

Farrell (1984) suggests that the narratives are designed to "delight, instruct, or move
the listener" (p. 174). Grandparents who tell stories to their grandchildren can be seen
as passing on family values and history. The tried-and-maybe-true story of the parents
or grandparents walking through the blizzard to make it to the schoolhouse is a way to
tell the progeny about the importance of getting an education—even in a blizzard. My
father used to tell me about "going to town" when he was a child twice a year from the
homestead in Wyoming and having five cents to spend on candy. Clearly, relationship
narrative (or "accounts," as the social science researcher prefer to call them), are "presentational"—they serve as a way to present an event (Duck & Pond, 1991).

As a listener to a narrative, you too have a communication role to perform. You
need to (1) agree to hear the story, (2) refrain from taking a turn except to make
remarks about the relationship under discussion, and (3) at the end of the storytelling,
demonstrate your understanding of it (Polanyi, 1985). In a sense, the active listener
("Yeah, I see; then what did he say to you?") participates as a "co-author," urging the
other on (Mandelbaum, 1989).

What about the accuracy of narratives? Rather than ask about accuracy, it is more
informative to focus on the degree of overlap in the two people's narratives. If Russell
and Susan tell similar stories about their romantic relationship, that is evidence that
they have some agreement about important relationship marker events. If both, for
example, tell about the time they went winter camping and didn't take enough food and
both laugh about it, then it indicates how they are "together" in this view. If the story
is a "collaborative effort" (Veroff et al., 1993), it indicates the cooperation between the
two. On the other hand, if they have relational difficulties or break up, you can rest
assured that Russell will tell one story and Susan another. The "narrative overlap" is an
indicator of the "we-ness" of the relationship; conjoint stories indicate more closeness
and agreement, while divergent stories indicate people who are defining themselves as
more separate and independent. One of the differences between men and women is
that, in recalling past events in relationships, women tend to have more vivid memories, which, of course, makes it difficult to have conjoint stories that are perfectly in tune
(Ross & Holmberg, 1993). In sum, narratives can be seen as varying between these two
poles: (1) individual, divergent accounts; and (2) conjointly agreed-upon accounts.

Finally, we really have not had enough systematic research to know about the frequency of narratives in day-to-day encounters. If you went to the student union, a local
coffee shop, into a private home, or some other place where people "tell their stories,"
what types of narratives would you hear? I would guess they would fall into these categories:

1 Telling about traumatic or transformational events in the relationship.
2 Discussing current difficulties, conflicts, or struggles in the relationship.
3 Talking about the future of the relationship.

Listening closely to other's narratives will give you a window into the person's desire to save face and be seen as acceptable, and will also give you information about how they got the state of their relationship. The narrative serves as both a reflection of the relationship and a force for the future of the relationship. And, finally, listen to your own narratives—and see where you are in your own relationships. Are you stuck and frustrated? Do you tell the same story over and over, unable to change over time? Does the narrative correspond with what the other would say? These and related questions about how you talk about your own relationships can give you insight into your reactions to the current situation.

Idioms in Relationship

Part of the narrative of a relationship involves personal idioms. They tend to develop in concert with the intimacy of a relationship (Bell, Buerkel-Rothfuss, & Gore, 1987) and are part of the "personalized" language used in close relationships. For example, saying "my honey" or "sweetykins" for your romantic partner cues both you and outsiders to the idea that the relationship is something special. Idioms are used both in private and in public, and come into being only after there is a certain degree of intimacy in the couple pairing (Hopper, Knapp, & Scott, 1981). Once used, they tend to both (1) reflect the degree of intimacy and (2) facilitate continued escalation of intimacies (Bell, Buerkel-Rothfuss, & Gore, 1987). Idioms are used in many types of close relationships, for example, among friends and family members, and between romantic partners.

Couple's idioms can be discussed as falling into the following categories (the categories and examples come from Hopper, Knapp, & Scott, 1981, and Bell, Buerkel-Rothfuss, & Gore, 1987):

Partner Nicknames: Where the partners refer to one another by special names only fully understood by the couple. Examples are "Boo," "Snuggle Bug," "Mopsy," "Izzy," "Applehead," "Caveman," and "Long Duck Dong."

Expressions of Affection: These idioms express love, reassurance or praise to one's partner. Examples are using "hunch nickel," "so much," "10 cents," or "huggle" to mean "I love you."

Labels for others outside the relationship: These are nicknames for specific people who are not in the relationship. Examples are "Pizza King," referring to the next door neighbor; "The Hood," to refer to members of the male's fraternity; calling the male partner's coach "Jock Strap"; and "grape" used to label a person thought to be a homosexual. The labels allow the couple to discuss others in public, usually in pejorative ways.

Confrontations: These idioms show criticism of the partner or displeasure about him or her. Examples are "Number Three" for signaling that something didn't work, saying "frightening" to signal the male partner to stop acting weird, using "Jello-Bitch" to let the female partner know she is being obnoxious, or the nonverbal twisting of a wedding ring to let the partner know "don't you dare say (or do) that."

Requests and Routines: These are ways to signal the partner. One common situation is when you let the other know you want to leave a party. Examples of this type of cueing were saying "L.L." (abbreviation for let's leave), blowing on the palm of your hand, or saying "what's new."

Sexual References and Euphemisms: Idioms that make a reference to sexual techniques, birth control, intercourse, breasts, or genitals. References to male genitals were "Bozo," "Boa," "Trouser Trout," and "USDA Choice." References to female genitals were idioms such as "The Oven," "Coochy," "Wuzzer," and "Marian." Breasts were referred to by saying "Baby Feeders," "Puppies," and "Bullwinkle and Rocky." Oral sex was called "torture," and sexual intercourse "boogie-woogie," "BOS," and "Legs."

Sexual Invitations: These idioms become code words for proposing sexual intercourse. The couples said such things as "Aren't you getting awfully hot?", "Let's go home and watch some TV," "I want some ice cream," and "wanna do a load of laundry?"

Teasing Insults: These idioms are used to derogate your partner, but in a spirit of play. Examples are "fat piggy" or "Hogmo" to refer to partner's poor table manners, and "H.H." (abbreviation for Hippo Hips) to refer to the other's large rear end.

In the Hopper et al. (1981) study and the Bell et al. (1987) studies, respectively, 57% and 43% of the idioms were used exclusively in private. About half the idioms used by couples, therefore, are not used or understood by outsiders. Friends, however, more often use idioms in public, and in the research by Bell and Healey (1992), friends' idioms were used 65% of the time by their other friends. So friends' idioms are less private and more public than those of couples.

Research has not yet uncovered the specific use of idioms in other close relationships, but we know they exist. One daughter, for example, used to send electronic mail (e-mail) to her father and address it to "Poppy." He picked up on this and started addressing her e-mail to "poppyseed," and they now refer to one another with these interlocked idioms. If this father–daughter use parallels those used by friends, other family members may soon learn of the new form of address.

Symbols of Relational Identity

Baxter (1987b) probed how participants construct relationship meanings. She found that relationship symbols are "concrete metacommunicative 'statements' about the abstract qualities of intimacy, caring, solidarity, etc. which the parties equate with their relationships. The symbols give the parties a sense of 'history' about the relationship; they serve to link the past to the 'forces of novelty and change' " (Baxter, 1987b). In addition, the symbols allow them to test their common conception of their experience and see if the two of them have agreement on the relationship. Baxter found five types of relational symbols, listed in the order of frequency, for same-sex friendships and opposite sex romantic relationships.

1 *Behavioral actions* are actions the participants do. They have three subtypes:
   a Jointly enacted activities—such as hiding Valentine's Day stuffed hearts from one another, playing sports, or other things jointly created.
   b Interaction routines unique to the pair, such as jokes and teasing.
   c Others such as nicknames, affection terms, or code words to refer to sexual matters.[2]

2 *Events or times that held special meaning* were very diverse but all "held special meaning as distinguishing the relationship as unique." Many of them represented "firsts"—first meeting, first time they "really got to know one another," and so on.

3 *Physical objects* include an even more diverse set of examples. Everything from strawberries, to a stuffed buffalo, to a broken string from a violin, to assorted pieces of jewelry" (Baxter, 1987b, p. 269).

4 *Symbolic places* were of two types. Some were symbolic because they were visual metaphors of the partner or something in the history of the relationship, such as a restaurant or coffee shop. Others were symbolic because they served as a meeting place for the partners, such as Kalispell, Montana.

5 *Symbolic cultural artifacts* were things such as songs, music, books, and films that are part of the surrounding culture that have symbolic meaning for the two people.

Baxter then assessed the symbolic functions of the relationship symbols. She asked the participants what meaning these symbols had that made them feel the relationship was unique and special. The following nine functions emerged in order of frequency:

1 *Recollection prompt*—to remind them about past events or thinking about the other in her/his absence.

2 *Intimacy indicators*—signs of closeness, trust, or affection.

3 *Communication mechanism*—promoting togetherness or sharing between the two.

4 *Stimulation/fun*—offsetting boredom or excessive seriousness.

5 *Seclusion mechanism*—to physically separate themselves from others.

6 *Exclusivity indicator*—providing psychological seclusion for the relationship.

7 *Management of difference/conflict*—using locations that were conducive to discussion or joking or teasing as a way to deal with difficult issues.

8 *Public tie-sign*—giving others a signal that the parties were in a relationship.

9 *Endurance index*—testifying to the relationship's endurance or strength in withstanding adversity.

This research establishes what we already know intuitively—that relationships contain symbolic elements. The meanings of events in a relationship, while showing some general patterns, are seen as unique and special by the two people involved. Once a symbolic marker begins being used in the relationship, people can make shorthand references to it. A romantic couple, for example, only need say, "Ah, Kalispell," to serve as a symbolic remembrance of events important to them.

One final finding is worthy of note. Baxter found that, even though males and

---

[2]These are the idioms discussed above. Since Baxter cast a wide net, idiomatic usage was just one of the features she found.

females did not differ in the type or quantity of relationship symbols, "females regarded their relationship symbols more positively than was the case for males. Further, there was a trend towards females finding their relationship symbols more important than was the case for relationship symbols reported by males" (Baxter, 1987b, p. 279). This is consistent with the often-noted finding that females value their close relationships more than do men.

PERSPECTIVES ON RELATIONSHIPS

Laing, Phillipson, and Lee (1966) discuss the interperceptions and interexperience of the relationship participants. They take as a fundamental postulate that the "world is peopled by others, and these others are not simply objects in the world: they are centers of reorientation to the objective universe." For each individual two aspects are related, namely, (1) the other's behavior and (2) your experience of that behavior. When Peter acts, Paul can react only in terms of his experience of that behavior. The meaning that Paul attaches to Peter's behavior in turn influences Paul's behavior. *The behavior of each toward the other is mediated by the experience each has of the other.* In fact, "The failure to see the behavior of one person as a function of the behavior of the other has led to some extraordinary perceptual and conceptual aberrations that are still with us" (Laing, Phillipson, & Lee, 1966). For example, we often "make sense" of someone's behavior, not by looking at the relational context in which it unfolds, but as a personality characteristic of the person, as if the person is not embedded in a relational world.

The *interpersonal perception method* (IPM) is a fine device for you to use to understand your own relationships. For example, if you find yourself unclear about what is happening in a relationship, the method can allow you to "unpack" it to see the focus of the difficulties. It can be used for any relationship you are in, ranging from work partners to more personal relationships such as friends, family members, and romantic partners. Basically, the interpersonal perception method highlights the three perspectives each participant has in a relationship. In the case of a romantic pair, for example, they are as follows:

Husband's view of object X	Direct perspective
Husband's view of wife's view of object X	Metaperspective
Husband's view of wife's view of his view of object X	Meta-Metaperspective

People use such perspectives (though they are often unaware of doing so), and the IPM system can heighten our awareness of the process. The following case illustrates the perspective of a romantic dyad. The woman and man have been seeing a lot of one another, and frequently the man has invited his roommate to join their outings. In this case, the man likes his roommate, and the woman does not. Their perspectives are:

He: "I sure like my roommate."   (his direct perspective)

He: "She likes my roommate."   (his Metaperspective)

He: "She thinks I like my roommate."   (his Meta-Metaperspective)

She: "I don't like his roommate."   (her direct perspective)

She: "He likes his roommate."   (her Metaperspective)

She: "He thinks I like his roommate."   (her Meta-Metaperspective)

This example illustrates how a relationship based on these perspectives will have some areas of conflict. The degree of matching of perspectives is crucial for any encounter. Liang, Phillipson, and Lee suggest that the following relational aspects are helpful in understanding relationships:

1 Comparison of one person's direct perspective and the other person's direct perspective on the same issue yields *agreement* or *disagreement.*

2 Comparison between one person's metaperspective and the other person's direct perspective on the same issue yields *understanding* or *misunderstanding.*

3 Comparison between one person's meta-metaperspective and the other person's direct perspective on the same issue yields the *feeling of being understood* or of *being misunderstood.*

4 Comparison between one person's meta-metaperspective and the other person's metaperspective on the same issue yields *realization* or *failure of realization.*

Using the sample case of the romantic pair, we can observe the operation of each of these relational statements. Figure 1-1 outlines the comparison of participant perspectives.

In this case, the direct perspectives do not agree. She correctly perceives that he likes his roommate, so she understands him on this issue (her metaperspective matches

FIGURE 1.1.
Degrees of agreement and understanding with the interpersonal perception method.

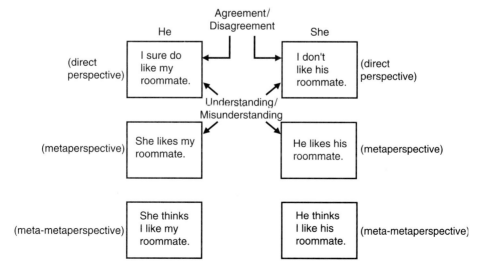

his direct perspective). Note, however, that he does not understand her on the issue (his metaperspective, "She likes my roommate," does not match her direct perspective).

Figure 1-2 completes the analysis. Here the feeling of being understood or misunderstood, and the realization or failure of realization, are sketched. If you were she, you would feel misunderstood, because what you thought (direct perspective) and what you thought he thought you thought (meta-metaperspective) do not match. On the other hand, his direct and meta-metaperspectives match, so he feels understood.[3]

Realization is when a participant knows the other person understands or misunderstands him. In this case, he realizes that she understands him. Correspondingly, she realizes that he misunderstands her. In each case, realization can be seen as follows: When he becomes aware of her metaperspective ("He likes his roommate"), he can compare that to what he thinks she thought about his roommate ("She thinks I like my roommate"). The comparison of the two allows him to realize that she understands him. The corresponding process can be followed for her, too.

Now that the fundamental elements have been covered, let's see how they apply to a *perception of a relationship.* In the following example, the "object of perception" is the relationship itself—a common event in all types of relationships.

Mario and Adelle have been dating for a year and, on Friday night, go to a mutual friend's house for a party. A number of Mario's former buddies are there, but Adelle knows no one at the event. During the evening, Mario is with his circle of friends and

---

[3]Note that the "feeling of being understood" is operating within one person's perceptions and isn't strictly relational. But it does illustrate that many of the internal feelings a person has in a relationship arise in response to the perception of the partner. Thus, even the feeling of being understood is generated relationally.

FIGURE 1-2.
Degrees of realization and feeling understood with the interpersonal perception method.

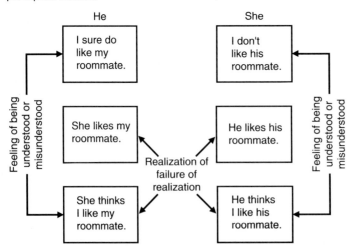

they are all kidding him about his seriousness with Adelle. One says, "Hey, Mario, we don't see you anymore. All you seem to do is hang around with women these days. Whatever happened to old hell-raising Mario?" Another chides him for stopping his former weight-lifting exercises. Then, when Adelle is just in earshot, he is asked, "Mario, how are you and Adelle getting along? Is this thing moving toward marriage or something?" Mario says, "Oh, we're doing OK, but nothing to write home about."

Later that evening, Adelle gives Mario a "what for." She begins by saying, "If this relationship isn't important to you, then you can just get out. I don't want to be associated with someone who takes advantage of others." Here is what is actually happening with their perspectives:

Mario	**Adelle**
"I like our relationship." (DP)	"I like our relationship." (DP)
"She likes our relationship." (MP)	"He doesn't like our relationship." (MP)
"She thinks I don't like our relationship." (MMP)	"He thinks I like our relationship." (MMP)

As the dialogue unfolds, Mario feels hurt and misunderstood by Adelle, and after lashing back at her for not having any faith in him, he tells her that he cannot show his buddies how much he really cares for her because they would continue to give him a difficult time. She responds by telling him that she felt foolish—she went to a party with him, didn't know anyone, then was devalued by him when he told his friends she was "not anything to write home about." After a long argument, it finally became clear that Mario *did* care for Adelle; in fact, he loved her very much. And they reached a new agreement about what to say in public (and they lived happily ever after?).

Notice, by rechecking the preceding dialogue, that the two of them are in agreement—they both think that the relationship is important. However, Adelle misunderstands Mario, she was thrown a curve by the statement he made to his buddies. She also realizes that he understands her—he thinks that she likes the relationship, and she does. And she has the feeling of being understood. But even with all this, she is angry—because she *thinks* they are in disagreement about the relationship. And, of course, Mario feels misunderstood by her and realizes that she misunderstands his intentions.

In general, we assume that the "best" combination of perspectives for a relationship is agreement, understanding, feeling understood and the realization of understanding. However, no particular combination of perspectives, metaperspectives, and meta-meta-perspectives makes for guaranteed success in relationships. The interpersonal perception method highlights the fact that relationships can be maintained on any number of bases. For instance, the participants may agree on an issue, yet one or both misunderstand each other. However, It is probably more often the case that people in relationships do *not* understand one another. For example, Baxter and Bullis (1986), after concluding their research, said that the low agreement between partners suggests that "relationship parties indeed coexist in separate phenomenological relationship worlds" (p. 488). And in committed romantic relationships it is usually the case that both people misunderstand the other—they overestimate their similarity on issues. They misunderstand each other and think there is agreement when there is not. Yet, the relationship may function perfectly well as do most with the partners overestimating their similarities.

The IPM allows us to see some of the complexity of relationships. For instance, when there is agreement on an issue, there are four possible configurations of understanding:

1 He understands her; she understands him.
2 He understands her; she misunderstands him.
3 He misunderstands her; she understands him.
4 He misunderstands her; she misunderstands him.

When (1) the feeling of being understood or misunderstood and (2) the realization or failure of realization are added in, the complexity of relationships becomes apparent. Some configurations are more functional than others for particular pairs. For instance, a perfect match of agreement, understanding, and so on may be less important in an employer–employee dyad, because the participants may "agree to disagree" on some items as long as they understand each other's position. And there are even cases where misunderstandings may be positive. For one thing, misunderstandings can cause two people, like Mario and Adelle, to work on their relationship and further clarify the nature of their commitment to one another. Many couples, working pairs, or family members have engaged in overt misunderstanding and argument as a prelude to a clearer perception of each other. This "working through" in a relationship can produce excitement, bring needed energy back into a relationship, and provide new impetus for working together to "make it go."

Furthermore, to say that agreement, understanding, realization, and feeling understood are always desirable goals is to overlook the sometimes negative consequences of the "perfect matching" of a pair. It can be argued that matching perfectly with another provides for a relationship that obscures the identities of each person. For instance, married couples sometimes get to the point of being unable to separate their individual personalities from one another. If you ask the husband, "Would you and Donna like to come over next Monday?" and he says, "Of course, we always like being with you," he has made a decision without checking Donna's preferences. *We* can sometimes be inappropriately substituted for *I*.

The effects of each relational configuration for a pair—whether marital dyad, generation pairs, friendship pairs, superior–subordinate pairs, or others, is still unknown. In general, however, relational satisfaction appears to be enhanced by more agreement, understanding, realization, and feeling understood. Liang, Phillipson, and Lee found, for example, that disturbed marriages, when compared with nondisturbed marriages, manifest more disagreement and more misunderstanding. However, research by Sillars and his colleagues illustrates that much of the research has confounded understanding with agreement. For example, two spouses, who often have the same attitude on a topic, would appear to "understand one another" yet they simply agree with one another. Their estimate of the other's attitude is based on their own attitude (Sillars et al., 1984). Furthermore, an understanding between spouses may be due to their non-verbal cues and other factors, so that "understanding (or misunderstanding) of the spouse is not related in a simple causal fashion to marital satisfaction" (Sillars & Scott, 1983; Sillars et al., 1984). Even given these reservations, the researchers conclude that understanding may be important to marital satisfaction when sharing is an important value for the spouses (Sillars & Scott, 1983). Whatever the final resolution of the understanding–satisfaction issue, it is very clear the IPM method can unpack underlying relational dynamics.

RELATIONSHIP PROTOTYPES

"Relationships" are a product of our mind-set within a particular cultural frame at a point in time. Our concepts of relationships, therefore, are subject to change both across time and context. The *Relationship Schemata Model* (RSM) is one organizing framework suggesting how people derive their notions of relationships.

The Relationship Schemata Model   The Relationship Schemata Model (RSM) is designed to demonstrate the following things:

1 The process of relationship defining.
2 The interconnection of communication and relationships.
3 The mechanisms for relationship change via communication.

The RSM suggests that relationships are defined, reinforced, and negotiated by the schemata participants have of them (Wilmot & Baxter, 1989; Wilmot & Shellen, 1990). People have schemata for understanding the social world in general and relationships in particular. A *schemata* is a "coherent conceptual framework" for relationships and how they grow and change (Craik, 1979). Schemata are "internal to the perceiver, modifiable by experience and specific to what is being perceived" (Neisser, 1976, p. 54). Our "blueprints" or schemata allow us to organize the world and process it. At the simplest level, for example, if someone gives us a piece of furniture with four legs and a back on it, we can sit on it, we instantly see a "chair." We have a *prototype,* an image of what type of things a "chair" must have to be classified as a chair. There has been considerable research on objects of our social world, but our discussion here will be limited to how we think about relationships.[4]

People mentally process relationships in a variety of ways. We have thoughts (1) about *kinds of relationships* and (2) about *relationship processes.* For types of relationships, we often start with "ideal" types, or *prototypes,* of relationships. One prototype is "friendship," another is "sister," and yet others are "spouse," "romantic partner," "colleague," and "ex-lover." And if you are Australian, "mate" is an important prototype. In addition to types of relationships, we have notions about how relationships move or change through time. For example, we have prototypes for how

---

[4]If you are interested in pursuing the general topic of schemata and prototypes, consult among others, Neisser (1987), Osherson and Smith (1981), Medin (1989), and Armstrong, Gleitman, and Glietman (1983).

relationships move toward more intimacy (Honeycutt, Cantril, & Greene, 1989; Planalp, 1985), for how they deteriorate, and for their overall trajectories (Baxter, 1988).

Where do we get our mental pictures of relationship types? Andersen (1993) accurately notes that we get them from (1) norms in our culture; (2) mass media portrayals; (3) information from third parties, for example, talking to others about your relationships; (4) observing friends interact; and (5) thinking about our own relationships between communication events. As Pavitt (1990) says, we come into relationship events with "preexisting conceptions," which McCall (1988) labeled as our "cultural blueprint" of what we consider characteristics of friends, colleagues, and so forth. When we solidify these social and personal learnings into an "objectified social form," we have a "prototype" (Davis & Todd, 1985). Our own experience in relationships, of course, affects how we think about present and future relationships (Zimmer, 1986). One particular study found that people's optimism about future love relationships was affected by their experience in past love relationships (Carnelley & Janoff-Bulman, 1992)—a carryover of different relationships within the same prototype.

All prototypes, regardless of their specific components, can be described as having three elements (Wilmot & Baxter, 1989):

1 Natural language label
2 Criterial attributes that typify the prototype
3 Communicative indicators of the criterial attributes

Natural Language Labels   Natural language labels were solicited in the research by Wilmot and Baxter (1989) where respondents were asked to describe their personal relationships and, further, to distinguish between types of "friends." people used from two to five labels to distinguish between types of friends. For example, one person said his friends were either "face-name" friends or "friend." Another said she saw friends as ranging from acquaintance to friend, close friend, and very best friend. There were an average of 2.6 natural language labels for the domain of "friendship." People do process relationships according to prototypes, their ideal images of different types of relationships (Rose & Serafica, 1986).

The relationship prototypes occur on two levels: (1) relationship-in-general and (2) relationship-specific (Surra & Ridley, 1991). The relationship-in-general prototypes are used within a given culture, for example, romantic relationships within western cultures. When one talks about "friendships" or "romantic partners" or "married" persons, one is invoking a general prototype. These prototypes are an "ideal form" of the relationship. When researchers, for example, ask for the qualities of a good romantic relationship, they are tapping relationship-in-general prototypes. For example, in western cultures, the label "friend" is most likely applied to (1) nonrelatives, (2) associates lacking other specialized role-relations with you, (3) people of the same age, (4) people known a long time, and (5)those who are primarily sociable involvements (Fischer, 1982).

Relationship-specific schemas, on the other hand, are grounded in a particular relationship. When you are describing a current best friend or the sister in the family you are closest to, you are referencing a relationship-specific prototype. Since research on relationship prototypes is in its infancy, we as yet do not know how people integrate their ideal prototypes with those for an actual relationship. What happens, for example, when one has a particular prototype for "best friend" and Joe no longer acts consistent with the prototype? Under what conditions do we alter the ideal type, and when do we become dissatisfied with the particular relationship because it doesn't match the prototype? If your current lover does not fit well with your ideal type, do you change romantic partners or alter the prototype?

Natural language labels vary considerably across time and cultures. A "friend" for a 3-year-old is someone who lets you play with her truck, yet to a 30-year-old "friend" has a much more complex meaning. Interestingly, people below the age of 22 hold more idealized views of relationships than older folks (Knapp, Ellis, & Williams, 1980), and for the elderly, the label "friend" might suggest more intimacy than "friend" does for a 17-year-old (Bettini & Norton, 1991). And just as the labels vary across our own lifetime, they change culturally as well. "Friend" currently in the United States is used in many ways—sometimes to refer to an opposite or same sex romantic partner, sometimes to refer to someone to just spend time with. An illustration of just how broadly a person may use this label occurred when I once asked Curt how many friends he had. This rather gregarious college student said he had 50!

The natural language label is only the first level in describing how people's prototypes are constructed for relationships. At the next level, the criterial attributes, clarify the detailed views people have of relationships.

Criterial Attributes

The RSM also specifies that natural language labels are connected to criterial attributes. A criterial attribute is some quality that must be met before one could be called "friend," "best friend," or any other prototypical category. These were the most common criterial attributes that must be met before someone would be called a "friend":

trust	general comfort
respect	security in other's presence
ease in communication	openness

Each relationship has its own criterial attributes—those elements that make up that relationship definition. If you were to list the criterial attributes of "family member" or "romantic partner," there would be (1) some overlap in the descriptions and (2) some distinctness in the descriptions for each prototype. In the research, the criterial attributes listed above for friendship were also often listed for romantic partners—they are *conjunctive attributes;* they apply to more than one type of relationship. "Trust," for example, is a conjunctive attribute that people often list for a wide variety of relationships—family, coworkers, friends, and romantic partners.

There are also *disjunctive attributes,* those that are reserved exclusively for one prototype. Romantic relationships, for instance, are more often characterized by "mysticism" or inexplicableness, are seen as more intimate especially in the sexual sense, involve more talk about the relationship per se, require more effort than do friendships, and are more fragile and exclusive (Wilmot & Baxter, 1989; Wilmot & Shellen, 1990). There are also prototypical disjunctive attributes about how to sustain friendships. Argyle and Henderson (1985) found that, across cultures, the six important notions about how to preserve friendship are:

1 stand up for the other person in his or her absence
2 share news of success with the other
3 show emotional support, trust, and confide in the other
4 volunteer help in times of need
5 strive to make him or her happy and
6 be happy when in each other's company.[5]

All relationships, whether one is thinking about relationships in general or a relationship-specific case, are constituted by criterial attributes. Yet this is not the end of the story, because relational participants will sometimes get into arguments about an attribute. Two romantic partners or a father–daughter pairing may get into a struggle. One says, "You don't trust me," and the other says, "I do too!" And the conflict ensues. More detailed specification of the criterial attributes will help illuminate these difficulties.

Communicative Indicators

Criterial attributes always involve some fuzziness. "Trust" is a rather ephemeral concept, as are *all* the criterial attributes people mention. For example, to say a friend is one who can be "trusted" doesn't tell us what communicative behavior connotes trust. The RSM model's third level details the "communicative indicators" of the criterial attributes. When people talked in open-ended interviews about their relationships, it was easier for them to generate natural language labels (friend, romantic partner) and criterial attributes (trust, mysticism) than to move to the third level. Wilmot and Baxter (1989) conducted a second study designed to tap the communicative indicators connected to the criterial attributes. The indicators for the attributes were wide-ranging and diverse. For example, to communicate 'trust' in a friendship, one could:

• be willing and able to be open
• let go of the other
• not do any 'put-ons'
• keep a secret
• defend the other if he or she needed it
• put one's life in the other's hands
• express anger with the other
• listen to the other's problems

---

[5]Note that this list mixes the two levels, criterial attributes and communication indicators.

The findings about the communicative indicators revealed that:

1 People have difficulty pinpointing communicative indicators without being specifically asked about them,

2 The indicators vary in their density; some are rich and complex, and some are lean and sparse, without any symbolic importance,

3 Across people, there can be a wide diversity of communicative indicators for the same criterial attribute, and

4 The same indicators may be connected to different relationship attributes. For one person 'no phoniness' indicates trust, while for another no phoniness indicates feeling comfortable.

A simplified diagram of the interconnections between the levels of the RSM is given in Figure 1-3. It shows, in truncated form, what one person (Molefi) might say about his or her prototypes, criterial attributes, and communication indicators. In other words, it shows *one person's* schemata for two types of relationships. The solid lines show the connections for Molefi for his view of "romantic relationships," and the dotted lines show the connections across the three levels for his "friendships."

By following the solid lines for "romantic relationships" and the dotted lines for "friendship," one can examine the conjunctive criterial attributes at Level 2 for friends and romantic partners (those specific to each prototype). Mysticism is used exclusively for romantic partners, as is relationship talk, as is sex. In this example, this person has no disjunctive attributes for friends—the attributes of trust and caring are for Molefi, shared by both his friends and romantic prototypes. Also note Molefi's Level 3 communicative indicators. For him, in a romantic relationship, one shows trust by (a) willingness to be open, (b) keeping a secret, and (c) listening to other's problems. For his friendship prototype, "keeping a secret" is the only communication indicator for the Level 2 criterial attribute of "trust." In addition, for his friendship, one shows caring by Level 3 communication behaviors of (a) keeping a secret and (b) listening to other's

FIGURE 1-3.
The RSM levels.

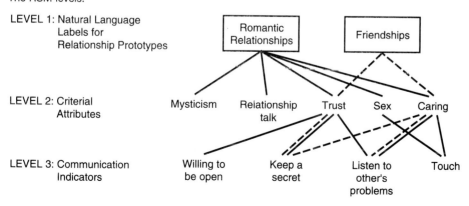

problems. But within his romantic relationship type, one shows caring by (a) listening to other's problems and (b) touch.

The pared-down Figure 1-3, of course, only shows part of what Molefi's schemata might be. And, if we talked to Molefi for a considerable length of time, we would find his prototypes are more complex than as represented in the figure.

We all have prototypes for each of our personal relationships, and they may be quite distinct from the next person's. If Carl sees friendship as composed of "face-name" friends and "best friends," and Julie sees friends as "very best," best, close, occasional, and beginning friends, Carl and Julie have very different schemata for the generic category "friends." And, others might not use any of these labels. Even if the natural language categories are the same, the criterial attributes and communication indicators may be quite diverse. It all depends on each person's schemas activated through the three levels. The RSM gives us an indication, in this streamlined form, of the levels people process relationships on.

Before we leave the notion of the prototypes, several points need to be made. First, the prototypes are loosely structured, flexible, and subject to change (Vangelisti, 1993; Neimeyer & Neimeyer, 1985). Second, as previously implied, the prototypes are "fuzzy"—they are not discrete categories totally separate from one another (Masheter & Harris, 1986). As we saw in the case of Molefi, his friendship categories shared much in common with his romantic relationship categories—there were many attributes common to both (the conjunctive ones listed above). If you expanded his chart to include work associates, his children, and his brother and other kin, the complexity of the chart would be overwhelming—and more and more attributes common to all the relationships would emerge. And, if we keep stretching to include "love of children, love of parent of a child, and other types of love beyond romantic love, the picture would get even more fuzzy" (Fehr, 1993; Aron, Dutton, Aron, & Iverson, 1989). As Fehr (1993) says, "the folk definition of love is complex and provides no sharp boundary between love and other, related experiences" (p. 435). As a final illustration of the overlap in categories, one piece of research found that, when people were asked to list their "best friend," 44 percent listed their romantic partner! (Hendrick & Hendrick, (1993).

Third, the culturally agreed upon definitions of "friends," "romantic partners," "spouses," and others will show considerable variation, depending on whom you are talking to and the interest of the researcher. All you have to do is consult the various pieces of research to see that a listing of *the* attributes and communication behaviors for friendship and romance is probably impossible, except at the most general level (for example, Sapadin, 1988; Rose & Serafica, 1986; Contarello & Volpato, 1991; Adelman & Parks, 1987a; Fisher, 1982; Fehr & Russell, 1991, Wilmot & Baxter, 1984; Fehr, 1993; Zimmer, 1986). For instance, in looking at the notion of love, one study found 93 different features, and another found 68 (Fehr, 1993). And, the general conclusion seems to be that, for love, "companionate features lie at the core" (Fehr, 1993, p. 11), with passionate features somewhere less central. If we describe love in such general terms, however, it will not come close to capturing the complexity that one person may have for it.

Fourth, the most important thing to know, rather than our general cultural prototypes, is *each individual's* prototypes—that is what, in real life, counts. If you are in a beginning romantic relationship with someone and you both agree that "trust" is extremely important, but for you "trust" primarily means not dating anyone else while for the other "trust" is indicated by "not telling secrets," the day could come when these different definitions come out. So, when you see your partner on a date with someone else, and you walk up and say (in a rather unpleasant tone of voice), "I thought I could trust you," and the partner says, "You can—I didn't tell anyone about what you did when you were ten years old," you both have some work to do on the relationship.

Fifth, we do not know how the prototypes are altered or changed. There is no direct research showing how we "adjust" our templates when we are in a real relationship. For example, how people handle definitions of "mixed relationships," such as step-families, a sister being your best friend, a family member who "breaks off" the relationship with you, or the work colleague with whom you have a romantic relationship, is an unresearched question. Our relational work is getting more complex all the time, and many relationships cross over the traditional boundaries of "relationship types." A second example of adjusting our prototypes is how we adjust the "real" to the "actual." What do you do if you find a friend or romantic partner who meets some of your criteria and not others? How do you reconcile the real relationship with your ideal prototype? One piece of research examined how people deal with behavior that is inconsistent with their relationship prototype. Surra and Bohman (1991) suggest that there are two models for change: (1) a bookkeeping model, in which gradual changes are made each time there is a lack of fit between the model and the behavior; and (2) a conversion model, in which sudden changes are incorporated as a result of a dramatic or salient events. We need much more research on how people adjust (or not adjust) their prototypes to adapt to a particular relationship.

Finally, we do not know the influence of the other's prototype on yours. If your best friend and you get really clear with one another about the meaning of the friendship, and you find that you see things differently, how do you each adjust to the other's prototypes? If, for her, punctuality is a key, but for you it is not, how do the two of you incorporate this difference? Are you always on time? Do you encourage the other to see you being late as "not part of the friendship?"

In sum, we currently know very little about (1) how stable the prototypes are, (2) how people reconcile their real relationships with the prototypes, or (3) how people adjust their communication and prototypes to the other person's prototypes. While these are intriguing areas for research and speculation, at a minimum, the RSM lets us see how individuals process relationship types on three levels. It allows us to see the areas of "mismatch" and lack of understanding between two individuals who get into difficulties with one another. It also gives us knowledge of how to begin processing relationships. So when your friend says, "You just can't be trusted as a friend," you can respond with, "What are the things I do or don't do that you classify as the lack of trust?" hopefully opening up dialogue about what can be corrected.

Process Trajectory Schemata

In addition to schemata for relationship types, we also have schemata for the processes relationships go through (Baxter, 1988). When someone says, "Well, I had to get out of the love relationship—it just wasn't going anywhere," he or she is revealing a process schemata about relationship growth. The relationship trajectory schemata allow the parties to "make sense" out of the episodes of their relationship; it gives them a mental framework for understanding. In our current mainstream culture, people have two major schemata for how love relationships develop. When asked about how relationships develop, they report two primary ways of viewing the growth trajectories for love relationships. The two broad categories are (1) *whirlwind* and (2) *friendship first* (Baxter, 1988). As you would guess, the growth trajectory for "whirlwind" is love that happens in a rapid time frame—you meet at a party, and it is "love at first sight." The other growth trajectory is "friendship first," which is the most common form of romantic involvement. Under this kind of schemata, the participants meet, become friends, and then develop a romantic relationship. Some people believe in one, some in the other, and some in both, but the two general paths are the schemata we "overlay" on romantic relationships to see how they develop.[6]

Research on the schemata people have for maintaining or rejuvenating their relationships is, as of this writing, not well organized. We don't know, for example, what the most common conceptual notions are that people use to make sense out of these acts. Chapter 5 details some of the research on specific strategies people try in rejuvenating their relationships, but specific work on the schemata is not yet completed. Given some of the difficulties in this culture for maintaining long-term relationships, it will be interesting to see what the overall schemata are that people have for infusing new life into a faltering relationship, whether a work situation, family, friendship, or romantic.

People also have schemata for the dissolution trajectory of relationships. The two general notions parallel the ideas about how romance develops. Baxter (1988) suggests that research demonstrates two general trajectories (1) *protracted indirectness* and (2) *swift directness.* These also parallel the ideas of Davis (1973), who suggested long ago that when people dissolve romantic relationships they use "passing away" or "sudden death." Baxter's research lends credence to these two schemata that we use to make sense of the demise of romance. For example, in using protracted indirectness, people who want to dissolve a romantic relationship know that they need to reduce disclosure and indirectness (Wilmot & Baxter, 1983). Similarly, those who chose the swift directness route talk about "getting it over with" and reduce interaction with the other suddenly.

Not only are there schemata for the development and dissolution of relationships (and probably for maintenance as well), but people have notions about how to change relational categories. Take the case of when people experience a "friendship first" trajectory in romantic relationships. Given that the boundaries between friendship and romantic types are "fuzzy," they need some notion about how to move from one relationship type to another. The work of Wilmot and Baxter (1984) found that the first display of physical affection, and the first "date," tend to signal such a category shift. A related set of schema pertain to the transformation of love relationships into friend-

---

[6]There are, of course, many classifications of how relationships develop provided by researchers. For example, Surra (1987) suggests that courtship trajectories are (a) accelerated type, (b) accelerated-arrested, (c) intermediate, and (d) prolonged. But the current book's approach to schemata asks how the *relationship participants* conceptually organize events.

ships. While most terminated love relationships do not move to friendships, some do. If the romantic partners were friends first, then became romantic partners, it is easier to move back to a friendship after the romance dissolves (Metts, Cupach & Bejlovec, 1989). This tends to suggest that the two people have a different set of schemata for how to maintain the postromantic relationship; their experience as prior friends helps them change back to that relationship type.

To date, our knowledge of relationship trajectory schemas is in its initial stages. You will note that most of the work has centered on romantic relationships, and on development and dissolution. Much work needs to be done to tap the "folk logics" (Baxter, 1988) that people have, their schemata, about all types of relationship events.

THE INTERPENETRATION OF COMMUNICATION AND RELATIONSHIPS

We have explored the fundamental features of relationships by first examining a definition of "what is a relationship." Then, the IPM model of participant perspectives was set forth and third, relationship schemas were explored by looking at natural language labels, criterial attributes and communication indicators. Within each of these perspectives we have seen the central role communication plays in relationships. This section will go a step further and probe the complex association between communication and relationships. We begin with some essential principles, slowly building a more complex view of the interconnection between communication and relationships.

Principle 1: Relational Definitions Emerge from Recurring Episodic Enactments.

An *episode* is a nonverbal and verbal communication event—a short discussion in the student union, sitting silently together and watching a sunset, a "Hi, how's it going" on the street, or an extended evening spent together. Relationships and communication episodes exist at different logical levels, and the episodes have a "building block" effect on the relationship; they are part of a chain of events. Communicative episodes build a relationship definition intermittently, over time, in spurts and with cumulative effects (McClintock, 1983). And each utterance and nonverbal action has force for creating a relationship (Hopper & Drummond, 1992; Duck et al., 1991; Goodwin, M. H., 1990). Although one individual episode does not predetermine the entire course of a relationship (Fisher & Drecksel, 1983; Hecht, 1984), the recurring episodes implicitly build a relational definition over time. For example, a number of recurring negative interactions early in a relationship appear to influence relationship satisfaction several years later (Markman, 1979). This occurs because we each react to episodes with our own "relational translations"—we attach relationship meaning to the episodes. When someone does you a favor, for example, you will tend to see that as a "friendly" act, supplying your own "relational translation" of the content of the act. You react to each act with an implicit relationship definition as you have repeated experiences with the person. As you and the other reciprocate more favors, spend more time together, and have fun you may gradually begin to see the other as a "friend." Figure 1-4 illustrates this process. Each episode is pinpointed with a small *e,* from episode 1 to infinity.

When you have your first experience with someone, it gives you a hint of what the

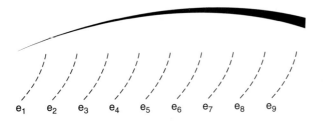

FIGURE 1-4.
Episodes accumulating into a relationship definition.

$e_1 \quad e_2 \quad e_3 \quad e_4 \quad e_5 \quad e_6 \quad e_7 \quad e_8 \quad e_9$

relationship will be. The first time I went to Vicki for a haircut, for example, we had a fine time joking around and laughing a lot. But it isn't until you have *repeated* episodes with someone that the relationship begins to have some resilience and form. Now that Vicki has cut my hair several times, it is well established that we have a fun-loving, jovial relationship. Similarly, the first kiss does not mean a romantic relationship will blossom; it has to grow past one episode for the relationship definition to gain strength. But each time we have an episode with someone we "re-achieve" our relationship (Hopper & Drummond, 1992)—the relationship is continually constructed through our episodes.

By the time you have multiple episodes with someone, the relationship definition begins to have some overarching power to define who the two of you are to each other. For example, your episodes with your family of origin were repeated many times, so altering these relationship definitions once you are grown may be difficult. The over-arching relationship definition, formed out of earlier interaction episodes, will propel your parents into seeing you as "the kid" because of the numerous experiences in the past. The subprinciple operating here is that *the more frequently a relational definition is reinforced by episodic enactments, the more potent it becomes.* Finally, not each episode has a demonstrable effect on the relationship definition—many episodes simply follow the usual pattern, which reinforces the relationship definition without anyone even noticing (Baxter & Wilmot, 1983).

Although communication and relationships are at two different levels, they are obviously linked (Capella, 1984; Fitzpatrick & Indvik, 1982). Gottman (1979) notes that the communication patterns of dissatisfied couples are characterized by more "cross-complaining" than those of satisfied couples. As you have repeated episodes of each person criticizing the other, they build a relationship that is dissatisfying. The more they criticize, the more the relationship is defined as one of mutual criticism. In sum, the first principle specifies that relationship definitions are constructed via the meanings we have for the episodic enactments.[7]

---

[7]The "levels" of relationships and communication can be charted a number of ways. Pearce and others, 1980 specify multilevels, whereas Wilmot and Baxter, 1984 discuss three levels. Although I prefer the three-level approach, it is a bit complicated for presentation here, and the straightforward levels of (1) relationships and (2) communication are retained in this discussion. For more detailed treatment of all these issues see Hinde, 1979, Baxter and Wilmot, 1983, Bochner, 1978, Bateson, 1979, Wilmot and Baxter, 1984, Pearce et al., 1979, Wilder, 1979, Knapp, Ellis, and Williams, 1980, Wilmot and Baxter, 1983, Hecht, 1984, King and Sereno, 1984, Capella, 1984, McClintock, 1983.

Principle 2: Relationship Definitions "Frame" or Contextualize Communication Behavior (Wilder, 1979; Wilmot, 1980).

Communication events cannot be properly interpreted outside their relational context. If you see two men, one 40 years old and the other 20, standing with their arms around one another, you will interpret their communication behavior quite differently if you think they are father and son rather than gay males. Similarly, the refusal of a good-night kiss on a date means something totally different if it occurs on the first date or 6 months into the relationship. The meaning of our communication behaviors is dependent on the relational frame where they occur. For example, a Valentine's Day message has different meanings in different relationships—for friends it is different than for lovers (Duck & Pond, 1991). As Gergen (1991) says, "What is rational in one relationship is questionable or absurd from the standpoint of another" (p. 78). From planning what to do in a relationship (Berger & Bell, 1988) to actual nonverbal and verbal behavior, the relational frame determines the meaning. What may be considered invasive in one relationship—standing close, intense eye contact, physically touching the person—is perfectly appropriate in another (Burgoon et al. 1989). Other research has demonstrated that new friendships are more impacted by negative behaviors than are established, close friendships (Hays, 1989). Further, what appears as silly or confusing to outsiders can make perfect sense to the insiders, because those with the relational history draw upon a history of experiences that is not available to outsiders (Burgoon & Newton, 1991). We can't "pin down" communication behaviors and study them in isolation—they always occur in some relational context.

Not only do relationship labels "frame" our interactions so that they make sense to us, but certain relationship types are associated with consistent patterns of communication within given cultures. The labels we learn to use for relationships have some commonality across people. For example, Knapp, Ellis, and Williams presented different relationship terms to large groups of people to see what they associated with the labels. They found, for example, that more intimate relationships (such as lovers or best friends) were associated with more synchronized and personalized communication activities.

Although these perceptions may be the result of our culturally learned schemas about what makes a "good" intimate relationship and may not actually happen in relationships, it is significant that some overall patterns did emerge (Knapp, Ellis, & Williams, 1980). In all cultures, there are certain qualities linked to particular relational definitions, since the relational definitions arise from repeated communication experiences. Most people know this intuitively and sometimes use it to their own advantage. Take the case of a young woman and man living together. They might choose to introduce each other as "my roommate" or "my friend" rather than "my romantic partner." The use of these natural language labels sets the stage for expectations for the participants and outsiders, and this linkage between relationship definitions and assumed communication behavior follows some regular patterns.

The cultural definitions for relationship types give us frames to guide and shape the ensuing communication episode. In mainstream Western cultures, for example, we know that romantic partners will act differently than will family members. And in China, the relationship is the basis for bonding rather than depending on the specifics of the interaction to determine whether a relationship will solidify (Chang & Holt, 1991). Relational frames define, circumscribe, and prescribe the appropriateness of communication as it occurs on the cultural level as well as between intimates. Therefore, Principle 2 states that communication is interpreted and associated within given relational definitions.

Principle 3: Relationship Types Are Not Necessarily Mutually Exclusive—Their Boundaries Are Often "Fuzzy."

When most people talk about their relationships, they treat them as if they were totally discrete from different types. For instance, a "friendship" is talked about differently from a romantic relationship or family relationship. However, as Wilmot and Baxter (1983) note, "Social relations in real life are rarely so stable and nonchanging." Relationships are more a process than a static state. And because of the process nature of relationships, many relationships are not "sharply and completely distinct" (Kayser, Schwinger, & Cohen, 1984).

The "fuzzy" boundaries between types of relationships is illuminated in the work of Wilmot and Baxter (1984). The conjunctive attributes of trust, respect, caring, ease in communicating, general comfort and security in the other's presence, and openness are used by people for both romantic and friendship relations. Turn back and look again at Figure 1-3, showing the overlap in friendship and romantic criterial attributes.

The issue is further complicated by the fact that many relationships move from one category to another. A friendship may evolve into a romantic relationship, and a romantic interlude that is unsuccessful may result in the participants redefining themselves as "friends." Some married people, for example, refer to themselves as each other's best friend, and two sisters may well be each other's best friend. While the prototypes may seem distinct on the surface, the qualities of each may overlap with another. Such "fuzzy" boundaries, of course, may bring confusion to the participants, when one person thinks close physical contact is a sign of developing a "romantic" relationship, whereas the other interprets the physical affection as "friendly."

Principle 4: Relationship Definitions and Communication Episodes Reciprocally Frame One Another.

We noted earlier that participants' interpretations of communication episodes set the forces in motion for arriving at a relationship definition. When the communication behavior is seen as fitting a prototype, such as helping the other being associated with friendship, the participants begin to see the relationship as forming.

But relationship definitions *do change*. Friendships deteriorate, romantic relations fall apart, family members become estranged, and work associates move closer and farther apart. The "frames" (relationship definitions) we use to interpret communication behavior are in process and do undergo alterations (Wilmot & Baxter, 1984). Although the relationship frame supplies the context for understanding the communication behavior, it only remains unchallenged while it works. For example, if your friendship is based on keeping confidences between the two of you and Sarah "tells all" about you to a third person, it challenges the existence of the friendship. One man, upon learning that his friend, now living elsewhere, was "bad-mouthing" him to others, wrote to him, saying, "Friends of mine don't go around getting social points by misusing the friendship. Consider yourself an ex-friend!" When the prototypes for the relationship have linkages to communication behavior, and when they are not fulfilled, the definition of the friendship is challenged. Put another way, while communication is always interpreted within the backdrop of the relationship, the obverse is also true—relationships are judged according to the episodic events that unfold (King & Sereno, 1984). There is reciprocal influence between the two.

You change a relationship by enacting episodes that do not "fit" the prototype for that relationship (Wilmot & Baxter, 1984, 1985; Lloyd & Cate, 1985). If you are in a committed relationship and begin staying out all night without the other, such actions erode the assumed definition of the relationship. Negative episodes, where the two people are constantly in unproductive conflict, is like a relational acid—it slowly "eats away" at the definition. Similarly, of course, if you are in a relationship that is not going well, *altering the communication patterns* is one possible way to begin bringing back a healthy relationship. Or alternatively, if you have a love relationship that has gone sour, it might be easier to redefine the relationship definition as "friends" rather than trying to alter the communication patterns. If you alter the behavior, you put pressure on the relationship definition to change; if you alter the relationship definition, you "re-contextualize" the communication that is occurring. Either way, the key is to have the relationship definitions and communication behavior match the expectations of the participants.

In summary, these principles demonstrate some of the complexity between communication and relationships. Relationships are created via communication, communication reflects relationship definitions, relationship types have some overlap, and you change relationship definitions by engaging in communication that does not fit the relationship definition. Both language and nonverbal communication (1) create the relationship definition, (2) serve as an indicator of the type of relationship, (3) serve as a medium for maintaining and changing the relationship, and (4) serve "as a consequence or outcome of the relationship" (Wilmot & Shellen, 1990, p. 415).

A THEORY OF EMBEDDEDNESS

No communication event, or any relationship, is an island to itself—each arises within a context of family influences, community connections, larger social groupings, and an overall national culture, as well as a world context. The "relational context" means the interconnectedness of both people—their individual and joint networks of friends, kin, work associates, and others throughout the country and world. There is no such thing as a contextless relationship, just as there is no such thing as a relationshipless person.

Of course, each of us will have varying degrees of influence from the diverse realms we are embedded within. For some, other friends and romantic partners, as well as their connections with others, will be central influences on your relationship. For others, you may belong to an identifiable subgroup within your community that is your prime source of influence on your primary relationships. Or your identity with a religious orientation or recreational activity might be forged on a regional, national, or even an international basis. While the specifics differ for us all, each of our important relationships are embedded or located within a broader set of connections—and they exert powerful influences on us. While it is impossible to accurately portray each potential level of embedded factors, Figure 1-5 does show some of the wider groupings that have an effect on our relationships. For purposes of illustrating, take the relationship between two best friends. Their relationship is embedded within these kinds of contexts:

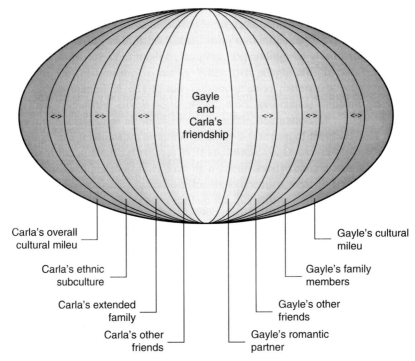

FIGURE 1-5.
Layers of embeddedness.
(adapted from a diagram used for other purposes by Ladd, 1991).

Note that, for Gayle and Carla, the most important relationships outside their friendship are (1) their romantic partners, (2) their other friends, (3) their families, and (4) the wider culture. And, notice that the order of embeddedness is different for each of them. Of course, if we were showing the embeddedness of romantic pairs, work associates, casual acquaintances, or others, we would require a different labeling diagram. And, for some people, their subculture would need to appear, because their subculture may divert from the mainstream American culture. Regardless of the specifics, however—*every* relationship is embedded within a larger context of relationships.

To illustrate the importance of understanding context, two prominent types of "outside" influences will be discussed showing their impact on relationships. First, relationship constellations—the network of other relationships you are connected to will be discussed. Second, some general observations about the impact of culture (or could be subculture as well) on communication and relationships will be offered. Of course, not all sources of influence are charted—these are for purposes of illustrating some of the influences that impinge on relationships.

Relationship Constellations

Each relationship is embedded within a larger *relationship constellation*—interconnected networks that form patterns. These constellations, or social contexts, exert considerable influence on each relationship (Wilmot & Sillars, 1989). As Parks and Eggert (1991) say, "personal relationships are inextricably intertwined with the participants' surrounding social networks of family and friends" (p. 5).

While much research ignores the overall relationship constellations and the mutual influence of intertwined relationships, some research is illuminating the overall web of relational influence. In terms of initiating relationships, the constellations exert influence in four ways (Parks and Eggert, 1991). First, whom we initiate with is influenced by the networks we both are in. Second, there are social norms within a wider network that impact our choice of possible romantic partners and friends. For example, if you are active in the same religion as your parents, that will become a screening criterion in selecting possible partners. Third, initiation is influenced by the location of the initiator and the potential partner in the network. Finally, relationship initiation is impacted by direct action on the part of others in your network and their approval or disapproval of your choices. While initiation in western culture is not as rigidly constrained as in more homogenous cultures, there is still influence nevertheless.

The influence of other relationships in an overall constellation doesn't end at the initiation stage. Parks and Eggert (1991), in studying romantic partners, found "nearly two thirds (66.3%) of the subjects had met at least one member of their partner's network of close friends, family and other close associates prior to actually meeting the partner himself or herself (p. 7)." And in work relationships, with one study of women working night shifts, "supportive interactions with the close friend outside of work . . . is linked to the psychological well-being" (Brand & Hirsch, 1990, p. 169). And, the success rate of romantic partners staying together is influenced by the network. As Parks and Eggert (1991) note, "those who had broken up . . . had significantly less communication with the partner's network, received less support from the partner's network" (p. 25). Across the developmental cycle, the network of relationships had a measurable influence on the romantic relationships:

> People who perceived that their own and their partner's networks were more supportive also interacted more, perceive their partner to be more similar, felt more intimate with their partners, and experienced greater commitment to the romantic relationship . . . the general pattern emerging from these findings bears witness to the strong association between internal, developmental dynamics of romantic relationships and the communication networks surrounding those relationships. (Parks & Eggert, 1991, p. 20).

The density of the network also makes a difference. As you and your partner's friends become friends, it strengthens the density of the overall constellation—and reinforces the relationship by promoting positive interactions and multiple friendship ties (Healey & Bell, in Cahn, 1990a, p. 125). And in terms of the romantic relationships mentioned earlier, the constellations promote the relationship by offering support such as money, create chances for joint interactions, and impose barriers to the breakup of the relationship (Parks & Eggert, 1991).

Interestingly, in our beliefs about the "declining family," we tend to underestimate the influence of the family context. Just stop for a moment and think of the people who are the most important to you. Amongst friends, romantic partners, family, and others. List their names in the spaces below, with #1 being the person most important to you and so on down to #5.

1

2

3

4

5

If you are like most people, in the "top five" will be included many of the members of your family—parents, sisters, brothers, and your own children if you have any. Kin are often "overrepresented" in the first three, closest levels of intimacy. It is easy to not see the importance of family, even in these times when much is being written about the lessening influence of families. Clearly, we are all heavily impacted by our network of family members.

There are, to be sure, "tugs across types." Friends influence romantic relationships, family reactions influence friends and romantic pairings, romantic and friend relations influence your work associates, and vice versa. Influence flows among all the categories in one's constellation of relationships. If, for example, you have a romantic relationship that is embedded within a dense constellation—you and your romantic partner's family and friends also know one another—it may enhance your relationship longevity. As Salzinger (1982, p. 143) says, "Dense networks limit the option and reinforce the relationships of their members, whereas loose networks are both less limiting and less stable." As a result, relationships within dense networks should be comparatively long-lasting, "since each relationship is reinforced by the presence of numerous others" (p. 120). And if you and your partner come from a situation where you lack close kin relationships, you are "free to engage in voluntary relationships" such as new friends (Palisi & Ransford, 1987). Some recent research demonstrates that it may not be actual actions on the part of the constellations members that affect you, but rather that you "anticipate or imagine the reactions of those close" to you (Surra, 1990, p. 852).

Since the "tugs across types" is not fully researched, we do not know all the types of influences that flow within constellations of relationships. There is one piece of research, however, which shows a man's relationship with his father affects the man's romantic partner. This intriguing finding is that the "son's perceived confirmation from their fathers" affects the female partner's reluctance about interacting with him! The more you see your father as confirming you, the more your romantic partner interacts with you (Beatty & Dobos, 1993).

The impact of the constellations, of course, varies according to where you are on the life cycle. Young, single adults, for example, are less influenced by their kin than are married adults of the same age (Shulman, 1975, p. 816). And, one typical event for many people is that the birth of a child brings some family members closer. And, when a couple gets married, the husband experiences a decline in his friendships (Tschann, 1988).

Before empirical work was conducted, much was made of the "Romeo and Juliet effect"—meaning that, if both sets of parents disapproved of a love relationship, it *strengthened* the bond between the lovers. But, in reality *most* people are directly influenced by the support or disapproval of the network—more support begets a stronger, more enduring romantic relationship. As Parks and Eggert say, "support from network members is positively associated with romantic involvement" (1991, p. 18).

It is important to note that many network members stay in the background until you have a crisis. For example, many an adult will maintain a minimal connection with his or her parents; then, with the onset of a crisis (divorce, heart attack, death of your child, loss of a job) the family will "rally around" and provide support. The constellation "gets activated," and the members move in closer. Interestingly, just "knowing" the family members are there and ready to respond if you need it "raises self-confidence and a greater sense of mastery" (Eggert, 1987, p. 102). Actually, under crisis situations it has been found that families and relatives provide much more help than friends (LaGaipa, 1990). And, as you might guess, the support of kin, friends, and formal mental health sources can "ameliorate the negative effects of life change and stress" (Buehler & Legg, 1993). One last finding of interest: When studying adults who had a parent who endured a crisis, it was found that they were more supportive if the parent did not have alternative sources of support (Dykstra, 1993). All the members of the network are affected by the others—if your parents have a crisis and a primary relationship, it affects how involved you will become.

We have only charted some of the rudiments of constellation effects, but before moving on to culture, it should be noted that the embeddedness can also have negative effects. For many "highly embedded" people, there is stress associated with juggling all the complexity of the relationships (Leslie, 1989). One can be overinvolved with family, friends, or work associates so that the competing demands create stress.

Cultural Considerations

Not only are relationships impacted by the overall constellations of other connective relationships, each relationship is encased within a cultural milieu. In western cultures it is easy to think that culture has no impact, because its influence is so diffuse and difficult to pinpoint. When, however, our media extol the virtues of romantic love, they are nudging us to make choices based on strong feelings. Our predominant messages encourage separation from family, mobility, and a sense that your individual self and relationship are the most important considerations. For example, in the United States, "childhood is chiefly preparation for the all-important event of leaving home" (Bellah et al., 1985). We want independent, self-sufficient selves as well as self-sufficient relationships that can stand on their own.

Such values are culturally derived—they don't just spring out of the air. In high-context cultures (Hall, 1959), such as Chinese and Japanese and many native cultures, there is a concern foremost for "social harmony" (Nakanishi, 1986). The prime value is to preserve the relationship harmony in the entire group, such as the family, rather than strike out on your own. As a result, Japanese disclose less and are more indirect as a way to preserve social harmony; self-expressiveness is seen as damaging to the overall harmony (Nakanishi, 1986).

One of the confounding features of low-context cultures such as the United States is that we are multicultural. You might grow up in a group that prizes family cohesion (whether derived from Slovenian, Native American, or other roots), while your best friend in school comes from a family with little connection. The diversity in our cultural milieu makes it difficult to generalize about "our culture," because we are composed of many cultures coexisting side by side. But whatever the particular influences on your values about relationships, they are derived from a wider cultural context. We all are influenced by our neighborhood (whether it is a close, connected neighborhood or one where no one knows anyone), our town or city, and the larger culture coming to us through media exposure. We can't escape cultural influences—whether diverse or not within a particular country, they are there. If you grew up in the wide-open spaces of Wyoming as a grandchild of two homesteaders, or in the inner city of Philadelphia—those cultural imprints help shape your views of relationships.

2

SELF AND OTHER
IN RELATION

One cannot escape perspective.

Gergen (1991)

Most of us have a definite viewpoint on relationships and our role in them—whether we talk about it or not. Further, most of us think that our way of viewing self, other, and relationship reflects "how it is." Yet, during struggles with others we often hear another viewpoint. Carl and Susie were dating, and one Tuesday evening Susie ended the relationship saying, "You just don't include others in your thinking—you are so selfish, it is no wonder no relationship has worked for you." She is articulating the difference between how she sees self and relationship and how he sees self and relationship. How we view self in a relationship context is of fundamental importance. Some view the people as independent who just happen to "be in relationship," and the most important thing is enhancement of oneself. For others, self is only defined within relationships—not something that is *ever* separated from the relationship constellations encompassing it. This chapter will highlight some predominant conceptualizations of self/other/relationship and illustrate the profound impact such views have on both the nature of self, relationship, and communication.

The western vocabulary for understanding both ourselves and our relationships has been "robustly individualistic" (Gergen, 1991). Most people see communication as operating between separate, autonomous units, with each person being a "unit." Such views presume that people "are dependent upon nothing outside themselves for their existence" (Wilder, 1980, p. 92–182). In our dominant western cultures, we prize individual achievement (Slugoski & Ginsburg, 1989), talk about "finding ourselves," and

35

exit relationships when they don't met our needs. The self is put at the center of the universe—we prize individual achievement, assign college grades to individuals, and chronicle individual lives. In short, we identify the person, not the relationship, as the starting and ending point. In fact, "Americans tend to think of the ultimate goals of the good life as matter of personal choice" (Bellah et al., 1985, p. 22). When people go for therapy, for example, it is usually to "change their self" or find another way of adjusting to the rigors and demands of life and relationships—all presuming that the "self" is the center—the causative force around which everything revolves. We have developed a sophisticated language of identifying the self—and the classifications of individual pathologies in the *Diagnostic and Statistical Manual* (used by psychiatrists and clinical psychologists), like the rest of our society, locates dysfunction in the individual. This has led, for instance, to more than 80 percent of the psychological studies of black Americans ascribing their problems to something internal to them rather than considering their circumstances (Sampson, 1989, p. 5).

The "self" is formed as an object to be studied, scrutinized, labeled, and worthy of a specific vocabulary to describe all its shortcomings. Thus, we talk of "low self-esteem," and use "compulsive," "paranoid," "mid-life crises," and a myriad other terms to characterize the "self" as the locus of all important events. In fact, the "vocabulary of human deficit has undergone enormous expansion within the present century" (Gergen, 1991, p. 13). Even the workplace takes up this mantle—when there is a conflict, both sides talk about how the other person is dysfunctional.

At the current time, to say "independent self" is redundant—independence and autonomy are at the heart of our very concept of "self." College students talk about "getting my stuff (or something else) together," assuming they can "find" themselves at the end of the quest. Sadly, research indicates that young college students experience more "intense feelings of boredom, depression and restlessness than do older persons" (Gerstein & Tesser, 1987, p. 358). The burden of taking the self as responsible for everything that happens might be related to such events—and the load too big to bear for an individual.

Stated another way, we "believe in the dignity, indeed the sacredness, of the individual. Anything that would violate our right to think for ourselves, judge for ourselves, make our own decisions, live our lives as we see fit, is not only morally wrong, it is sacrilegious" (Bellah et al., 1985, p. 142). Wilber (1983) captures the double-edged results of this focus and responsibility for the "self":

> In a sense, each child growing up today has to pass through this same process of building up an "I, me and mine". The child has to become his own person, or his own property and his own author, or responsible agent of his own actions. First he has to become his own property by prying his self-hood out of its initial embeddedness in the material environment, in maternal fusion, in animism, magic and myth. He has to transfer the ownership of his consciousness from other to self. Second, he then has to assume responsibility for that ownership. He has to become author of his actions, and cease giving authorship of his life to mother, to father, to king and to state. (Wilber, 1983, pp. 275–276)

This view, presuming the self to be independent, self-contained, and the causative agents behind events (Harré, 1989) carries over to how people see communication and relationships. As Sampson (1989, p. 5) notes, "the ideology of autonomy and individuality remain carved deeply in the subjective consciousness of the culture." It is to this first view, or paradigm, that we now turn.

PARADIGM I: INDIVIDUAL SELVES LOOSELY CONNECTED

This view of how self and other are related presumes the person is the center and an integrated whole in and of himself or herself (Sampson, 1989).[1] As Geertz notes:

> The Western conception of the person as a bounded, unique, more or less integrated motivational and cognitive universe, a dynamic center of awareness, emotion, judgement and action, organized into a distinctive whole and set contrastively against other such wholes . . . is a rather peculiar idea within the context of the world's cultures. (Geertz, 1979, p. 229)

As he notes, such a conception, thoroughly familiar to all of us raised in the west, is "a rather peculiar idea within the context of the world's cultures." Yet firmly rooted in it we are. Such notions stress that there are Descartian atomic units "dependent upon nothing outside themselves for their existence" (Wilden, 1980, p. 92). Graphically, such views would be expressed as in Figure 2-1.

Note the Self and Other are independent units loosely connected by the relational thread. Paradigm I emphasizes the self, deemphasizes the other, and reduces the relationship to a fragile connecting mechanism. Those who view relationships from such a perspective would be prone to emphasize individual growth, individual responsibility, and want to look inside the envelope of the individual for explanations (Harré, 1989). Further, individual achievement is the goal, and so ego identity requires the person have some control over the process, and anything less than a separated individual identity would be seen as deficient (Slugoski & Ginsburg, 1989). Such an ideology of individualism necessitates specializing in looking at our own reactions, determining if a relationship is "worth the effort" based on whether we are happy or satisfied. The "bridge" between people is precarious at best and ineffectual at worst. The assumptions of such a view are clearly highlighted by Chodron (1990, p. 107):

> We think things exist in a way they don't. We have a wrong conception of who we are, thinking we are a permanent, concrete, findable entity. Then, we cherish this illusory 'real self' dearly. The one thought in our minds from morning to night is, "I want hap-

---

[1]The use of "self" in this section is consistent with the much broader use made popular by Jungian psychology. Normally, there is confusion between "ego" or "persona" and "self." Self, as used here, refers to the complete aspects of one, not just the presenting, conscious aspect. For clarification of this use of the term, see Stevens (1990).

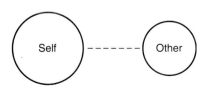

FIGURE 2-1.
Paradigm I: Individual selves loosely connected.

piness and my happiness is the most important." We think and act as if we were the center of the universe, for the thought "my happiness, my suffering" is foremost and ever-present in our minds. Our concern for others comes after our concern for ourselves.

It is interesting to note that the entire concept of "self" arose during the middle ages when people were, for the first time, seen as having separate rights and obligations (Wilber, 1983). The word "self" in fact didn't appear until from about 1595 (Slugoski & Ginsburg, 1989).

One of the ramifications of Paradigm I is that, in contemporary western culture, relationship difficulties (whether between lovers, friends, or family members) can be identified by the degree of *blame of the other*. Since the two persons are seen as loosely connected, separate entities, if there are difficulties, the first line of defense is to blame the other, taking great care to show how the disturbances traveled down that thin wire of the relationship to cause your behavior. Our concrete view of self also extends to a solid view of the other—who causes all our problems. Paradoxically, in such a self-oriented culture, the self is the last object for analysis for many people in times of relationship difficulty. The person seldom blames the self, or interconnected communication patterns or other features, but rather blames the other. If one subscribes to Paradigm I, then during times of difficulty the first impulse is to take care of one's self at the expense of the other, and during such times the relationship threads are not vital enough to hold the two together. This is reflected by appearances on TV talk shows such as Oprah and Donahue. As Carbaugh (1990a) noted, after intensive study of the Donahue show, "the presentation of the 'self' is the preferred communication activity" (p. 123). It is, in mainstream western cultures, taken for granted, not only that we have a 'self,' but that it is seen as normal to publicly present it.

The prevalence of Paradigm I is displayed in most studies of relationships. For example, the popular "social exchange" model rests on the assumption that you try to maximize profit in relationships (Roloff, 1981). Talk of profits, rewards, and costs connotes an image of investing in something not connected to you. If the payoff isn't high enough, you switch investments. Such views, of course, set difficult standards for relationships, because the prime value is *self-satisfaction,* not enhancement of the relationship. Lay persons who do not subscribe to Paradigm I often criticize those who do as "selfish," trying to make the point that there is an overemphasis on the self. It is a value question, of course, but it may be that our cultural stress on individualism has grown "cancerous" (Bellah et al., 1985).

Scholars who adopt perspectives such as social exchange (e.g., Roloff, 1981) are merely reflecting a prevailing Paradigm I view endemic to our culture. The choice of this perspective is to judge relationships from the standpoint of the viability of *individual* growth. It is said, "She is finding herself," not "The relationship is finding itself."

Before proceeding to the next paradigm, there is a common variation on the "Individual Selves Loosely Connected" Paradigm that is worthy of mention (see Levinger & Shoek, 1978). While the diagram appears different from Paradigm I sketched above, it does share the most basic assumption that the locus for understanding relationships is lodged in the separate individuals. Figure 2-2 illustrates another version of Paradigm I:

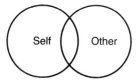

FIGURE 2-2.
Paradigm I variation.

The relationship context arises from the mere overlap of the two separate, autonomous selves who just happen to have enough in common to create a relationship. Such a view, while appearing to give more emphasis to the relationship elements, still rests on the assumption of two discrete selves as the starting point. After all, all the selves have to do is pull away, and the relationship withers to nothing.

To move from these paradigms of the self as loosely connected is very difficult and "awkward and confusing" (Gergen, 1991, p. 240). It is easier and less of a stretch in our dominant U. S. culture to continue to see self and other as only minimally interdependent. And the attendant communication behaviors are often a Monologue Of The Self—telling stories, regaling others with our individual exploits (individually taking full credit ourselves for anything positive that happens to us). As Yum (1988, p. 376) says, "each communicator is perceived to be a separate individual engaging in diverse communicative activities to maximize his/her own self-interest."

Across the Postmodern Divide.[2]

- "Identity is combined in a context of relationship" (Gilligan, 1982)
- "Without others there is no self" (Gergen, 1991, p. 178)
- "Finding oneself is not something one does alone" (Bellah et al., 1985, p. 85)
- "We appear to stand alone, but we are manifestations of relatedness" (Gergen, 1991, p. 170)
- "There is no more monstrous punishment for a person than to be thrust into society all by himself and left absolutely unnoticed by all its members" (Watzlawick, Bevin, & Jackson, 1967, pp. 18–19)

Writers in the postmodern era are challenging the notion of independence and individualism that is so deeply ingrained in the American psyche and treated as truths by many (Sampson, 1989; Stewart, 1991). By definition, postmodern approaches call attention to "constructedness"—the recombination of elements (Gitlin, 1989). In terms of relationships, a postmodern approach goes beyond assumptions of a linear order (Gitlin, 1989).[3] We begin to see people as "forming" and "reforming" their selves within each relationship.

---

[2]See Borgmann's (1992) book with a similar title for treatment of some of the macro issues of postmodernism.

[3]Postmodernism is a very large and complex topic, especially regarding art and literature. For our purposes, discussion of relationships, this brief foray is necessarily very limited and incomplete. For another application to communication, see Albrecht and Bach (in press).

When you begin to observe people talking about themselves, for example, they will speak as if they are more isolated and arbitrary and separate than they really are (Bellah et al., 1985, p. 21). It may well be that our individualism has gone rampant and become cancerous, but at a minimum, our individualism propels us to not see the relational forces that shape us. But most of us raised in the West see the entire goal of life to become a "self-sufficient" person, not bounded by relationships and contexts. The very meaning of life for most Americans is to "become one's own person," to in a sense "give birth to oneself." (Bellah et al., 1985, p. 83). Individual achievement is the final barometer of growth, and we see the lack of establishing a separate identity as a deficit (Slugoski & Ginsburg, 1989).

Of course, as one leaves home, moves away, establishes a separate identity, it is easy to overlook the tremendous social support for such an exploration. Even those breaking free from the family and community still have support and nurturance—from new friends, from romantic partners, from teachers and mentors, and from others. As Bellah et al. note, "our sense of dignity, worth, and moral autonomy of the individual is dependent in a thousand ways on a social, cultural, and institutional context that keeps us afloat even when we cannot very well describe it" (1985, p. 84).

The postmodern view of self suggests that the very notion of "self" is not correctly conceived—the self is not an independent, findable, essence whirling through life unconnected to others. As Gergen notes, "In the postmodern world there is no individual essence to which one remains true or committed. One's identity is continuously emergent, re-formed, and redirected as one moves through the sea of ever-changing relationships. In the case of 'Who am I' it is a teeming world of provisional possibilities" (1991, p. 139). Such a view insists that we focus on the interconnections and interdependencies that have created the "self" we like to see as independent. As Wilden says, " 'do your own thing' is a useful metaphor to play with when the things are doing you" (1980, p. 2).

This move to the *relational self* takes a step back, examining the cultural assumptions and blind spots regarding how we see ourselves as individualistic and separated. We change from the "isolated" to the "relational" self with our focus. In this view, we only have the "self" because we have others who support that view—your very definition is cast within a broader framework of family, friends, lovers, work, and the broader culture.

The postmodern view of a relationally connected self is similar to how we see the conscious and unconscious mind. When we speak of the mind we usually imply the conscious ego—that everyday pattern of thinking we know as the mind. Yet the most powerful aspect of the mind is the unconscious—the aspects we do not control and of which we cannot be aware. Similarly, the individualist stress in our society finds us talking about each one's personality as if it is a findable, immutable entity. Yet the backdrop—the entire network of connections and relationships—just like the unconscious, is probably the most profound source of influence on us. Our very definition of "self" is done in a culture that tells us that is how to make meaning out of our lives and "self."

The deconstructionist position on these conceptual issues questions the individual as a transcendent entity—and specifies that the notions of the person as autonomous and self-contained are an illusion (Sampson, 1989, p. 3). In a very real sense the "selves" become manifestations of the relationship, thus "placing the relationships in the central position occupied by the individual self for the last several hundred years of Western history" (Gergen, 1991, pp. 147–148).

The influence of postmodern thinking is reflected in the next two paradigms, which specify the move from an individualistic perspective to a more broadly conceived notion of self, other, and relationship.

PARADIGM II: THE EMBEDDED SELF

With a fundamental shift in thinking we move from the individual as a separate, non-affected self to a self embedded within relationships. Note in Figure 2-3 the essential self cannot be described outside a relationship context.Thus, though you might talk about the self, its very definition hinges upon the relational context from which it arises. Research conducted from the Paradigm II perspective assumes that "studying individual members of dating couples does not do justice to the dynamics of their interpersonal relationship. Simply providing a detailed explanation of the structure and function of an individual person will not lead to an adequate account of social behavior and the structure of the social order" (Senn, 1989). Moreover, it will not give much insight into the "self."

Paradigm II explains self-esteem by seeing it composed as a "system of mutual exchanges," dependent on others for its creation and maintenance, where self and other are in a sense "created by" one another. Or as one set of researchers say, "the person acts as if some or all aspects of the partner are partially the person's own" (Aron et al., 1991, p. 242). As Wilber (1983, p. 272) says, "the identity of 'I' is possible solely through the identity of the other who recognizes me, and who in turn is dependent upon my recognition." In a sense we spin the self within the relationship web, and the relationship web is spun with the other. The self is developed always within the context of the other (Bellah et al., 1985). Or, in the terms of the deconstructionists, there is an "interpenetration" of the society (relationships) and the individual (Sampson, 1989). Such views bring with them a very different research agenda than Paradigm I, such as the call for examining "Relationship Constellations" as a needed step in our understanding of personal relationships (Wilmot & Sillars, 1989).

Paradigm II assumes that relationships serve a transcendent function. The relationship itself is treated as an entity; it has an identity (Hecht, 1993). If one assumes that

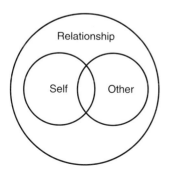

FIGURE 2-3.
Embedded self.

the relationship has an identity, it, like the participants, can have influence. It is created by the participants yet goes beyond them. Stewart (1990, p. 26) has called it a "Spiritual Child" of the two people. And just as when two people create a child, the child comes to have a life of its own. Such a creation by two people, of course, can becomes destructive as well. If the relationship takes on negative power and is damaging for the individuals, it can become a "Demonic Child" that devours the parents. Whether becoming a positive or negative force, the relationship has become an entity both arising from and existing separately from the two participants. Paradigm II allows us to see that the relationship is the overarching connective force that allows self and other to experience somewhat permeable boundaries. Relationship allows the overlap of selves.

Relationship participants who subscribe to some of the variations of this major Paradigm II would talk about "our relationship" being in trouble, suggesting that the relationship has an entity or even self-esteem. They also likely stress collaboration, the interweaving of self/other into ongoing complex patterns of unfolding. When they have faith in the relationship and believe in it, especially if they think it has a future, then they have a relationship (Leatham & Duck, 1990).

Some typical differences in male/female communication could arise from different paradigms of relationships, with males more often relying on a Paradigm I position and females using a Paradigm II stance. It has been clearly demonstrated that females do value and monitor their relationships more than do males (Baxter & Wilmot, 1985). And in terms of maintenance or rejuvenation, females more often see the need for proactive relational work and are more motivated to invest energy to maintain the relationship (Dindia & Baxter, 1987).

Participants, when a relationship becomes "suffocating" or "constricting," are ascribing power to the relationship entity itself, noting its impact on their choices, often explaining how they can't move or make independent choices. Critics of marriage would ascribe considerable power to the relationship itself; thus one should avoid or jettison a marriage because of its power to deform the self (Guggenbuhl-Craig, 1977). And when participants begin to feel that the relationship can bring lasting happiness and cling to the relationship, they are assuming that the relationship has a real findable essence (Chodron, 1990).

Paradigm II adherents would argue for relationship rejuvenation work per se, because the relationship has a definable essence of its own that transcends the two individuals and with relationship improvement comes a different set of forces on the self.

One perspective that both stretches our current thinking and still adheres to a findable self is the dialectical perspective. It is a type of Paradigm II thinking and, while not moving all the way to Paradigm III, does challenge some of the assumptions of the independence of self and other.

The Dialectical Perspective

It is an illusion to think you can have right without left, good without evil, women without men, the rose without the garbage. (Murdock, 1990, p.171)

At almost any level of human experience, contradictory and opposite elements occur. American society, for instance, supports dichotomous values. On one hand, materialism is valued; on the other, moral behavior is stressed (Rushing & Frentz, 1978; Fisher, 1973). On the individual level, our minds support contradictory abilities. The left hemisphere of our brain gives us the ability to think logically and methodically in a step-by-step fashion, and the right hemisphere lets us perceive totalities, the gestalt, in metaphoric and analogic terms (Watzlawick, 1978).

The dialectical approach to relationships stresses that phenomena that appear to be opposites are bound together, and that there is a dynamic *interplay* between such opposites (Baxter, 1984, 1994). It presumes that polarities that appear unconnected in nature mutually presuppose one another (LaGaipa, 1981). Heraclitus taught that there is a "dynamic and cyclic interplay of opposites" and that there is a unity of opposites (Capra, 1983). Or as Werner & Baxter (1994) note, there is a dynamic tension between unified opposites.

An example of recognizing connectedness where one previously saw opposites comes from Jim, the son of one of my colleagues. When he was 7 he was asked, "What is the similarity between the first and the last?" He replied, "They are opposites, but they are related. Because if you push on the first kid in the line, the last one also has to move back."

Those of us raised in western cultures are often not sensitized to thinking in terms of the dialectic of opposites. In the west we tend to think in either/or fashion rather than in terms of both/and (Sampson, 1989). Perceiving the unity of opposites allows one to see that "each person is both male and female possessing qualities of both maleness and femaleness; an event is both good and bad; food is both sweet and sour; a person is both weak and strong" (Smith & Williamson, 1977, p. 170). We pay for the exactitude of our factual language with the price of being able to speak from only one point of view at a time. We often deal with the world in a dualistic way, which sets us apart. Even "dealing with the world" presumes we can be separated from it (Dell & Goolishian, 1981). Our cultural "frame" promotes the view that elements are opposite and not connected, rather than seeing the dialectical interrelation of opposites.

The dialectical perspective always insists on seeing the end-points as interconnected. For example, if you put (1) individual autonomy on one end and (2) relational connectedness at the other end, they are not only opposites, they are part of an "interdependent unity" as well (Werner & Baxter, 1994; Baxter, 1994a). Relational connectedness presupposes the existence of unique identities, and connectedness with others is necessary "in the construction of person's identity as autonomous" (Werner & Baxter, 1994, p. 351).

The dialectical viewpoint brings fresh insight into how personal relationships operate. For example, the dialectical perspective emphasizes *process and contradiction* (Baxter, 1990). Thinking dialectically brings the presence of the paired opposites into focus and looks at growth and change—how relationships grow over time. Basically, rather than seeing relationships as moving in a linear line toward improvement (or toward dissolution), the dialectic perspective lets us focus on the swings—now close, now far—in all relationships. Even the healthiest relationships are characterized by instability and detachment at times (Masheter & Harris, 1986).

The prime polar opposites in relationships have been identified variously by many authors (see, for example, Rawlins, 1992, 1994; Masheter & Harris, 1986). Baxter (1990, 1994a, 1994c) has identified some of the opposites in personal relations, and they will be used for purposes of illustration, though other writers in the dialectic framework identify slightly different lists of the opposites (see, for example, Rawlins, 1992, 1994; Hatfield & Traupmann, 1981; Spitzberg, 1993a; Werner & Baxter, 1994).

Before discussing the dialectic tensions occurring in relationships, we need to note that the dialectical tensions are presupposed to exist both (1) external to the relationship and (2) internal to the relationship. External dialectics are when, for example, a couple faces the contradiction between autonomy as a couple and integration with others as a couple (Werner & Baxter, 1994). Another external tension would be between (1) being a marital couple and (2) in a parenting role (Cissna, Cox, & Bochner, 1990). Internal dialectics are the focus for the rest of our discussion—they are the forces that occur internal to all relationships.

The most frequently cited set of opposites in personal relationships is that of *autonomy–connection,* or stated another way, the tension between separateness and connectedness, or between *me* and *we,* or, if you prefer, *independence* and *interdependence.* Regardless of your chosen label, the two are dialectically bound together, because as one of them is stressed in a culture, the other is "always hauntingly there in the background" (Fisher, 1973). For example, each person in a close relationship wants (1) connection mutuality with the other, and (2) separate "breathing space" for the self independent of the other. Pat's personal choices reflect this well. She is in a committed romantic relationship with Sol; while they were living together, she found herself always "wanting to get away"—to get more separateness. When she moved into her own apartment, she had the "breathing space" to allow herself then to be closer to Sol, or as she said, "Now that I know who I am, I can deal better with the two of us!" Such opposites between me and we also occur on the organizational level. As Peters and Waterman (1982) wrote, we seek self-determination and, simultaneously, security with others. People often have ongoing struggles in their jobs over whether to "adopt the organization as your identity" or "develop your own identity" separate from the job. Both of these reflect the classic me–we dichotomy.

The dialectical tension between autonomy and connection is manifested in numerous ways. In the 1970s for example, the emphasis was on *me,* with many writers arguing for "looking out for number one." People were encouraged not to let their relationships bind them, to discover themselves, assert themselves, and downplay their dependence on others. We were in an age of narcissism, with enhancement of the self being the goal for many. Of course, this came on the wake of a previous social emphasis on the connection of people, downplaying the individual for the good of the relationship group.

The tension between autonomy and connection is also present within each relationship. In families, for instance, one of the main ongoing struggles is between the growing child becoming an individual and being loyal to the needs of the family (Bowen, 1965). In romantic relationships, "Everyone feels an intense conflict between the desire to be free and independent versus the desire to merge with others" (Hatfield, 1982). This "dynamic tension" is present and tends to have an ever-present influence on the relationship. The friend who drops out of sight for a few days, and the romantic part-ner who professes close, enduring love but then suddenly retreats, both illustrate attempts to deal with the opposites. As we get closer to the other, it can trigger a fear of being "swallowed," which causes a need for more autonomy. Some of the "crazi-ness" and unpredictability in close, intimate relations comes from the oscillations between autonomy and connection. As we get farther away, we miss the other, and when we feel at "one" with the other, we sense a loss of the self. These alternating pat-terns of close–far respond to the dialectical nature of opposing needs in a relationship for autonomy and connection. Of course, the issue is made sharper by the fact that the two people probably feel the polarities at different times and with different intensity. Just as your romantic partner is trying to "get some space," you may feel the need for more closeness and intimacy, or vice versa. Robin, one of my students, said it this way: "He wants to be closer, I back off. He tries harder, I move farther. He gives up, I move closer. He responds, I back up, and on, and on it goes." Such contradictory needs, felt at disparate times by the partners, fuel the inherent difficulty in close personal relations. Both ends of the dichotomy are true—we need to be independent from others and we need to have a connection with them in order to be fully human.

A second dialectic identified in personal relations is that of *expressiveness–protec-tiveness,* between openness and closedness. In all our relations, we have needs to share information with the other and to withhold information from the other. Our relation-ships can be characterized as differing in terms of openness and closedness, and open-ness is taken as the single most important quality in intimate relationships. Most of our relationships are, in fact, not close and intimate, and even among those we withhold some information (Bochner, 1982; Parks, 1982). On the other hand, intimacy and closeness are built by disclosure of important information. The tension between candor and restraint underlies our relationships, just as did the dialectic of autonomy and con-nection. Rawlins, in an intensive study of friendships, highlighted the expressive-ness–protectiveness dimension well (Rawlins, 1983). He found the contradictions implicit in all friendships because the person faces the contradictory tendency to pro-tect the self by restricting disclosure *and* to strive to be open by confiding in the other. Family members, friends, work associates, and romantic partners cope with the con-tradictory poles by a variety of means—emphasizing one pole over the other or oscil-lating between poles to balance out over time. When someone says, "You have to always be open and honest in all relationships," and another says, "You can't trust anyone with private information about yourself," each is stressing one pole of the dichotomy. Some people construct entire lives based on their feeling that one pole of the expressiveness–protectiveness dichotomy is preferable. For example, in many close relationships partners try to find out information by using "secret tests," a clear preference for using a closed strategy to try to get information (Baxter & Wilmot, 1984).

Rather than choosing one pole or the other, some people engage in an oscillation between the poles. A person who gets a divorce at age 30 often becomes totally dis closive with a brother, sister, or parent for a period of time. Once equilibrium is estab-lished, however, he or she then retreats from the openness and returns to not sharing much information. And as with the first dichotomy, each person's preferences for how to deal with opposites can run counter to the timing or desires of the other. While one person wants to share all, the other feels like retreating and being less open.

The third type of dialectical opposites in personal relationships is that of *pre-dictability–novelty,* or between stability and change. Some writers on interpersonal relations stress that we want to "reduce uncertainty" (Berger & Bradac, 1982). The opposite is also true—too much certainty is often avoided. We want relationships that have some stability—for continual flux is unsettling—but a boring relationship also is to be avoided. Many relationships, once they are defined, go on "automatic pilot," with little change occurring in them. In attempts to bring some predictability to our personal world, many of us define the relationship as a way to get some certainty. Saying "we are friends," or "we are married," are just two examples, for without some stability, you never know "where you are" with the other. However, without some risk and change, a relationship can become so predictable as to be boring. As with the other dialectical dichotomies, individuals have different solutions to the opposing needs. For given relationships, Lorraine may opt for complete stability and sacrifice excitement, change, and risk. Or Shelley may choose to have a series of relationships, each "risky" and full of change, and sacrifice stability. Of course, another option is to oscillate between stability and change in the same relationship. As the friendship becomes predictable, you throw some change and alteration into it. When the romantic relationship becomes too unpredictable, you get married in order to provide stability.

Coping with Dialectical Tensions

The three dialectics of autonomy–connection, expressiveness–protectiveness, and predictability–novelty underlie all our relationships. It may be there are other central dialectical forces yet to be identified that operate in the same fashion. Regardless of the particular dialectic, however, the participants in a relationship have some choices for dealing with them. We cannot "solve" the dialectical opposites, but we do have some options for dealing with them (Capra, 1983). Some even argue that the index of our adulthood is the ability to deal with the "contradictory demands" of relationships (Selman & Selman, 1979). Research is just beginning to illustrate how people cope with the tensions inherent in the dialectic nature of relationships.[4]

Emphasis and Cyclic Alternation   When one engages in dialectical emphasis, one of the poles is stressed over the other, ignoring that the opposite also exists in the background (Rushing, 1983). For example, when one emphasizes his or her autonomy, argues for complete openness in relationships, or acts totally predictable, one pole of each of the three dichotomies has been emphasized. Such choices, from a dialectical point of view, will lead to the emergence of the opposite later. As Baxter (1990) says, "in attempting to extinguish these contradictions by ignoring one of their respective dialectical aspects, relationship parties are likely to grow frustrated with the unmet need for the ignored aspect" (p. 87). The person who prides himself or herself on com-

---

[4]Note that, in the following discussion, the labeling originating with Baxter (1990) and followed by Masheter (1994) has been changed for ease of presentation.

plete autonomy, for example, later discovers that friends or close relations with family members do not exist and then must deal with loneliness—the opposite side of the coin. Similarly, if you are totally predictable, introducing no change into your most important relationships, the net result will be boredom with the relationship. Or, take my friend Simeon, who was living the life (as he described it) of a "free-wheeling bachelor," reveling in his autonomy. One morning he awoke and said to himself, "This is not working," and joined the Benedictine Monastery, where he has had a long and fruitful career serving others. He jumped from autonomy as a life course to connectedness literally in a day!

Research examples of how parties move on the dialectic tensions are provided by Baxter (1990). She found that, in college student romantic relationships, people who reported the dialectic pulls of autonomy–connection (interdependence) have two major ways of coping. Most frequently they reported "cyclic alternation," moving from one pole to another, from autonomy to connection. As one student reported, "We kind of kept floundering around together . . . drifting towards each other and drifting apart again . . . kind of a cycle" (Baxter, 1990, p. 80). With ex-spouses, Masheter (1994) discusses one woman who moved from being an abuse victim to planning a divorce—swinging from the connection end to autonomy.

Cyclic alternation can also be evident on a more macro level. Often, gray-haired college students (from age, not stress) often say, "I finally decided to do something for myself after so many years of serving others." One of my students was quite dismayed because her mother decided to go to college, too—and to the same school as the daughter. As she said, "I didn't expect her to strike out on her own, and worse yet, to come *here*. I'm supposed to be independent of her, and here she is moving to *my* town."

The second most frequent coping strategy with autonomy–connection was when they legitimated only one of the contrasts (dialectic emphasis). As one male respondent said in response to autonomy–connection, "We decided, well, we're going to give this a shot" (meaning they were committing themselves to the connection or relationship) (Baxter, 1990, pp. 80–81).

In terms of coping with the dialectic of openness–closedness, Baxter (1990) found that emphasis of one pole occurred the most often, resulting in total openness (which was the most common) or total closedness. And, Masheter (1994) found ex-spouses moving to one end and not discussing some topics, which allowed for the same type of emphasis.

Finally, in dealing with predictability–novelty, people would emphasize one pole and go through cyclic alternations, swinging one way then another (Baxter, 1990).

While more research will eventually discover if there are regularized patterns of coping with the tensions, we do know at this time that, during the initial stages of development of a relationship the tension of openness–closedness is mentioned more often by respondents than the others (Baxter, 1990) and that, during the subsequent stages of development, autonomy–connection and predictability–novelty were reported with increasing frequency. With more detailed work, we may well discover that the methods of coping with the tensions show variation across relationship types and across time in a given relationship.

Pseudosynthesis, Reframing, and Relational Transcendence   This second clus-
ter of coping strategies all share a conceptual attempt to deal with the dialectical opposites. First, as the scholars Fisher (1973) and Rushing and Frentz (1978) have noted,
"pseudosynthesis" can occur when the two disparate elements are "brought together
effortlessly, glossing over their inherently contradictory nature" (Rushing, 1983).
Someone who says, "Well, I can be independent, and so can you, and we still can be
close to one another all the time," is engaging in pseudosynthesis. Refusal to see the
power of the opposing forces can, of course, seem like a viable alternative, but from a
dialectical point of view, the opposites are still operable. The net result will be an
unclear accommodation—neither will the individual needs be met nor will the need for
connection or community be satisfied.

Finally, reaffirmation of the contradictory nature of relationships is one method for
dealing with the three dialectics. In using reaffirmation, one recognizes the opposites
and believes that they are truly contradictory and cannot be easily explained away
(Rushing, 1983). In reaffirmation you expect the relationship to oscillate between the
two poles on each of the three dimensions, and you see that as a natural process. You
might, for instance, say, "Well, when times are stressful at school, you can't expect to
be close and helpful—but once vacation comes, we can get back together again." You
see the relationship in a state of dynamic tension between the poles and see continual
fluctuation as bringing the balance (Capra, 1983). Put another way, you see that relationships are not "fixed," that they do vacillate between contradictory poles, whether
those be autonomy–connection, expressiveness–protectiveness, or predictability–novelty. If in your judgment the relationship is moving too far toward one of the poles for
a period of time, you make an effort to move it in the other direction. Out of this new
balance of forces, you have essentially created a new "synthesis," which then sets up
forces for the next fluctuation. As Capra (1983, p. 131) says, a relationship arises from
the opposites, and the conflict between them "can never result in the total victory of
one side, but will always be a manifestation of the interplay between the two sides."

The second kind of mental rearranging comes in the form of "reframing," where one
attaches new meaning to the behavior. You literally transform the meaning of the opposites, in a way that brings more relational satisfaction. Baxter (1990) found that, for
romantic relationships, reframing was positively associated with relationship satisfaction for the autonomy–connection and predictability–novelty contradictions. Masheter
(1994) cites an example of ex-spouses who move from predivorce combativeness into
postdivorce cooperativeness. When people "reframe" their relationship from "spouses"
to "joint parents of the children," for example, it allows them to deal with the tensions
in a new way. Divorce mediators often help couples redefine their relationship as "co-
parents" or "businesslike partners" to help them deal with the postdivorce needs of
their children. Reframing, Baxter (1990) notes, was not used much by her respondents
because of the short relationship histories and may be more prevalent among relationship participants who have longer relationships.

The other conceptual movement to deal with dialectic tensions like the autonomy–connection dialectic is to see relationships as serving a *transcendent function.*
How we are "together" is through the relationship (Wilden & Sands, 1980)—"this WE
embraces the I and the THOU" (Arnett, 1986, p. 158). Seeing relationships as transcen-

dent allows us to overcome the sharp distinction between self and other (Bellah et al., 1985) and begin to see our common destiny—that the "self" and "other" are inextricably tied. And as self and other float away, then back, the common relational bond allows for such movement and change over time. On way to conceptualize such transcendence is diagramed again in Figure 2-4, which shows self and other "contained" by the relationship and identical to the embedded self described earlier.

Imagine that the line encircling self and other is elastic, allowing self and other to be at different distances from one another. Note the differences in closeness and overlap between the two persons in the figure. This week Sam and Sally are fairly close and coordinated; next week they have a spat over use of the car and drift a bit farther apart but are still connected by the relationship. The following week, they are very close and intertwined. Such a view captures how Chris Baril, one of my students, and his wife see their relationship as "encompassing" their individual selves, with the relationship being fluid and moving upward. So as they each change individually, the relationship has fluid boundaries that adjusts to accommodate their changes, sort of like a big glob of fluid that contains them but doesn't constrain them. The relationship, by being flexible yet providing some boundaries and form for their connectedness, allows each of them to grow and change while staying in the relationship—it serves a "transcendent function" for the tension between autonomy and connectedness.

One final note regarding the transcendent function of relationship. It has been noted by Chang and Holt (1991) that, ironically, the social harmony of Chinese society is in fact a means through which the Chinese achieve their individual goals. If one maintains social harmony (connectedness), then one is able to pursue individual goals within that frame, individuation within a relational context.

One of the prime advantages of viewing relationships from a dialectical framework is that the natural fluctuations can be seen as normal, useful, and temporary processes, and that each individual has a stake in (1) his or her interests, (2) the other's interests, and (3) the relationship as the interplay between the two. Furthermore, seemingly impossible, contradictory views can be held to be true. For example, which of the following do you believe?

FIGURE 2-4.
Relationship as a transcendent function.

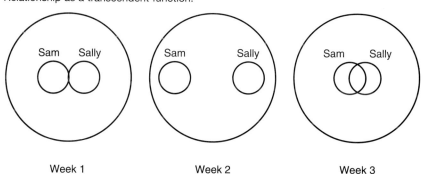

Week 1   Week 2   Week 3

1 "Get yourself together first, then get into a relationship with someone."
2 "You improve yourself through your important relationships."

Is one of these more true than the other, or are they contradictory yet equally provocative beliefs, both of which can be true?

One final note. It may be that the entire notion of dialectic is dependent upon a western mind-set that tends to divide things. For example, young children first developing language in the United States often say *mine* among their first few words. Such views imply we are separated from others and that our interests are not the same as those of others. In some cultures, the forces at work may be different. Eiji, a native Japanese student in one of my classes, expressed it this way:

> I have been culturally trained not to aggravate any existing relationship one has. The Japanese society, it seems to me, emphasizes among others, the following two things: (1) There is no such thing as dichotomy, and (2) anyone you see suffer today can be the image of yourself tomorrow. The result is that people in a relationship behave in a certain way: They intuitively pay attention to the dynamics of the relationship and are ready to put themselves in the shoe of anyone they are dealing with at any moment.

Our understanding of dialectics is in its infancy, and further work on the fundamental forces of relationships will clarify their nature. Until then, dialectical tensions can be recognized as one form of relational intricacy that helps explain the complexities of relationships.

PARADIGM III: NONSEPARABLE SELF/OTHER/RELATIONSHIP

> A human being is part of a whole, called by us the "Universe," a part limited in time and space. He experiences himself, his thoughts and feelings, as something separated from the rest—a kind of optical delusion of his consciousness. This delusion is a kind of prison for us, restricting us to our personal desires and to affection for a few persons nearest us. Our task must be to free ourselves from this prison by widening our circles of compassion to embrace all living creatures and the whole of nature in its beauty. Albert Einstein (1954)

Whereas Paradigm I and II both represent a separable self (though with differing degrees of overlap with the other), Paradigm III moves onto a view of the nonseparability of self/other/ and relationship. Rather than taking the individual as a sacred and separate entity to be preserved and nurtured at the exclusion and in isolation from others, it challenges the very notion of an identifiable "I." And, beware, it is no easy jump for those with a Cartesian bent! Here is how David Mace, the pioneer of couples' enrichment work, perceives his work:

> Was its foundation the individual? It seemed so at first, but I had to abandon that view. An individual human being has not significant separate existence, but is the product of a complex and elaborate system of interactions with other individuals. (Mace, 1985, p. 81)

When we peer at self from this third paradigm, we see self, other, and relationship so inextricably tied that to take care of one necessitates taking care of the other. Hanh

(1987) once noted, "I am, therefore you are," which can be extended. Examine the following statements and how they tend to stretch our concepts about the interrelation of self, other, and relationship. The first two are from Thich Nhat Hahn (1987, p. 87) to which a third can be added:

I am, therefore you are.
You are, therefore I am.
Our relationship is, therefore we are.

In a word, we are constructed in our transactions with others. We are not something that exists before contact with others, we "come-into-being" in our transactions (Stewart, 1991; Baxter, 1994a). Such an approach suggests we go outside and observe our relationships, and that duality itself is an illusion. And while we cannot obviously wholly enter into another person's subjective world, neither can we be separate from it (Bugental, 1978). Yet, while rejecting the either/or aspects of self/other, Paradigm III embraces the essence of the interweaving of self/other/relationship. They are seen as *not* separable. As we try to move conceptually from the earlier paradigms and into seeing self/other/relationship fused, we can begin to see the changes in Figure 2-5 as reflecting changes in our concepts. Note how self, other, and relationship begin as separate, then become intertwined and integrated. Does this happen in real relationships? Some evidence suggests that it can. For example, Sillars and Zietlow (1993, p. 251), in studying marital couples across the life span, noted that young couples often focus their conversations on individual differences and separate identities, yet retired couples "focused extensively on shared activities, common interests and beliefs, similarities, communication together, and similar communal themes." A married couple of 30 years, if they are close, will often finish statements for one another, with each one representing the mutual reality; each "me" is only defined in the context of "we." In addition, recent work on intimacy suggests that a feeling of being "at one" with the other is one of its characteristics (Register & Henley, 1993). And in cultures such as Japan, where individualism is not taken as the desired end-state, husband and wife are viewed as "a unit fused into one body" (Kamo, 1993, p. 567).

Let's try yet another visual interpretation of the essence of Paradigm III. It could be represented as in Figure 2-6. Note that, as in Figure 2-5, the self, other, relationship demarcations tend to become fuzzy and blended.

FIGURE 2-5.
The nonseparable self/other/relationship.[5]

[5]Thanks to Betty Jo Maughan for suggesting this representation.

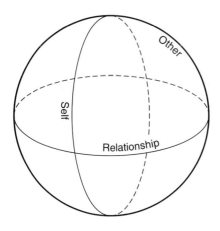

FIGURE 2-6.
Another version of Paradigm III.[6]

Adherents to Paradigm III would find themselves struggling not to default to the "I" but rather seeing self and other as inextricably tied. Instead of thinking, How can this relationship fulfill my needs, one would think, What can I give the other? (Chodron, 1990, p. 43). Relationship work would reflect a fundamental premise that it would not be undertaken to benefit "self" but would be chosen as a way to enhance relationship, other, and self, all interwoven. In a sense, we don't "do" relationships, they "do" us!

Such views, given that they do not align with our current cultural assumptions, necessitate some mental gymnastics. Researchers have yet to probe any of the variations on this theme. For example, in a culture bent on searching for the independent "I," how do individuals transcend that dominant perspective? The usual reaction to such a representation is that "it is impossible" or "you will lose yourself." Proponents, of course, would argue that the "self" is an illusion, a handy creation from our particular place in time, and that Paradigm III more accurately reflects what is happening in relationships—we just are unable to see it from our western perspective that anchors everything in the "self."

COMMUNICATION: CONJOINTLY CREATED

The three paradigms have dramatic impacts on the role we each see communication playing. Paradigm I thinking—two individuals as discrete units sending "messages" to one another—is probably the most dominant view in the United States today. Most of us think that (1) individual minds represent reality, (2) each person's individual reflections are communicated with his or her words, and (3) individuals use their words to represent the world as it is (Gergen, 1991). The prevalence of the individualistic focus of Paradigm I has us most often talk about the individual as a "relationless" being—moving through space and time as an independent unit that communicates "out" to others. Both in our culture at large and in some research studies in particular, commu-

[6]Thanks to Nicole Prevost for suggesting this diagram.

nication is treated as a static, linear, noninteractive event. For example, some research on persuasion still talks about the "target" of the message—as if that person can be reduced to a nonactive component of an event (Kharash, 1986). The prevalence of such views of how communication operate flows directly from Paradigm I thinking—that the independent, self-contained self is the center of what needs to be understood.

There are, of course, alternative ways to view the operation of communication in relationships. One can chose to view communication corresponding to the continuum from Paradigm I to Paradigm III. Our cultural focus has been so close to Paradigm I that we miss most of the richness and challenge of the other perspectives. Communication is most productively seen as a *conjoint reality,* created by two people in relation to each other. When we blind ourselves to the relational realities, we miss the dynamics of the interpersonal relationship (Senn, 1989). And though we have an impoverished language of relatedness, such an expansion of our view allows us to see the real power of communication.

Seeing communication conjointly, as the joint product of two persons in relation, opens our eyes to (1) the transformative potential of communication and (2) seeing dialogue, not monologue, as the heart of the process. Communication is transformative for both participants. Whether one is focusing on a business transaction, a family gathering, or someone in therapy, both participants in nonverbal and verbal connections experience some effects. At a minimum, even when one person is doing most of the talking, change happens because of the presence and actions of the listener. Often we hear about people needing to "get it off their chest"—and that "expression" is the key to personal change. Actually, we undergo significant personal change by expression *within a relationship.* One way to help heighten our awareness of "self talk" that brings about change is to see it as follows:

TRANSFORMATION = EXPRESSION + CONNECTION

It isn't just "getting it off your chest" that makes the difference, it is doing the expression in the presence of someone who validates, nudges, and assists you. People in crises don't just sit and talk to walls, they seek out family members, friends, priests, and counselors to have someone to listen to them.

As noted in the section on dialectical thinking, self and other develop over time within a relationship context. And the communication that occurs is less than perfect. Rather than two people verbally and nonverbally sending "accurate" messages about their feelings and thoughts to one another, we have two people generating meaning conjointly—and hoping for a productive development with the other. And, understanding is more elusive than often thought. Chodron says it well:

> How strange to think we completely understand another person! We don't even understand ourselves and the changes we go through. We don't understand everything about a speck of dust, let alone about another person. The false conception that believes someone is who we think he or she is makes our lives complicated. On the other hand, if we are aware that our concept is only an opinion, then we'll be much more flexible. (Chodron, 1990, p. 40)

We should, at a minimum, move from a view of communication as monologue to *communication as dialogue* (Stewart, 1991; Arnett, 1986). If we had a more rich relational vocabulary, we could describe communication as "relation-logue," but given our deep grounding in Paradigm I, taking communication as dialogue will suffice. The dialogic approach stresses the emergent, interdependent nature of communication—arising from the relationship between two persons. We respond to the other, not as an object, but as a cocreator of the communication event—not as an "it," but as a "thou" (Stewart, 1991; Arnett, 1986; Kharash, 1986). We stress connection with the other rather than individualism.

The contrast between monologue and dialogue can perhaps best be seen by giving specific examples. The following examples illustrate difference in talk between married couples. For some people, marriage is seen as a product of separate identities; for others, it is seen as a product of joint or interdependent relationship investment (Sillars, Weisberg, Burggraf, & Wilson, 1987).

Individual Talk

"You have your friends, and I have mine."
"You bitch all the time."
"I'm not good at communicating."
"Individual decisions are made individually."
"You're just a conscientious person."
"You have your things to do, and I have my things to do."

Joint Talk

"We enjoy the same things."
"We talk out disagreements so that we don't confuse the children."
"We talk all the time."
"Lack of affection stems from people marrying for the wrong reasons."
"If you're irritable and I'm feeling irritable, then that makes it worse."
(Sillars et al., 1987)

At a minimum, seeing communication through a dialogic lens, stressing the interdependence of both persons, opens up avenues for effective relationships, especially during times of conflict.

Our views of how self and other communicate and form relationships set in force a frame for what we see in communication events. With a Paradigm I view, you will default to seeing all difficulties in relationships as "caused" by persons' personalities. With a dialogic lens, coming from Paradigm II or III, you will experience difficulties between people as co-emerging, as them co-creating the reality that occurs. As we travel through the various aspects of relationships and communication in the subsequent chapters, you will hopefully be sensitive to the framework being advanced—that of a dialogic, "all in it together" perspective.

3

THE EBBS AND FLOWS OF RELATIONSHIPS

Peggy was in her office when Cathy, the supervisor, walked in and sat down. Cathy began the conversation by saying, "Peggy, you know we value you here, but you are just not doing the writing work the way I want it done." As Cathy critiqued Peggy's writing style, Peggy came to tears, stood up, and left the room by saying, "I just can't talk when I'm crying. I'll talk to you later." The next day Peggy telephoned and resigned.

Peggy's coworkers were shocked when they heard of the disruption in the office. Things had seemed just fine; then all of a sudden they heard Peggy had resigned. Over the next 10 days, friends of Cathy's got involved, Peggy sought counselling and took a trip with her husband to the coast, and finally Peggy and Cathy began discussing the details of the work situation. After 2 weeks, Cathy asked Peggy to return to work. She did, but only three-fourths time. Her duties were changed, and Cathy took over the disputed writing job that had caused the difficulty. The fellow workers were relieved that Peggy was coming back.

Such twists and turns in relationships are more common than not. Romantic partners "break up," then are back together the following week; a family member swears he will *never* be close to his sister, then 2 years later he is spending the fourth of July with her; and friends drift in and out of one another's lives.

Relationships have many paths and trajectories, yet most models for explaining relational growth and decay impose a linear, step-by-step view on the process. These mechanistic views of relationship development and dissolution tend to blind us from seeing the ongoing dynamism inherent in most relationships. Most models of relationship growth and decay:

1 Presume our relationships develop systematically and incrementally.

2 Focus on the initial stages (how people meet, how they begin conversations, etc.) and on the stages of dissolution (the events that lead to termination).

3 Assume that movement towards more closeness or movements toward dissolution are more linear, sequential, and incremental than people actually experience them as being.

A CREEPING INCREMENTALISM MODEL

As Baxter and Bullis (1986) note, two of the most useful and well-known models of incremental development and dissolution are those by Altman and Taylor (1973) and Knapp and Vangelisti (1992). For example, Knapp & Vangelisti specify that "movement is generally systematic and sequential" and "forward or backward", imposing some order on the development and dissolution of relationships.

There *are* some times when a step-by-step, predictable pattern unfolds. For example, telephone openings follow ritualized formats (Hopper, 1989a; 1989b), and the interaction of strangers shows "more predictable patterns of talk" than the spontaneity of intimates (Hopper & Drummond, 1992, p. 186). Similarly, the initial stages of relationships tend to be more regularized than an ongoing relationship that is already formed. Kellerman, for example, studied the conversational topics during initial conversations. She found that, in initial conversations, people use memory organization packets (MOP); they see regular sequences of topics. Figure 3-1 displays the initial conversation MOP for people. These are the topics that are typically recognized in the early stages of a conversation with someone. In a typical conversation, you would begin with "greeting" (#1 bracket) and not then jump to evaluating the encounter (#6 bracket). Rather, you would more or less move sequentially down the topics.

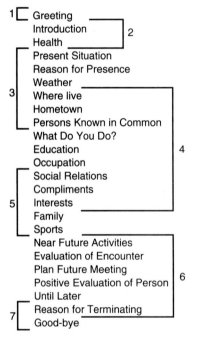

FIGURE 3-1.
Informal initial conversation MOP.
Source: Kellermann, K. The conversation MOP II. Progression through scenes in discourse. *Human Communication Research, 17,* 3, 388. Figure 1, copyright © 1991. Reprinted by permission of Sage Publications, Inc.

Each "bracket" (#1–7) is a subset that is linearly ordered. Within each subset are dialogue options. For example, when you are in the third subset, you might talk about the present situation, the reason why you are there, the weather, where you each live, hometown, or persons you know in common (Kellerman, 1991).

The step-by-step development of conversational topics in initial relationships allows the participants to incrementally move to more intimate topics over time, which was noted by Altman and Taylor (1973). When people are asked what they expect to happen in a developing romantic relationship, many of them see a step-by-step series of developments. Honeycutt and Cantril (1991), for example, asked participants who were in early-stage male–female relationships to list the actions they thought were typical in developing romantic relationships "when two people go from a first meeting to expressing a long-term commitment." Figure 3-2 lists the expected relational actions

FIGURE 3-2.
Expected relational actions for escalating Meta-MOP.

Relational Meta-MOP Action	Proportion of Subjects Mentioning Action
1. Meet for the first time (party, class, bar, etc.)*	.97
2. Ask for other's phone number and call later*	.57
3. Small talk* (discuss weather, school, etc.)	.69
4. Show physical affection** (kiss, hug, touch, etc.)	.43
5. Formal dating* (dinner, movie, etc.)	.92
6. Informal joint activities* (informal time spent together)	.64
7. Self-disclosure of intimate information*	.52
8. Overcome relational crisis (jealousy, uncertainty)	.13
9. Meet parents*	.26
10. Talk about future plans as a couple	.10
11. Verbal expression of love	.18
12. Bonding ritual* (give flowers, gifts, jewelry)	.30
13. Verbal commitment (stating a desire for an exclusive relationship)	.49
14. Cohabitation (living together)	.07
15. Sexual intercourse*	.26
16. Other-oriented statements* (stating interest in each other's goals, orientations, etc.)	.54
17. Marriage*	.28
18. Miscellaneous	.21

*Protypical meta-MOP actions in which 25% or more of subjects mentioned the behavior.
Source: Honeycutt, J. M., & Cantrill, J. G. Using expectations of relational actions to predict number of intimate relationships: Don Juan and Romeo unmasked. *Communication Reports, 4,* No. 1, 17, copyright © 1991. Reprinted by permission of the Western States Communication Association.

for an escalating relationship which Honeycutt and Cantril (1991) labeled "Relational Meta-MOP Action." This simply means a memory organization packet, the patterns imposed by our minds on events. The patterns reconstructed retrospectively by the subjects in Figure 3-2 are from cross-sex developing romantic relationships. So, just as in the sequence of topics in Figure 3-1, these activities in cross-sex romantic relationships are seen as ordered and sequential. Note the proportion of subjects mentioning each action, and that some of the actions occur infrequently. Even within an orderly view of relationship development, the sequence of actions is highly variable, with some of them mentioned by fewer than one-fifth of the people.

Knapp's and Vangelisti's (1992) model of relationship growth and decay suggests that relationships develop and decay according to stages of development. They further note that the stages are reflected by different conversational activities. The stages are:

1 *Initiating.* This stage includes small talk, opening lines, and initial reactions to the other (such as attractiveness as a romantic partner, usefulness as a business associate, and the like). The stage is dominated by the conventional modes of address: Greg says, "Hi, how are you?" and Brooke says, "Fine, and you?"

2 *Experimenting.* At this stage we begin to try to discover the unknown and engage in a lot of small talk in order to uncover topics and areas about the other that we can relate to effectively. Small talk serves these functions:

a It is a useful process for uncovering integrating topics and openings for more penetrating conversation.

b It can be an audition for a future friendship or a way of increasing the scope of a current relationship.

c It provides a safe procedure for indicating who we are and how another can come to know us better (reduction of uncertainty).

d It allows us to maintain a sense of community with other fellow human beings. Most of our social relationships do not progress past this point; we exchange basic information, maintaining the relationship at the experimenting level.

3 *Intensifying.* Just as the word suggests, during this stage the participants begin to delve into the deeper areas of each other's personality. Each person begins to expose more of his or her vulnerable areas to the other. A disclosure by Clyde that his father is an alcoholic, for instance, usually occurs in a more intense relationship than during social chitchat. Often intensification is so slow that we do not even recognize the deepening relationship. But sometimes deeper information is revealed that calls for a response at its level. In a class dealing with communication skills, the class members were engaging in small talk when one person turned to the instructor and said, "I tried to kill myself a year ago and was committed to the state hospital." The rapid move to intensification shocked the class into silence. During intensification, the participants begin to use special language, which is more informal, and begin to communicate in ways that are more coordinated to the other (Knapp, 1984).

4 *Integrating.* When a pair, such as business colleagues, brothers and sisters, romantic partners, family members, and friends, achieve a sense of "coupling," they have integrated. Integration is evidenced by a "we-ness," where the two act as a unit, develop a shared history, and merge their social circles. Part of each person is blended into the relationship. Once a pair has integrated, others will also treat them as a unit. If your college roommate is also your best friend, when one of you gets invited to a party the other will probably also be invited. Integrating is easily seen in the case of romantic couples. More decisions are made jointly because the two persons have an identity as a single unit.

5 *Bonding.* This final stage in development occurs when the couple undergoes a public ritual and formally contracts their relationship. Marriage is the most common form of bonding, yet in other cultures there are also public ceremonies that link friends in a committed relationship much like the friendship oath in ancient Greece. Other public acknowledgments of bonding are christenings in which godparents are named, adoptions, business partnerships, and ceremonies of unity for homosexual couples. The symbolic importance of bonding should not be underrated. For example, you don't "just get married." The public ritual moves the relationship to a new dimension. Witness the extreme disapproval that often greets gay and lesbian couples who invoke a public ceremony to celebrate and sanctify their relationship. All forms of public bonding serve important functions regardless of the culture. In the West, for instance, if a young person announces an upcoming marriage, others react with congratulations and talk about "taking the big plunge." Making a public commitment to share your future with another person is no small step. Many contemporary people (especially college students) resist the bonding stage longer in their romantic relationships than used to be the case. Some feel that the process of bonding will mean death to the relationship, and that if bonding occurs, each individual will "suffocate." Others delay bonding because they want to make a commitment that has the best chance of success. Still other people totally avoid bonding with another. Whether one engages in, delays, or avoids bonding, it is a significant stage in the development of a relationship.

6 *Differentiating. Differentiating* is the process of beginning the uncoupling, just as integrating was the process of coming together. Former joint endeavors take on an "I do this" rather than "we do this" connotation. The possessions of each take on a more individualized cast: It is "her" house and "his" camping equipment. The participants work to get more space from each other and establish separate identities. Especially when the bonding stage was rushed, the couple needs to differentiate from each other in order to feel a sense of individual identity. Differentiating, of course, does not necessarily lead to the termination of the relationship—it can perform the function of establishing more separate identities, so that the individuals then fuse back together again.

7 *Circumscribing.* During *circumscription* the communication becomes constricted, decreases in amount, and is restricted to certain topics. The communication tends to focus on more public and superficial topics with less breadth and depth. If one of the partners ventures into a topic, the other will close it off by saying something like, "Don't talk about that" or "It's not worth discussing."

8 *Stagnation.* As the pair moves through circumscribing, the next stage is *stagnation,* where the relationship is "put on hold" and discussion of the relationship becomes taboo. Married couples in the stagnation phase feel that they know exactly what the other will say, so there is no sense discussing important topics. Of course, with little effort going into the relationship, it does tend to wither away slowly. Parents and teenage children, as well as any other pairs, demonstrate stagnation by low levels of communicative exchange. The participants will often sit in the presence of the other for long periods of time and have nothing to say. This is painfully evidenced by the boredom and silence at some family holiday dinners.

9 *Avoiding.* In the *avoiding* stage the participants go out of their way to not be together. They spend energy actively making sure that they will not have to interact with the other person. Most often, the two try to avoid one another physically. I once observed a married couple sitting in a restaurant for 50 minutes. The man never once made eye contact with the woman or answered her questions. Finally, when he returned from the restroom, she moved to the chair next to his to capture his attention. He just raised his newspaper between the two of them and kept reading.

10 *Terminating.* During the terminating stage, one or more of the participants makes it abundantly clear that the relationship is over. This can occur, of course, in short-term relationships or in long-term commitments of many years. The participants signal the termination of open access and usually indicate what they want the future of the relationship to be. The typical lover lament, "She doesn't ever want to see me anymore," reflects a common termination condition.

Knapp and Vangelisti's (1992) contribution to the understanding of stages of relational development can best be seen by summarizing how they think participants move in and out of the stages. First of all, movement *is generally systematic and sequential.* When a relationship develops and dissolves, participants usually experience each stage in sequence. Knapp and Vangelisti (1992), however, say that the process is not linear and fixed, but that there are trends in this direction. As Altman and Taylor wrote, we can sometimes skip steps, but that makes the relationship more fragile at the core areas. For instance, if a man and woman meet, engage in close physical contact, "fall head and heels into love," and get married 14 days later, after the bonding experience they will probably have to recycle through the early stages in order for the relationship to survive the natural strains of living together. Similarly, committing oneself to a business partnership quickly will probably necessitate some effort to get to know the partner better.

Not only can people skip steps, but they can go through the steps in a very rapid fashion, an idea advanced earlier in this chapter. Many conditions lead to such developments. Summer romances are legendary, because the processes of moving to integration and bonding are speeded up. Facing the end of their time together, a couple will speed up the process of getting to know one another. Also, an external threat such as a crisis will often speed up the process of development through the stages.

Second, *movement may be forward or backward.* Movements forward are toward greater intimacy, those backward are toward less intimacy. As specified by Altman and Taylor (1973), we become more intimate and close by building on our past experiences together. And, of course, if a dyadic pair moves toward dissolution, they are moving "backward" toward less intimacy (even though the move may not be "backward" for the individuals).

Third, *movement occurs within stages.* As Knapp says, "There will always be a certain degree of instability associated with any stable relationship" (1984, p.2). As a result, being at one stage is not necessarily a sign that the next stage will follow automatically. Many relationships will encounter considerable variation within one stage. It is common, for example, for married couples to go through what Davis (1973) calls "reintegration ceremonies" as a way to supply some of the energy spent on accomplishing the original bonding. Similarly, work associates, friends, or any other set of participants can move in and out of these stages more than once. A counselor and client may move to integration each time they meet. Friends who reestablish contact also recycle through the early stages. There are even cases in which the entire sequence from development to dissolution is repeated more than once. One couple was married for 6 years, went through a divorce, and 18 months later remarried. Their experiences would, of course, not be the same the second time, but the stages might be speeded up. Quite an experience in relational stages!

Finally, Knapp and Vangelisti (1992) specify that movement *is always to a new place.* Our experiences with others are not repeatable—we cannot totally erase our previous interactions with them. A man and woman who begin as friends, become romantic partners, and then attempt to move back into friendship discover that it takes considerable effort to "move back" to where their relationship was initially. Even at that, the friendship can never be identical to what it was before. As time changes, so do our relationships.

The Knapp and Vangelisti model (1992) has its origins in the earlier book by Knapp (1984). His work was an extension of the Altman and Taylor (1973) book called *Social Penetration,* which specified the gradual, sequential movement toward intimacy as reflected in communication behaviors. The Knap and Vangelisti model (1992) allows us to (1) see the overall development of relationships across time, and (2) see the interconnection between "stages" of a relationship. It has the liability of a bias toward romantic relationships. It is unlikely that the model fits work relations, family relations, or even friendship as well as it does romantic relationships. And, further, it is probably most accurate in describing relationships in middle-class western culture. In other cultures, for example, the lack of verbal expressiveness would mean that a romantic couple could bond and live their entire lives without engaging in significant self-disclosure. A word of caution is in order, however, for the work by Gudykunst, Nishida, and Chua (1987) on Japanese students in American universities shows that they tend to increase disclosure as a relationship develops.

A PLATEAU/CHANGE MODEL

An alternative model, the "plateau/change" model, would argue that the creeping incrementalism does not capture the most important dynamism of relationships. As Bugental (1987) says, "linear reasoning and dependence on explicit formulation . . . do not accord with the reality of human subjectivity." Participants tend to experience relational change in terms of:

1 Periods of stability punctuated with times of rapid change. The "periods of stability" can be (1) a satisfying relationship or (2) a dissatisfying relationship, but in both cases the changes happen as "turning points" rather than incrementally and slowly over time. For example, Peggy at work in the opening example thought the supervisor was relatively pleased with her work until the day of the conversation. Romantic partners often feel that things are "fine" until some unfolding event challenges the relationship. For example, you may feel estranged from your family and move to another state; then, with the death of a parent or birth of a child, the entire family dynamic shifts as you move back home.

2 Relationships tend to oscillate back and forth, now closer, now farther (as we discussed in the dialectic section in Chapter 2), and over time, this may bring enough pressure for change. Gradual dissatisfaction with your job may eventually lead to your resignation, with many swings back and forth in your desire to stay or leave.

3 Relationships are continually changing, expanding, or contracting, even if the definition of the relationship is stable. When two people are "friends" for example, tremendous fluctuation in day-to-day communication patterns occurs without challenging their friendship. Likewise, families, work associates, romantic partners, and less personal relationships all tolerate considerable fluctuation.

4 Change in a relationship seems to be more a function of the *quality* of interaction rather than of the quantity (Baxter & Wilmot, 1983). As Duck (1988, p. 49) says, "We rise from plateau to plateau rather than up a continuously rising gradient of intimacy."

5 Change in relationship definition (lovers to enemies, strangers to friends, and others) follows these same criteria, except that the qualitative jump entails a change in the definition of the relationship. In terms of the Relationship Schemata Model, the communication indicators and criterial attributes diverge so much from the expected definition that "force" is placed on the relationship definition. For instance, two friends can have no contact for weeks usually with no problem (especially if they know they will meet again). Yet, if two friends part and don't have contact for years, at some point they cease to be called "friends" by the participants.

6 Relationships often develop a predominant mode around which they fluctuate, and most of our relationships do *not* have intimacy as their central point. If you do an index of all your relationships, you will find that most of them are not "intimate"—they do not manifest deep disclosure on the part of either person. As Wilmot and Shellen (1990) wrote, "friendships . . . stabilize at different levels" (p. 415). Most family relationships probably do not fit the mode of intimacy outlined by researchers, nor do many friendships and certainly not the multiple relationships we have at the work place. And as Neimeyer and Neimeyer (1985) note, nonintimate relationships differ in some major ways from intimate ones. Relationships both develop a central mode and fluctuate considerably in terms of actual communication behavior.

The work of Baxter and Bullis (1986) gave us a glimpse of how people operate in relationships by examining "turning points" in relationships. They asked participants what events, beginning with first meeting the other, led them to their current level of commitment in the relationship. Figure 3-3 chronicles the turning points mentioned. Note that the turning points are the times of maximum change; passion, for example, moves a relationship forward.

Relationships tend to have periods of stability and have "turning points" where the oscillations get to the point that some qualitative change occurs. The change happens

Supra-Types and Subtypes	Frequency (N = 759)
I. Get-to-Know Time	144
A. First Meeting	80
B. Activity Time	46
C. First Date	18
II. Quality Time	117
A. Quality Time	85
B. Meet the Family	17
C. Getting Away Time	15
III. Physical Separation	76
IV. External Competition	70
A. New Rival	39
B. Competing Demands	16
C. Old Rival	15
V. Reunion	57
VI. Passion	48
A. First Sex	23
B. First Kiss	10
C. "I love you."	9
D. Whirlwind Phenomenon	6
VII. Disengagement	46
VIII. Positive Psychic Change	42
IX. Exclusivity	34
A. Joint Exclusivity Decisions	23
B. Dropping All Rivals	11
X. Negative Psychic Change	29
XI. Making Up	25
XII. Serious Commitment	24
A. Living Together	13
B. Marital Plans	11
XIII. Sacrifice	23
A. Crisis Help	14
B. Favors or Gifts	9
XIV. Other	24

FIGURE 3-3.
Distribution of turning point types.
Source: Baxter, L. A., & Bullis, C. Turning points in developing romantic relationships. *Human Communication Research, 12,* No. 4, copyright © 1986. Reprinted by permission of Sage Publications, Inc.

due to something other than pure frequency of interaction—and all this happens within the current relational frame. Conville (1988) suggests that at times of transition, what changes are beliefs about themselves and the relationship. And of course, if such changes are large, they will eventually change the relationship definition. People experience turning points in other relationship types as well—two friends go through a flood together, two colleagues land their first book contract, or an employee receives a new job assignment. It is almost like a relationship is able to "contain" many changes until some noteworthy event pushes it to a new level.

People who experience the dissolution of a relationship also recall central turning points—the discovery of an affair, a lie ferreted out, someone getting ill, or one person moving out of state. Turning points in other relationships, such as work relations, family, and friend contexts, need systematic investigation too, so we can compare the differences and similarities of turning points across relationship types.

Which model, "creeping incrementalism" or "plateau/change," best captures both the communication and relational events that unfold? Since so much of the research depends on retrospective accounts by asking "what events led to the two of you to decide to marry," for example, participants may be creating both of these models as memory artifacts. We do not have sufficient research tracking people across time to know definitively. The longitudinal research we do have, such as that by Baxter and Wilmot (1983), tends to show more change and fluctuation in ongoing communication and feelings than is represented in most models of relational development. Certainly, as more research comes to bear, we find even more exceptions to the "clean" models such as uncertainty reduction—which specifies that, as people interact initially, they strive to reduce uncertainty, and that, as they reduce uncertainty, they are more attracted to one another (Berger, 1986). We now know, for example, that people prefer some uncertainty in their relationships, and we should not expect to find, in established relationships, a continual reduction of uncertainty (Duck, 1993; Kellermann, 1986). Uncertainty reduction, which arose out of studies of initial interaction, does not accurately capture the complexity of ongoing relationships; it illustrates the imposition of a linear, sequential, always-moving-toward-intimacy model that is not accurate for most of our relationships.

When we attempt to establish order or steps on the development, continuation, and dissolution of relationships, we run the risk of *not* seeing the more intriguing, challenging, and nonlinear aspects of their life course. The idea of clean-cut stages, while convenient for research, does not capture the complexity of relationship changes. Baxter (1984), for example, in studying heterosexual romantic relationship dissolutions, found that most people made many attempts to move toward dissolutions, recycling through phases many times. They were indirect, not telling their partner openly about their disaffection, but persevered, recycling many times until the relationship dissolved. The next most frequent dissolution scenario was when people, also indirectly, could make an attempted "repair" of the relationship, yet moved back into disengagement and eventually dissolution. This research relied on people's retrospective accounts; the relationships were already over. It is a fair guess that even more complexity would be evident if you could know that was happening day by day.

Regardless of your preference for viewing relationships—as changing incrementally or as going through periods of stability punctuated by rapid change—it is helpful to focus on the *process* over time rather than static views. The following perspective emphasizes the change and fluctuation of all relationships across time.

COMMUNICATION SPIRALS

A communication spiral occurs when the actions of each person in a relationship magnify those of the other. Communication spirals are evident almost everywhere, happening between humans, between us and other species, and among other species as well. A human–animal illustration should clarify the essential nature of spirals. My son Jason at age 3 saw a sleek, shiny cat. With the reckless abandonment of a child his age, he rushed at the cat to pet it. The wise cat, seeing potential death, moved out of Jason's reach. Not to be outdone, Jason tried harder. The cat moved farther away. Jason started running after the cat. The cat, no dummy about life, ran too. In a short 10 seconds from the initial lunge at the cat, Jason and the cat were running at full tilt. Luckily, the cat was faster and survived to run another day. Similarly, spirals occurs in many contexts:

- A child disobeys the parent, the parent acts more punitively and harshly, and the child becomes even more unruly.
- A parent and 22-year-old son embark on a foreign adventure for 2 months—just the two of them. As the trip draws to a close, they both note on the plane ride home how close they feel to one another, and how easy their communication has become.
- An employee may be quiet and not forthcoming to the supervisor, the supervisor puts pressure on him to talk, and he becomes even more silent.
- Two guys are sitting in a bar; one accidentally touches the other, the first pushes him, an insult is uttered, and within a minute the two are fighting in the street.
- A supervisor is dissatisfied with an employee's performance but doesn't tell the employee. The employee is complaining to others about the supervisor. Both the employee and supervisor keep doing more of the same—the employee withdrawing and talking to others, the supervisor getting more annoyed and not telling the employee. Then 6 months later during the performance appraisal, the supervisor says, "We are reorganizing the office, and you won't be needed anymore."
- Two close friends buy a cabin midway between their two towns. Each time they go to the cabin, their relationship is reinforced, and not only do they ski better, they enjoy one another's company more.
- Two romantic partners feel that the other is pulling away. So each shares less, harbors grudges, and spends less time with the other, until there is a fight during which they end the relationship.
- Two opposite-sex friends spend a lot of time with one another. As they spend more time, they exclude others and feel closer and closer. It gets to the point that they don't want to begin other friendships because this one is so fulfilling.

All spirals, whether building in a positive or negative direction, tend to pick up a momentum that feeds back on itself—closeness and harmony builds more closeness and harmony; misunderstanding and dissatisfaction creates more misunderstanding and dissatisfaction. The responses produce a lock-step effect in relationships (Leary, 1955; Kurdek, 1991). Quality relationships, like close friendships, develop an "end in themselves"—quality—and become self-sustaining (Rose & Serafica, 1986).

Communication spirals, whether they head in positive or negative directions, are characterized by these elements:

1 The participants' meanings intertwine in such a way that each person's behavior accelerates the dynamism of the relationship. The relational synergy builds upon itself in a continuously accelerating manner.

2 *Each* person's actions contribute to the overall dynamic. Whether you talk, retreat, engage, reinvest, or disinvest in the relationship, your communication (or lack of communication) directly impacts the other person, and vice versa. Each person reacts to the other (Kurdek, 1991).

3 Bateson (1972, 1979) noted long ago that spirals manifest either (1) *symmetrical* communication moves or (2) *complementary* communication moves. In symmetrical spirals, as Person One does "more of the same" Person Two also does "more of the same"—for example, two people shouting at each other. In complementary spirals, as Person One does "more of the same" Person Two does "more of the opposite"—Person A shouts and Person B withdraws in silence (Wilden, 1980).

4 At any given period of time, a spiral is contributing to the relationship in either generative or degenerative ways. Generative spirals promote positive feelings about the relationship and more closeness; degenerative spirals induce negative feelings about the relationship and more distance.

5 Both generative and degenerative spirals tend to continue accelerating until the participants check the movement by some action.

6 Spirals can be changed, their pace quickened or slowed, or the direction reversed by the participants' actions.

7 Based on the communication spirals that unfold, relationships expand, wither, and repeat patterns of close-far.

A diagram of the nature of spirals in Figure 3-4 shows how the dynamics of the communication for both persons tend to increase over time. Notice how the cycles get larger and larger across time—which is the nature of all communication spirals.

Generative Spirals

When communicative behaviors interlock to produce more positive feelings about the relationship, the participants are in a *generative spiral.* For instance, the teacher who can be open and accepting of students often experiences such spirals. Searching for the positive in a student and rewarding him or her appropriately can open a student up for teacher influence. The more genuinely the teacher relates to the student, the better the student performs; the higher the quality of his or her performance, the more positive the teacher becomes.

Generative spirals are obviously not limited to teacher–student relationships. A highly motivated worker illustrates the same ever-widening nature of spirals. As one improves working conditions, the worker's motivation increases, which cycles back and makes for an even better climate, which increases. . . .

In generative spirals, the perceptions of the partners become more productive and their mutual adjustments continue to build. In romantic couples, "love generates more

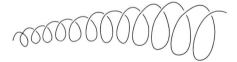

FIGURE 3-4.
A communication spiral.

love, growth more growth, and knowledge more knowledge" (O'Neill & O'Neill, 1972). The favorableness builds upon itself. Trust and understanding cycle back to create more trust and understanding. The relationship is precisely like a spiral—ever-widening.

We all experience generative spirals. The student who begins doing work of a high caliber earns better grades and becomes self-motivated enters a generative spiral. Each piece of work brings a reward (good grades or praise) that further encourages him or her to feats of excellence. And if conditions are favorable, the spiral can continue. Teachers who retrain and become more knowledgeable discover that they have more to offer students. The excited students, in turn, reinforce the teachers' desire to work hard so they can feel even better about their profession. In generative spirals, the actions of each individual supplies a multiplier effect in reinforcement. The better you do, the more worthwhile you feel; the more worthwhile you feel, the better you do. The effects of a simple action reverberate throughout the system. An unexpected tenderness from your loved one, for instance, will not stop there. It will recycle back to you and probably come from you again in increased dosage. A good relationship with your supervisor promotes you to want to please more, and the supervisor seeing your increased involvement, gives even more recognition to you.

Degenerative Spirals

Degenerative spirals are mirror images of generative spirals; the process is identical, but the results are opposite. In a degenerative spiral misunderstanding and discord create more and more relationship damage. As with generative spirals, degenerative spirals take many forms.

The inability to reach out and develop meaningful relationships is often compounded. The person who has reduced interest in others and does not form effective relationships suffers a lower self-esteem (because self-esteem is socially derived), which in turn cycles back and produces less interest in others. "The process is cyclical and degenerative" (Ziller, 1973). Or if one is afraid to love others, he or she shuns people, which in turn makes it more difficult to love. Also, such degenerative spirals often happen to people with regard to their sense of worth concerning work. People who have not established themselves in their profession but have been in the profession for a number of years may get caught in a spiral. They may spend time trying to appear busy, talking about others, or using various techniques to establish some sense of worth. Behavior that can change the spiral—working hard or retraining—are those least likely to occur. It is a self-fulfilling prophecy with a boost—it gets worse and worse. With each new gamut or ploy perfected (acquiring a new hobby, joining numerous social gatherings, etc.), the performance issues become further submerged.

A simple example of a degenerative spiral is the case of a lonely person. Lonely people tend to be less involved, less expressive, and less motivated in interactions. As a result, their partners in the conversation see the lonely person as uninvolved and less competent, and are less likely to initiate and maintain conversations with them. As a result, lonely people become further isolated from the social networks needed to break the cycle (Spitzberg & Canary, 1985).

Degenerative cycles are readily apparent when a relationship begins disintegrating. When distrust feeds distrust, defensiveness soars and the relationship worsens, and such "runaway relationships" become destructive for all concerned. In a "gruesome twosome," for instance, the two participants maintain a close, negative relationship. Each person receives fewer gratifications from the relationship, yet they maintain the attachment by mutual exploitation (Scheflen, 1960). When the relationship prevents one or both partners from gratifying normal needs, but the relationship is maintained, the twosome is caught in a degenerative spiral. Recent marital research demonstrates that, as love declines, negative conflict increases—a clear degenerative spiral (Lloyd & Cate, 1985).

Degenerative spirals, like generative spirals, occur in a variety of forms. A typical case involves the breakup of a significant relationship such as marriage. During a quarreling session one evening the husband says to the wife, "If you had not gone and gotten involved in an outside relationship with another man, our marriage could have made it. You just drained too much energy from us for our marriage to work." The wife responds by saying, "Yes, and had you given me the attention and care I longed for, I wouldn't have had an outside relationship." The infinite regress continues, each of them finding fault with why the other caused the termination of the marriage. The spiraling nature is clear. The more the wife retreats to an outside relationship, the less chance she has of having her needs met in the marriage. And the more the husband avoids giving her what she wants in the relationship, the more she will be influenced to seek outside relationships. One of the most common negative spirals between wives and husbands occurs when (1) the husband withdraws emotionally and (2) the wife expresses dissatisfaction to the husband (Segrin & Fitzpatrick, 1992).

Degenerative spirals are not limited to romantic relationships—they occur in all types. Parents and children often get caught up in spirals that create a dysfunctional system. The more dependent the child is on the parent, the more responsible and overburdened the parent is. And the more the parent takes responsibility for the child, the more this promotes dependence on the part of the child. It works like this: "One's actions toward other people generally effect a mirror duplication or a countermeasure from the other. This in turn tends to strengthen one's original action" (Leary, 1955).

There are many everyday examples of degenerative spirals. Take Jackie and John as examples. They started dating and went together for about 2 months; then the generative spiral reversed direction. John notes that Jackie is "emotional" and not "logical" in making her decisions about work time. Jackie, in turn, sees John as "controlling" and "cold and aloof," and as the days pass, they each see the other as more extreme. As John becomes more "logical," pointing out to Jackie how "anyone" would make a better decision about work times, she accuses him of "not understanding people." The spiral continues until the two of them stop seeing one another, with John telling his friends, "She is quite an airhead," and Jackie letting her friends know that John is an "automaton—not a real person." One former student of mine, Arlene Baltz, gave the following example of a degenerative spiral between two romantic partners. The spiral in Figure 3-5 shows how perceptions and communication accelerate over time. What

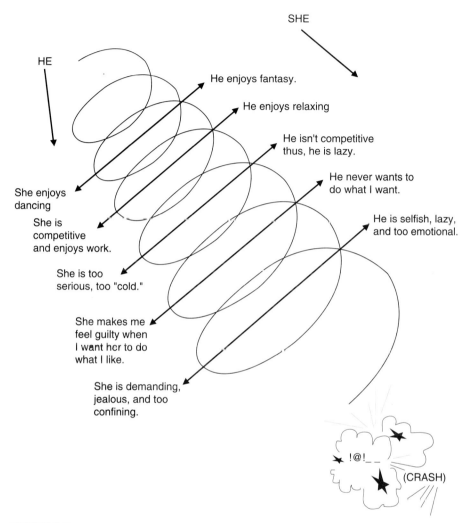

FIGURE 3-5.
A degenerative spiral.

begins as a descriptive statement of each about the other's communication becomes more evaluative and negative. Concomitantly, of course, each person acts in a more negative way because of his or her perception of the other's behavior.

Degenerative spirals come in many shades and hues; examples are literally endless. One thing is apparent. Unless degenerative spirals are modified or limited, they lead to the dissolution of the relationship—quitting the job, leaving the family, drifting away from the friend, or breaking off the romance.

Oscillations

Figure 3-5, although it accurately portrays the ever-increasing nature of both generative and degenerative spirals, has one major weakness. It gives the impression that a spiral, once begun, has no limits and continues unabated. All communication spirals, however, have boundaries. An individual's high self-concept promotes positive responses from others, which in turn enhances his or her self-concept. Such a generative spiral, however, has limits. If people's self-concept continues to be encouraged, they will eventually reach the stage at which they consider themselves superior to others. At that point, negative responses from others will go to work on them to lower their self-concept. Either a generative spiral will whirl away unchecked and break a relationship, or degenerative phases will occasionally slow it down. In either event, it is clear that generative spirals cannot continue unabated.

Degenerative spirals also have limits. A conflict, if unchecked or without redeeming features, will lead to the dissolution of the relationship. The employee can only stand so much disregard from the supervisor before resigning, and the supervisor has limits for toleration of poor performance. A person with a low self-concept can suffer only so much continuing maladjustment with others. A romantic pair caught in a degenerative spiral will eventually move back to less destructive behaviors or else dissolve the relationship. Even the special case of the "gruesome twosome" is similar. In this case the constant bickering and quarreling are still done within limits, albeit more negative and damaging than most of us would tolerate.

Dyadic relationships fluctuate between generative and degenerative spirals and at any one point in time can be typified as primarily generative or degenerative. Take the case of a marital dyad. The relationship begins as a generative spiral. The two are in love, and the mutually rewarding behaviors of both participants keep the system healthy. But because of more and more separation, for instance, degenerative spirals, rather than being an occasional event, become the norm. In Figure 3-6 the fluctuation of the relationship can be seen.

The relationship continues to disintegrate into ever-degenerative stages until the critical limit of the degenerative spiral is reached. As the relationship begins passing the critical limit, the patterns of degeneration become more and more difficult to arrest. After the relationship is on the verge of total collapse, the participants manage to reverse the direction of the relationship patterns. Through active participation in marriage enrichment programs, self-examination, and a job change, the couple is able to

FIGURE 3-6.
Generative and degenerative spiral phases of a marital dyad.

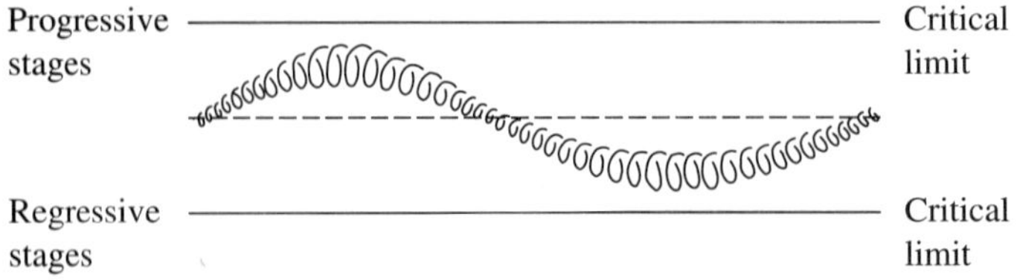

begin building generative spirals. And because they recognize some of the techniques for altering spirals, they can help other couples in their counseling programs to check the ever-damaging course of degenerative relationships.

The particular patterns of oscillation between the generative and degenerative stages of dyadic relationships vary across relationships. Figure 3-7 illustrates a case where another couple experienced many changes in the relationship over a 5-year span of time. This relationship was characterized by an initial generative spiral for the first 2 1/2 years, then a dramatic downturn, followed by an up-and-down pattern, until the final crash just before the termination of the relationship.

In another case an employee was not valued by her superior, yet she managed to build up a slow, ever-improving situation over an 9-year period. The progress of their work relationship is demonstrated visually in Figure 3-8.

This relationship example demonstrates that a dyad does not necessarily always wildly fluctuate between the extremes. It can move along with a predominant overall pattern that slowly changes over time. For example, it is amazing how much people can tolerate long-term negative interactions. Those in dissatisfying marriages and jobs, for example, may stay there for years, unhappy, adding their own venom to the system and just grinding away unproductively. We all know of people who endure an incredible amount of pain and distress, yet continue the predominant mode of the spiral, firmly stuck in destructive patterns. And at times, there is a "breakup to make-up cycle" where romantic partners recycle between making up and breaking up, but the cycle itself, while sometimes looking like it will move to a different predominant mode, keeps the participants less than satisfied overall.

And of course, a relationship can take on a predominant form for many years and then take a dramatic and unexpected turn. One of the common experiences of parents

FIGURE 3-7.
Oscillating spirals leading to termination.

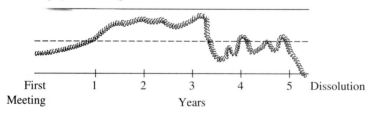

First Meeting   1   2   3   4   5   Dissolution

Years

FIGURE 3-8.
Spirals in a work relationship.

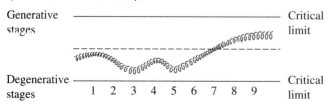

Generative stages   Critical limit

Degenerative stages   1 2 3 4 5 6 7 8 9   Critical limit

is that, when the last of the children leave home, there is a drop in satisfaction and a series of "rough times" while they work to redefine their relationship. After this transitional period, if they stay together, they often enter a period of very positive relations—they develop new hobbies, begin to spend more and more time together, and rekindle the flame that got started so many years ago. This pattern is illustrated in Figure 3-9.

Our relationships are always moving and changing, either toward more satisfaction or toward more distress. When people's behaviors interlock such that each one's behavior and view of the other are intensified, they are in a spiral. A relationship may not look any different today than it did yesterday, but over a year's time, you can see overall improvement or disintegration. While long-term spirals are more difficult to pinpoint by the participants, you can compare the relationship to a much earlier state. It is often an "imperceptible decline"—each turn of the spiral is unnoticed, but the cumulative effect over time is large. The two friends who used to share everything 18 months ago and who now just say "hi" on the street both know that relationship has declined over time. But in any given day or week they might not be able to point to noticeable changes in the relationship. Nevertheless, most relationships are in spirals over time—often oscillating through phases as we saw above.

Altering Degenerative Spirals

Spirals, obviously, do change, with people going in and out of generative and degenerative spirals over the course of a relationship. And, as a relationship participant, you can have impact on the nature of the spirals—even altering degenerative spirals once they start. There are specific choices you can make that can alter the direction a relationship is flowing.

First, alter your usual response—do what comes unnaturally. For example, if you are in relationship where you and the other tend to escalate, call each other names, you can stop the spiral by simply not allowing yourself to use negative language. Or, you can say, "This will just lead to a shouting match. I'm going to take a walk and talk with you when I come back," then exit from the normally hostile situation. Or say you have a roommate who is not very talkative and over the past 2 months you have tried to draw him out. You see that the more you talk, the more he retreats and the less he talks. Doing "more of the same" does not work, so do "less of the same." Don't act on

FIGURE 3-9.
Marital oscillations.

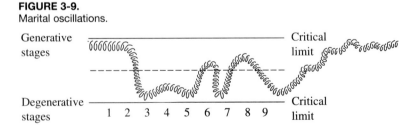

the natural inclination to talk when he is silent; in fact, talk less and outwait him. Similarly, if you are often quiet in a group of four friends, people adapt to that by sometimes leaving you out of the decisions. Then, for the first time, begin to tell them what you would like to do. Change the patterns, and you change the spiral.

Wilmot and Stevens (1994) interviewed over 100 people who had "gone through a period of decline," and then improved their romantic, friendship, and family relationships—basically pulling out of a degenerative spiral. When asked what they did to "turn it around," it was found that a potent way of altering the patterns was to change behavior. The changes of behavior, of course, took many forms, given the particular type of relationship spiral that had occurred. Some people became more independent, some gave more "space" to the other, others changed locations or moved, and still others sacrificed for the partner or spent more time together. But the basic principle is the same—when in a degenerating or escalating set of communication patterns, change!

One last anecdote about changing patterns. I know one parent whose 11-year-old daughter was getting low grades in school. The parent had been a superb student, and the daughter, in the past, had done well. But, in the middle of the school year, the daughter started getting lower and lower grades. As the grades went down, the parent's criticism went up. Pretty soon, both the girl's grades and the mother–daughter relationship were in the cellar! After some help from an outsider, the mother took a vow to *not* talk anymore about grades, regardless of what happened. It was very difficult, for each evening the two had been arguing about grades; grades had become the focal point of the entire relationship. It only took 2 weeks, and the daughter's grades made dramatic jumps. The mother, who found "giving up" very difficult, had taken her negative part out of the communication system—and it changed.

One final note on changing your behavior. The people in the Wilmot and Stevens (1994) study noted that "persistence" was one important key to bringing about a change in the relationship. If the parent above had only stopped her criticism for one night, as soon as she resumed it, off the spiral would have gone again. The other person will be suspicious of your change at first, probably question your motives and other negative interpretations. But if you are persistent in bringing the change, it will have effects on the other person, for his or her communication patterns are interlocked with yours.

Second, you can use third parties constructively. Friends, counselors, relatives, clergy, and others can sometimes provide a different perspective for you to begin to open up a degenerative system for change. Third parties can often make specific suggestions that will break the pattern of interlocking, mutually destructive behaviors that keep adding fuel to the degenerating relationship. In one case, a husband and wife went to a marriage counselor because they had come to a standoff. He was tired of her demands to always talk to her and pay attention. She was tired of his demands for more frequent sexual activity. As result, they became entrapped in a degenerative spiral—he talked less, and she avoided situations of physical intimacy. Upon seeing the counselor, they both realized that they were getting nowhere fast. Each was trying to get the other to change first. With the help of the counselor, they renegotiated their relationship, and each began giving a little bit. Over a period of a few days they found themselves coming out of the degenerating patterns.

Third, you can reaffirm your relational goals. Often when people get stuck in negative patterns of interaction, the other automatically assumes you want to "jump ship." If you are in a downward spiral, whether with your parents, boss, lover, child, or friend, reaffirming what you each have to gain from the relationship can promote efforts to get it back. The couple who saw the counselor found that they both had an important goal to stay together—for if either one had "won" the fight and lost the relationship, neither would have gotten what he or she wanted. Relational reaffirmation can help you focus on all the things you can do to get the relationship back to a more positive phase. Good relationships take energy to sustain; similarly, making a commitment to the relationship obvious to the other will help pull you out of the debilitating negative patterns.

Fourth, you can alter a spiral by metacommunicating. Wilmot and Stevens' (1994) respondents reported having a "Big Relationship Talk"—talking about the relationship and what had led to the degenerating series of actions. When you comment on what you see happening, it can open up the spiral itself for discussion. One can say, "Our relationship seems to be slipping—I find myself criticizing you, and you seem to be avoiding me, and it looks like it is getting worse. What can we do to turn it around?" Such metacommunication, whether pointed to the conversational episodes or the overall relationship patterns, can set the stage for productive conflict management and give participants a sense of a control over the relationship dynamics. Metacommunication, especially when coupled with a reaffirmation of your relational goals ("I don't want us to be unhappy, I want us to both like being together, but we seem to. . . ."), can alter the destructive forces in a relationship. And, of course, you can use metacommunication in any type of relationship, such as on the job. J.P., for example, says, "Sally, it seems to me like our work enthusiasm is slipping away. What might we do to get that sense of fun back like we had about 6 months ago?"

Firth, try to spend more or less time with the person. If you are on the "outs" with your co-workers, you could begin to spend more time with them—go to lunch, have coffee, take short strolls together. It is amazing what kinds of large changes can be purchased with just a small amount of time. Likewise, relationships often suffer because the people spend more time together than they can productively handle. So Tom always goes on a 3-day fishing trip with me in the summer as a way to both get more distance and independence in his marriage (and, coincidentally, to reaffirm our relationship with one another). Getting more distance and independence can bring you back refreshed and ready to relate again. Interestingly, Wilmot and Stevens (1994) found such "independence" moves as an important way to alter a degenerating spiral.

Finally, we all recognize that changing an external situation can alter a degenerating relationship. One parent has a son who got into an ongoing battle with the principal of the junior high school. The feud went on for months, with the principal (according to the mother) tormenting her boy and the boy retaliating by being mischievous. The mutually destructive actions were arrested only when the boy switched schools. He (and the principal) had a chance to start over, not contaminated by the previous interlocking patterns.

Another way to change the external situation is to stay in the presence of the other person but move to a new environment. Many married couples have gone for extended vacations in order to give themselves time to work out new solutions to relationship problems. If the relationship is important to you and you want to preserve it, effort expended to help the relationship reach productive periods is time well spent. Retreats, for business partners, romantic partners, and friends, can allow an infusion of fresh energy into a declining relationship. Because once the degenerative phases are reached, the behaviors of each person tend to be mutually reinforcing and damaging. Each person can blame the other and claim his or her own innocence, but that will not alter the degeneration. It sometimes takes long hard work to alter a negative spiral, and it may be successful if both put in some effort. But as every counselor knows from experience, one person alone can usually not change the relationship. If that person makes changes, and the other reciprocates, you have a chance to turn the spiral around.

TURNING POINTS AND SPIRALS

When participants talk about the turning points in their relationships, they are probably referring to the sharp *changes in the spiral*—either positive or negative. Even though a relationship is always pulsing and moving, either toward improvement or toward degeneration, we tend to go on "automatic pilot" and not actively process it. For example, you may work at a job for 15 years and not notice a slow decline in satisfaction until some triggering event happens; suddenly you become aware of the difficulties. We tend to track our relationships most *during times of the largest change*. The turning points, therefore, are simply parts of the spirals that are easily remembered—they become the focus for our memory of the relationship. If you go back to the various diagrams of the relationship spirals, where the spiral changes direction the most, is at turning points remembered by the participants. It is like people telling you about their childhood—they had thousands of meals, but tell you the story of the time they ate peas and then threw up on the family dinner (a turning point for everyone!). We remember relationship events depending on their impact on our views of self, other, and the relationship and tell narratives to dramatize the turning points.

Figure 3-10 illustrates how Lamar recalls his friendship with Randy. It is hypothetical, but shows how our memories of events tend to focus on turning points that (1) mark a decline in a relationship and (2) mark improvement in a relationship

#1: When he and Randy first worked together on a project and they discovered just how much they had in common.

#2: When he and Randy tried many times to take an outdoor trip together and couldn't schedule it; first one couldn't go, then the other.

#3, #4, #5, #6: Through a period of months, he and Randy kept trying to spend time

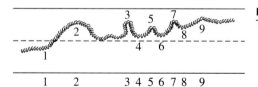

FIGURE 3-10.
Turning points and spirals.

together; sometimes they would, and other times they found it to be too difficult to arrange.

#7, #8, #9: When Lamar began a marital crisis, Randy became his confidant and, over a 9-month period, they kept getting closer and closer.

#10: When he and Randy did an extensive backpack trip together.

This sequence of turning points, of course, will continue for the length of the relationship. It demonstrates the ebb and flow of relationships over time—closer, farther, at a state of equilibrium, and onward and onward.

Relational flow and change illustrate a number of points concerning all relationships.

1 Relationships never stand still—they are constantly changing. Even "stabilized" relationships, once you examine the communication events and feelings of the participants, fluctuate between varying stages of generative and degenerative spirals. The actions of each participant either accelerate a spiral in progress or provide pressure so that the direction of the spiral will change.

2 People remember most vividly the events that have the most impact on the spirals—those that bring them closer and those that drive a wedge between them.

3 All spirals have limits, and once the critical limit is reached, if the spiral is not reversed, the relationship will encounter so much strain that it will dissolve.

Woody Allen captured the essence of relational change when he said, "Relationships are like a shark. They either move forward, or they die." Our relationships are dynamic, always moving and changing either toward or away from improvement. Participants' behaviors interlock so that each one's behavior influences the others, and the mutually conjoined behaviors intensify the other's reactions.

People look at their relationships using different time frames. Some people tend to only look at the macro perspective, charting the changes in yearly units such as "do I feel as good about my job today as I did a year ago." A relationship may not look any different today than it did yesterday, but over a year's time, you can see either overall improvement or disintegration. The long-term spirals are identified by comparing the relationship to a much earlier state.

Other times one may process and categorize a relationship on an hour-by-hour basis. For example, when Jan's romantic partner announced that she wanted to "call it off," Jan spent the next 2 weeks thinking about the relationship, talking to her partner, and doing endless processing of all the changes coming her way. Rapid relational change, especially if it is unexpected, can cause intense processing of the relationship, sometimes to the point of overload. Those who suffer from an unexpected firing, termination of a romance, or disinheritance from the family find themselves processing at a depth they didn't think possible.

What is important, is to begin to sensitize yourself to the ebbs and flows inherent in all relationships, so you can make informed choices. Becoming attuned to the nature of communication spirals can increase your understanding of these processes.

4

RELATIONSHIP ENHANCING COMMUNICATION

One central issue facing contemporary people is, "How can I have satisfying relationships?" While much time is spent examining the initiation of relationships (everything from finding a new romantic partner to interviewing for a job) and the ending of a relationship ("How can I tell him I want to leave?"; "Should I quit this job even though I don't have another one?"), most of our time is spent neither developing nor dissolving relationships—it is spent sustaining them (Duck, 1988). If you look at the life course of any relationship, the bulk of the time you spend is in one already past the formative stages. Even in a 6-month, short-term romance, the day-to-day activities after the beginning of it are what occupy us. And, in jobs, long-term friendships, lifelong family relationships and committed romantic relationships, the most recurring questions have to do with how to *sustain* and *enhance* them. Sustaining a relationship means to "keep it going," while enhancement refers to efforts to improve the relationship. Of course, the line between sustaining and enhancing is rather blurry, and if people watched you from the outside, they might not be able to tell if you were "sustaining" or "enhancing" a relationship when you do favors for your best friend. Thus, the focus of this chapter will be on how we can enhance or improve our relationships.

One word of caution is in order. Most of the research on relational enhancement focuses on romantic relationships, primarily because those are the ones that people tend to talk about the most. As a result, we know little about other relationships that also present enhancement issues. For example, you may have been drifting away from your brother for years, yet research is not very helpful in telling us what we might do to enhance family relations. Similarly, while we spend an incredible amount of our adult life doing jobs, little research addresses what we might do to improve work relations. And what about our connections with our neighbors, those in our spiritual communities, and people we see only occasionally yet are important to our sense of belonging? While the research on marital and romantic relationships will be overviewed, there are other relationships that we wish to improve. As our view of relationships expands to concentrate on all types of relationships, we can rethink about enhancement from a broader perspective.

Why should we be interested in relational enhancement? Canary and Stafford (1994, p. 7) note that, if relationships are not sustained, they will deteriorate. Vangelisti and Huston (1994) summarize other research that demonstrates that, by the second year of marriage, there is "some disenchantment" and lessening of satisfaction in contemporary marriages. When one makes efforts to improve the relationship, you are signaling to your partner (whether romantic or otherwise) that the relationship is important to you. For couples, the hallmarks of effective couple functioning are (1) a strong commitment and (2) equal experience by the partners (Rusbult, Drigotas & Veritte, 1994). Effective enhancement efforts can be the avenue to both partners recommitting themselves to the relationship.

We often assume that the large amount of turnover in relationships means that focusing on enhancement is not worth the time. At all times, however, when you look across relationships there is a large amount of relational stability. Even though you have been fired from your job, your best friend remains the same. When you go through a sequence of romantic partners, your kin relationships are there throughout. Even among young people who are in a high turnover era (going away to college and changing locations), there is considerable relational constancy. In one study, for example, of college students' "nonkin" relationships, 57 percent had been in existence for longer than 11 years (Shulman, 1975).

It is easy to underestimate the constancy of relationships when we focus on turnover. The average person may change jobs during his or her lifetime, yet each individual job may last for years. And, even though the divorce rate fluctuates between 40 and 50 percent, what of the years you *do* spend with a particular partner? Is the quality of the relationship worth some effort? Furthermore, it probably is the case that the high degree of relational turnover is due to too few relational partners coping effectively with relationship enhancement (Dindia & Baxter, 1987).

When writing about relationship enhancement, some use the terms *relational maintenance* and *relational repair,* referring to (1) keeping a relationship at a current satisfactory state, and (2) repairing a relationship to a previous satisfactory state. "Maintenance" and "repair" metaphors imply a static state—a relationship is at a certain point and you want to either keep it the same or "fix" it with a repair.[1] We "maintain" and "repair" our cars and clothes, keep them in an original state or "fixing" them so they return to an original state. Synonyms for *repair* are words such as *fix, mend, patch*—all of which undermine the central notions of flux, alteration, and ever-changing dynamics of relationships in this book. Therefore I prefer the word *enhance-*

---

[1]If you want to explore this issue in greater depth see the articles in the excellent book by Canary and Stafford (1994) on *Relational Maintenance.* The articles by Wilmot, Rawlins, and Baxter argue that "maintenance" and "repair" are inappropriate metaphors while the other contributors suggest they are appropriate metaphors. Montgomery (1993) suggests we not use maintenance metaphors, because they "denote the preservation of a steady state" (p. 221). Throughout this chapter, I am substituting *sustain* where others have used *maintain,* and *enhancement* in place of *repair.*

ment, which emphasizes that all relationships can be improved, regardless of their current state. Further, enhancement efforts are not limited to the middle state of relationships—they can happen during the entire course of a relationship. Even after a relationship has "ended," such as a divorce, if you are parents of children, you will be affected by the quality of the postmarriage relationship, and enhancement efforts may well be needed. Many divorced people spend considerable effort trying to figure out how to improve the now-changed relationship with their former spouse. Therefore, as Baxter (1994c) suggests, *maintenance* as a word tends to limit our view to the middle stages of relationships, which is too narrow.

CONTEXT-SENSITIVE COMMUNICATION

Obviously, if you buy the notions in Chapter 1 that our relationships are created via our communication, then the road to relationship enhancement also resides in communication behavior. Relationships don't just change all by themselves; they change due to the actions and interpretations of the participants.

Even though communication is the central ingredient in the relational stew, it is not so simple to just say "do this and that" and you'll have a good relationship. The meaning of communicative moves always is dependent on each relationship context. For example, if you come from a culture where direct talk is not done, to improve the relationship by "talking about our problems" would be counterproductive—others will react to you breaking the norm. In most families, for example, direct talk about the concerns is not the accepted way of dealing with difficulties. And, on the opposite end, some relational cultures require talk. Contemporary romantic relationships, for example, are now under the "you oughta communicate" belief—that direct communication nurtures and enhances the relationship. In this type of relational context, to *not* communicate is against the rules.

Context-sensitive communication is adaptive to the particular relationship, factoring in the cultural and personal preferences of the participants. A context-sensitive approach validates silence, symbolic and metaphoric moves, *and* relationship talk as avenues for enhancement. The next section will examine mundane routines, ritual actions, and other indirect ways to enhance relationships. Then, direct talk as an avenue of improvement will be discussed. Subsequent sections on metacommunication and constructive conflict management will further elaborate on the "talk" theme. As you read these sections, you may find yourself saying, "Ah, no way, that wouldn't work." Such reactions can give you information about the values you hold—whether to enhance relationships indirectly, to sit down and talk as the chosen strategy, or to never even be concerned with enhancement.

One final note. Research on enhancement is still rather embryonic. We do know, however, that the level of relationship satisfaction is unrelated to any particular strategy choice, and that people often use only a narrow range of choices (Dindia & Baxter, 1987). It is important, therefore, to fully examine available options for enhancement; in your work relationship you might try one approach, in a family situation something entirely different. Regardless of the communication choice, however, the focus is on activities that enhance the relationship.

The largest component of a context-sensitive approach is to recognize that not all relationships have to be close or intimate to be fulfilling. Such an "ideology of intimacy" (Parks, 1982) is, in fact, not how most of us lead our everyday lives. If you do a survey of your own relationships, ranging from work, to classes, to friends, romantic partners and family, *most* of those relationships will not be intimate in nature. Most people actually have very few close, intimate relationships, and to impose an "intimacy" model onto other perfectly healthy and functional relationships distorts them and brings unnecessary dissatisfaction.

A second component of a context-sensitive approach is to grant that, even when you want a sense of "intimacy" or closeness, it can be accomplished in diverse ways. Lots of jokes currently abound regarding guys doing "male bonding": when two male friends are planning a back country ski trip together, they might say, "We are going to do some male bonding—ski into the thoroughfare region of Yellowstone for 2 weeks." Clearly, males (and others) *do* bond through activities, and it is a perfectly legitimate way to build a relationship of quality and substance. We overgeneralize if we see intimacy only as *talk per se.* Intimacy is probably more accurately defined as appreciation, warmth, and affection rather than as a synonym for self-disclosure.

Context-sensitive communication standards also are adaptive to particular relationships. For example, if one imposes an "intimacy" model onto all marriages, many successful marriages fail the test. Some interesting research by Guisinger et al. 1989 showed that the prognosis for a good remarriage is more related to (1) the husband contributing more equitably to child care, (2) the couple sharing tasks, (3) the stepmother developing good relations with the children, and (4) the couple not being too negative about the former wife. Clearly, the central importance of these features should nudge us a bit on using intimacy as the sole criterion.

Another aspect of the tendency to use intimacy as the only criterion is spending too much time on every relationship. Each relationship will have features that are positive and those that detract from it, so why spend time on trying to make a work colleague into the perfect companion? You can just as well have a functional work relationship. As Mada says, "it is appropriate to be concerned about relationships, but not *consumed* by them!" Wanting to improve your relationships is fine; being obsessed with their continual improvement so that you can't sleep at night probably is counterproductive—bringing nighttime tossing and turning rather than relational change.

Being context sensitive means being sensitized to some of the cultural variations in communication patterns. The following section, which details some cultures that adopt more indirect approaches, does not tell the entire story. For example, African American styles of communication, while not indirect like those in the following section, do diverge from mainstream patterns. In order to get along in mainstream situations, some African Americans learn to "code-switch"—speak both Black English and Mainstream American English (Hecht, Collier, & Ribeau, 1993). Below, based on their studies, are a few selected examples of communication differences between African American culture and European American culture.

• European Americans look at their conversational partner more frequently and for longer duration than do African Americans.
• African Americans prefer authority figures who avert their gaze.

- African American children move around more than European American children and exhibit a greater variety of movements.
- African American children speak to each other less than do European American children.
- European Americans tend to talk to males for longer periods, while African Americans spend more time talking to females. (Hecht, Collier, & Ribeau, 1993)

A context-sensitive approach openly asks what the cultural norms are, and thereby opens our eyes to diverse ways of communication. For many cultures (and subcultures) indirect and symbolic forms of communication are the most important to master in most contexts. It is to those indirect, subtle, symbolic, and powerful forms of enhancement and enrichment that we now turn.

INDIRECT AND SYMBOLIC COMMUNICATION

As noted in Chapter 1, most relationships are built implicitly from recurring interactions—building the relationship definition indirectly and implicitly from the behaviors. Everything we do in a relationship has symbolic significance—both actions and talk. Each behavior and conversation implies a relationship meaning; we signal to the other the construction and sustaining of a relationship.

One potent form of relationship enhancement is, of course, what we do. As Wilmot (1994) says, people signal the other by "watch my behavior" as well as "listen to what I say." Talk, while important in some relationships and cultures, is not the only thing happening, and we need to attend to the indirect ways people communicate. As Burleson and Samter (1994) state, "there may be substantial segments of the population for whom achieving accurate and sensitive understandings through verbal interaction just is not that important" (p. 85). Planalp (1993, p. 354) suggests that "intimate self-disclosure is much less common in everyday interaction than we think it is." Huston et al. (1986) found that the most frequent activity of married couples is completing household tasks. And Dainton and Stafford (1993, p. 267) note for us that romantic couples sustain relationships primarily by "simply being in each other's presence."

Indirect forms of enhancing relationships occur in all cultures, and in some cultures it is the only avenue for improvement. The following section will illustrate some diverse ways people improve their relationships via indirect and symbolic behaviors. Some of the examples illustrate indirect talk, while others focus on indirect actions, but in both cases they illustrate forms of communication that are not direct.

Cultural Considerations

Tannen says it well:

> Entire cultures operate on elaborate systems of indirectness. Only modern Western societies place a priority on direct communication, and even for us it is more a value than a practice. (Tannen, 1990, pp. 226–227)

In societies where the protection of the other's "face" is a central value, communication needs to be indirect. Indirect communication occurs when you communicate to the hearer more than you actually say "by referring to some mutually shared background information or rely in the listeners powers of rationality and inference" (Yum, 1988, p. 381). Social harmony is preserved by not using explicit verbal communicating; you and the other share such a common context (high-context cultures), and you *know* what is meant by someone's indirect speech act. For example, "Chinese avoid direct expression of feelings as a means to preserve social harmony" (Xing, 1993, p. 9). Indirect speech acts are the result of a predominant concern for the other's face. Xing (1993, p. 16) expresses it this way:

> In Chinese culture, one has to be very sensitive about gaining or losing face as it is concerned with shame, reputation, prestige, dignity and security. . . . In China, on the other hand, the best way to punish or take revenge is to humiliate the person publicly. As a result, Chinese people, in a sense, are more self-conscious and anxious about self-esteem in their interactions with others.

Of course, as we noted in the second chapter, the entire conception of the "self" is different in high-context cultures. "Face" is a "projected image of oneself in a relational situation" (Gudykunst & Ting-Toomey, 1988, p. 85). For people from individualist cultures such as the United States, Australia, and Germany, the "public presentation of face is expected to correspond to an invariant 'core self' within the individual (p. 85). But in collectivist cultures, the very definition of the "self" is "linked to their relationships with other human beings and does not emerge from the individual alone, as it does in the individualistic cultures" (p. 82).

In high-context cultures, talk is often seen as obtrusive, and being reticent is often interpreted as a sign of emotional strength and trustworthiness (Nakanishi, 1986). Often, East Asian foreign students in the United States are puzzled why they are constantly being asked what they want when they are visiting American homes. In their countries, the host or hostess is supposed to know what is needed and serve accordingly (Yum, 1988, p. 385). Similarly, in Ilongot society direct talk is seen as authoritarian and exclusionary" (p. 383). Indirect talk is seen in such cultures as reflecting a concern for the other—you automatically adapt to their needs and concern for saving their face (Katriel, 1986).

Norms for indirectness can, of course, become rather extensive. Native Japanese, for example, do not want to say "no" to someone, and there are 16 maneuvers that can be employed to avoid saying "no" to someone (Imai, 1981). An American from the United States (or an American from Canada) might ask you, "Please shut the door," or if trying to be indirect, say, "The door is open." In Japan, the indirectness would come out as, "It is somewhat cold today," more indirect because the door is not even referred to (Yum, 1988). If you properly understood this indirect speech, you would get up and shut the door. Another form of indirectness occurs when, in East Asian cultures, "it is very important . . . to engage in small talk before initiating business and to communicate personalized information, especially information that would help place each person in the proper context (p. 381). It is presumed that each person is engaged in an ongoing process; that the relationship in continually in flux (Yum, 1988). Finally, the indirectness is also evidenced with corporate situations. As a director of training for people going to Japan on business summarized it, "In Japan, the rules aren't made explicit, and the more you ask about them, the more vague the answers become" (Shine, 1993, 26).

One more extended example from a nonwestern culture. The Aboriginal people of central Australia have evolved a different form of public discourse than western cultures. For the Aborigines, consensus is to be maintained in all relations. An Aboriginal child will be embarrassed to stand up and address a class (Liberman, 1990). Here is how Liberman (1990, pp. 180–181) characterizes the communication norms:

> In Aboriginal society, it is impolite to look directly into another person's eyes; looking aside, speaking moderately, and even covering one's face slightly with one's hands are all actions that demonstrate a commendable self-depreciation and respect for others. Silence is not viewed to be insolence; on the contrary it is evidence of good manners. What is more, egoistic behavior is out of place.

As you might guess, when there is a class of cultures, the communication norms come into sharp contrast. Liberman (1990) cites this poignant example of an Aboriginal's appearance before a court of law. Remember that the Aboriginals communication preferences are to remain silent, which makes even taking an oath difficult.

Clerk: The evidence you shall give will be the truth, the whole truth and nothing but the truth, so help me God? Do you understand that?
Aboriginal Witness: (no answer)
Clerk: Please say, "So help me God."
Aboriginal: (no answer)
Clerk: Say, "So help me God."
Aboriginal: (no answer)
(Court accepts the Aboriginal's silence)
. . .
Magistrate: He didn't say "So help me God."
Clerk: Say, "So help me God."
Aboriginal: So help me God (Liberman, 1990, p. 181).

As you can tell, to try to improve this type of relationship through direct talk would be counterproductive—direct talk violates the Aboriginal's entire set of communication norms.

Even in Western cultures, there are many forms of effective indirectness. For example, the British share with the Chinese a norm that you do not discuss with your friend family matters or hurt feelings (Goodwin, 1990b). Nordbook (1987, p. 46) gives riveting accounts of "how to talk man-to-man" with uncles if you are an American of Scandinavian descent:[2] When you grow to within one foot of your uncles' heights and are old enough to stop dancing around from one foot to the other all the time, you qualify for Man-to-Man Talks with your uncles.

---

[2]My apologies to our other American brethren. Those of us in the United States have an unfortunate habit of referring to ourselves as "Americans," when Canadians and Mexicans are just as "American" as are we.

- Go out to the lawn (summer) or barn (winter).
- Plant your feet firmly, spread about as wide as your shoulders.
- Cross your arms and lean back slightly. (If you are holding something, like a coffee cup, put your free hand in your pocket and hold the cup at about mid-stomach.)
- Second option: Put both hands in back pockets, and both of you stare at the ground as if addressing your feet.
- Always mirror his posture.
- *Never* square off against him so that the planes of your shoulders are parallel. If you must face him, face him at an angle, Most comfortable: Stand *next* to him, facing the same direction.
- Stare at the horizon or at your feet while talking, except at the end of a question. Then stare him briefly right in the eye.
- Keep it short. He doesn't need to know every detail of your private life.

There are elaborate codes, as well, for women of similar descent. Here is how Nordbook (1987, pp. 46–47) suggests females talk to an aunt:

> Scandinavian/American women find that the Woman-to-Woman Talks with the aunts come somewhat earlier than the Man-to-Mans with the uncles do. Generally, girls are considered mature enough to be admitted to serious discussions with the women of the family (excepting discussion of s-e-x, of course) when they are old enough to become the primary dishwasher in their family.
>
> Sit next to your aunt (but not TOO close) at the table of her choice.
>
> Stop the conversation and look at everyone who walks through the room.
>
> Write down every recipe someone else writes down, no matter how awful it sounds. Better to throw away a recipe card than risk ill will.
>
> Ask the aunts to identify people in the family photos. No one will ever resent being asked to retrace the family tree, no matter how often they've explained it before or how often you've forgotten it. It's bound to be more interesting than hearing the uncles retell the same jokes.
>
> Do not ask embarrassing questions when you're looking at family photos. You cannot expect candid answers to questions like, "Wasn't Great-Aunt Christina Gay?" or "Didn't Great-Grandpa Nils have a wife and kids in Norway when he came over here and married Great-Grandma Mina?"

It may well be that indirectness is *the* most common mode of relationship enhancement, even in western cultures. Many a young person has been dismayed when he or she goes home and asks for a "talk" with the family only to find that the family members are not willing or able to talk directly about an issue. One's parents may have grown up in a time (or place) where the popular emphasis on open communication and direct expression of conflict was not present. Many marriages, rather than being based on open expression and verbal intimacy, depend on the competent performance of role expectations—she cooks and he earns a wage. And marital couples in the United States and Australia (both individualistic cultures) who are "separates" are low on openness, rarely discussing things openly (Noller & Hiscock, 1989). Rather than conducting marriage based on negotiation, many couples have a high respect for tact and discretion and a distaste for direct conflict expression (Zietlow & Sillars, 1988). For the elderly couples in the Zietlow and Sillars (1988) study, "communication appeared to be a reflection of the relationship, not a tool for adjusting it" (p. 243). When these couples had conflict, rather than discussing an issue they would be bitter and complain.

The implicit and symbolic forms of communication in our culture are quite obvious once we begin to look for them. Jean is a member of a family with five grown children; the family is close but not very verbally disclosive with one another. Here are some of the ways they indicate indirectly and implicitly relational importance:

- Jean travels to Boise to see Toni's new baby.
- Jean has two daughters, Kerry and Mindy, and Jean's parents drive for 2 days each way to attend Kerry and Mindy's graduations from college.
- When any important family event happens, someone pays a visit to show support.
- Each holiday a significant portion of the original children (and the grandchildren) travel to the hometown and spend the holidays with Jean's parents.
- Whenever someone has a birthday, brothers, sisters, and parents call.

Such implicit communication "tells" the family member of their importance; yet it is not stated directly. The importance of these implicit forms of communication becomes evident when someone violates the norm. In one middle-class family it was expected that each holiday the children come home from college. When Wallace was a sophomore in college and lived only 3 hours drive from home (and had a car), he called and said he was "too busy" to come for Thanksgiving (staying at college to see his girlfriend). The family was clearly upset at his "lack of consideration"; his implicit communication was, "You aren't important enough to for me to drive home for Thanksgiving."

Within mainstream North American culture there are a few findings about gender differences that will sharpen our focus on indirect and symbolic communication.

Gender Effects

In many cultures derived from European roots, such as in North America, males often are less expressive than females. Yet these inexpressive males *do* develop relationships! In one study, males and females were asked to describe opposite-sex romantic relationships. Males emphasized proximity, while females emphasized communication (Helgeson, 1987). For many males, relationship talk is not valued as an end in itself. For example, when things are going well, "there is no need for such talk" (Acitelli, 1988, p. 197). Males seem to value their close relationships differently and react to intimacy and control differently than do females (Cline, 1989). The clear differences communicatively between men and women was explained well by Helgeson (1987).

> Male intimacy involves proximity rather than communication. Because words can provoke conflict and expose vulnerability, communication is somewhat frightening for men. Male silence is discomforting to women, however, they require words for intimacy and feel distant from their partners in the absence of verbal sharing. (p. 195)

If a male operates according to these generalized notions, it would be easy to dismiss an inexpressive male as "not caring." I'll never forget Virgil, a 55-year-old male in a workshop. We were getting into some intense issues at times. Barbara, for example, spent time crying and showing her dismay over her family. She was adopted and abused by a family, and when her adoptive father died during the workshop, she was in a bind—wanting to be a family member and yet not wanting to be in their presence. She was in a state of severe inner turmoil. All the members of the group, except Virgil, talked with her, gave her support, and spent time showing they understood. All the while Virgil only said, "I don't do feelings!" It wasn't until 4 days later that Barbara revealed to the group that Virgil had offered to fly to Missouri with her at his own expense for the funeral and accompany her as an escort to help her face the family. The images of "nonexpressive" Virgil took a rather dramatic turn, while he said, "No big deal." Barbara will never forget that offer of kindness and indirectness. She ended up going by herself and credited Virgil's offer as the turning point to give her the strength to face the family by herself.

If we make "intimacy" synonymous with verbal disclosure, we bypass seeing the richness and complexity of symbolic, indirect moves made by males (and females, too). As Wood and Inman (1993, p. 280) suggest, we have developed a "non-inclusive view of closeness in which feminine preferences for verbal disclosures are privileged, while masculine tendencies toward instrumental activity are devalued. We have to be careful of putting such value overlays on relationships, and if we only look at verbal disclosures we will miss many of the important events that carry relational meaning, such as in the case of Virgil just mentioned.

Finally, there is some evidence to suggest that male inexpressiveness is a preference rather than an inability. In general, men are less interested, thoughtful, and communicative about relationships than women, and they think that "relationship talk is a response to a need, not something done for its own sake or to let someone know how good he feels about the relationship" (Acitelli, 1988, p. 196). Verbal expressiveness of feelings is just less common for men than for women (Dosser et al., 1986). As you might expect, men typically disclose less than women (Shimanoff, 1988), but this does not mean that relationships are not important to them.

There is current work suggesting that gender differences are overrated. For example, Dindia and Allen (1992) surveyed over 200 studies on disclosure, which involved 23,702 subjects. They found that *whom* you disclosed to made a critical difference. Women were found to disclose "slightly more" than men but in more close relationships. In terms of strangers, women and men disclosed about equally. Citing the work of Maccoby, Tavris (1992) suggested also that the disclosure of boys and girls depends on the gender of the child they are playing with. And when men disclose, it seems to be with female partners in their marriage.

A number of studies are beginning to show, not only that is disclosure dependent on the relationship, but that, when there are male/female differences, they are small. Dindia and Allen (1992) found that women only disclose "slightly more" than men. Ragan (1989, p. 180) says "we can make few claims about substantive, generalized sex differences in communication interaction across context." Similarly, Canary and Hause (1993) concluded that the differences due to gender are minimal. Further, Maltz and Borker (1982, p. 215) think that many of the observed gender differences of boys and girls tend to learn to "overcome at least partially some of the gender-specific cultural patterns typical of childhood." Tavris (1992) summarizes our focus on gender:

> One problem is that many people persist in believing that men and women differ in important qualities in spite of innumerable studies that have failed to pin these qualities down and keep them there. For instance, we've seen that former (average) differences in intellectual skills, such as mathematical, verbal, and spatial abilities have gradually vanished or are too trivial to matter. Other differences have faded quickly with changing times, as was the fate of "finger dexterity" (when males got hold of computers) and "fear of success" (when females got hold of law schools). But people LOVE sex difference, and not just the familiar anatomical ones. They love to notice and identify ways in which the sexes seem to differ psychologically, and then to complain or laugh about what "women" or what "men" do. (pp. 287–288)

Gender considerations can obscure the real relationship issues. The real issue is, what does each partner do, how does she or he adjust to the other's forms of communication, and what are the avenues they can use to improve their relationship? In a particular relationship, it does not matter if the man or woman is less disclosive; what matters is valuing multiple routes to relationship satisfaction. We need to be sensitive to the fact that many relationships function perfectly well without direct verbal disclosure and spend our time focusing on the mismatch between any two people rather than trying to decide if men or women are the best communicators.

Not attending to the values of indirectness, it is easy to jump into "marital enrichment" or "job enhancement" programs that do not fit the needs of people who want to avoid discussion of sensitive issues. For example, getting distressed couples to sit down and discuss their disagreements may not be the most effective route to enhancement. One mediator dealing with a family where the mother of two young children refused to let her parents continue seeing the grandchildren broke the stalemate by convincing the mother of the children to go bowling with her father. This indirect move reassured both of them of their importance to one another; the mother of the children was hurt that her parents showed more love for her children than for her. She and her father went bowling and, without discussing their feelings, turned around their relationship, and she permitted them to see the children again.

Indirect communication has import because it is *symbolic*—it has a rich meaning that transcends the simple acts being performed. "Being there" carries a lot of weight, especially when everyone understands its importance. In ministerial circles, it is often called the "ministry of presence"—just sit with the person at the hospital, and they know you care for them. Showing up on time, doing small favors, going out of your way to help someone, are all ways to relationally say "I value you."

We imbue our relationships with many symbolic acts—those that make it unique and different from other relationships and hold special meaning for the people involved. Families that take vacations to "Seven Brothers Lakes," business partners who put their names on a building they have constructed, and romantic partners who remember where they first made love all are keying into the symbolic nature of indirect acts. Baxter (1987b), after seeing that people had "symbolic" remembrances, studied them in opposite sex romantic and same-sex friendship relations. Relationship symbols serve as concrete "metacommunicative statements about the abstract qualities of intimacy, caring, solidarity. . . . which the parties equate with their relationship," serve to link the past, present, and future, and allow people to test whether "they share a common perception of their experience" (Baxter, 1987b, pp. 262–263). Baxter found these types of symbolic elements (which were discussed on page 11, and are worthy of repitition):

1 Behavioral Actions—Something people jointly did, interaction routines such as "verbally fencing with one another" and using nicknames (such as code words for sex). Recall our discussion earlier in Chapter 1 about idioms in relationships? Those can be examples of symbolic acts classified by Baxter.

2 Events or Times—Special events or times such as special ski weekends, spots where romance flourished, or even seeing a movie together they didn't like (as proof of how much they liked being together). Of course, just "being there" is an important symbolic reminder of the importance of this relationship to you—you chose it over other things to do, and the other knows that. Presence is an indirect form of communication—"I'm still here, aren't I?"—that many times is not talked about. Family members who are available to one another during crises (even if they live thousands of miles apart) show their concern by their availability. Friends who make efforts to get together 25 years after having been roommates are trying to enhance their relationship, too. And one person I know shows his commitment to the family by always being supportive of his daughters' tennis matches. Parents support their children and work daily to improve their relationship by showing up at games and events.

3 Physical Objects—Items such as strawberries, a stuffed buffalo, or broken violin string can have significance. Workers who retire receive plaques, friends send funny cards, family members send joke gifts back and forth, and spiritual practitioners wear objects to show their connection (relationship) to the spiritual approach.

4 Symbolic places—Some places serve as visual metaphors for the relationship, some quality of the relationship or some prior time in the relationship's history. We noted examples of these above, but favorite restaurants, hiding places for children when they were growing up, and special locations where two friends travel together all reinforce and add import to the relationship. Places are not "just" places, if some important event occurred there; going to "Tepee" for family vacations takes on symbolic value. Each time a family member refers to "Tepee," it recalls the importance of this family unit to all.

5 Cultural artifacts—Music groups, songs, books, and films can all serve as identifiers of the relationship.

Of course, what is being symbolized is quite diverse. Baxter (1987b) found that these major types of symbols serve these nine functions: 1) recollection prompt, (2) intimacy indicators, (3) communion mechanism, (4) stimulation/fun, (5) seclusion mechanism, (6) exclusivity indicator, (7) management of difference/conflict, (8) public tie-sign (signal to others about the relationship), and (9) endurance index.

At this juncture, research on the symbolic nature of our acts and how they serve to reinforce and enhance a relationship is just beginning. The basic types outlined above need to be expanded for all types of relationships, so we can understand the symbolic nature of indirect acts of all types. Further, we need to come back to some basic concepts such as "commitment"—how does one communicate commitment to a romantic partner, family, work associates, and friends?

We need to do comprehensive research on the components of how we indirectly indicate commitment to our relationship partners. There is evidence that the key variable in marital happiness, for example, is commitment per se. Likewise, perceptions of commitment in friendships may be the key ingredient to success (Griffin & Sparks, 1990). For romantic partners, the more they are in love, satisfied with the relationship, and committed to the relationship, the more they minimize the partner's faults and plan to continue the relationship (Kingsbury & Minda, 1988). In another study, "commitment was the most powerful and consistent predictor of relationship satisfaction" (Acker & Davis, 1992). Sprecher (1987) also found that "commitment to the relationship" was the best predictor of the expectation that one's partner would stay involved and of a willingness to stay in a relationship with a HIV positive partner. Often one's commitment to a relationship can be seen in the instrumental functions rather than the talk. While a man may sound independent, self-assured, and not needing others, on another level he may be providing for a family—showing his caring indirectly by his constancy. The sense of obligation to a relationship is often a very powerful force that keeps us in it (Duck, 1988). At this point, however, we do not know all the ways that commitment can be expressed, both indirectly and directly. You can probably recall specific events in your relationships, friends, family, and romantic, for instance, that show commitment, or lack of it. For instance, performing services, traveling to see you, going "above and beyond" what is normally expected, and spending money on phone calls and other forms of contact seem to be highly symbolic acts to the recipient.

One example of how a concept can be unpacked for its symbolic significance is play. Play also serves an indirect function of relationship building. Elaine and Mike can play and giggle for hours—and their marriage is strong and growing. The sense of mutual understanding, building a shared reality, and release of tension all make play very effective. Play at work can serve indirectly to support relational closeness. It may work like this:

> First, play is thought to be an index of intimacy. . . . Second, play is posited to function as a successful moderator of conflict and tension, allowing the relationship parties to manage sensitive or conflict issues without fear of jeopardizing the underlying relational stability. . . . Third, play is . . . a low risk or safe communication strategy that allows parties to undertake a variety of actions that might otherwise prove embarrassing to the parties, such as playfully escalating one's emotional attachment to the other in order to test for reciprocated emotion. (Baxter, 1992a, p. 337).

All behavior is potentially communicative; it conveys meaning to the partner. In fact, the "symbolic" nature of our communicative acts is what builds the relationship. The gruff father saying, "Want to come along?" to the 9-year-old boy may be sending symbolic messages just as effectively as the person saying, "I love you." The 60-year-old son-in-law who faithfully goes to the family cabin and drains the water pipes at the end of the season so they won't freeze is sending a clear message to his mother-in-law, and they both know it.

One final comment about indirect, symbolic communication. It has, of course, a power of its own, and in addition it often is at work when it is taboo to talk about certain topics. Baxter and Wilmot (1985) asked people in opposite-sex romantic relationships about what topics are "taboo"—that can't be discussed. They found that state of the relationship, relationship norms, prior opposite-sex relationships, conflict-inducing topics, or negative self-disclosure were topics best avoided.

How then does one "signal" to a partner their importance to you? Through indirect, symbolic acts that you hope will make the point to the other without having to talk about it. Indirect and implicit forms of communication need far more study; we have tended to downplay them in our focus on talking, dialogue, and "working through" issues. Clearly, relationships are built and enhanced through indirect acts.

CONNECTION THROUGH CONVERSATION

In everyday relationships we are usually performing *both* indirect, symbolic moves and conversational actions (that also serve as symbolic acts). While the above section is an attempt to heighten our awareness of everyday actions that often go unnoticed by those interested in verbal exchanges, it is important to see that all forms of exchange— silence as well as conversation—have a place in relationship enhancement.

If you believe in the "therapeutic" approach (open communication and disclosure; direct talk and negotiation), and your parents follow a less explicit approach to communication, you may have reactions similar to those of contemporary college students.

> (They) long for the unquestioning commitment their parents seemed to have, yet they are repelled by what they take to be the lack of communication, the repression of difficulties, and, indeed, the resigned fatalism such commitment seems to imply. These respondents both envy their parents and vow never to be like them. (Bellah et al., 1985, p. 103).

If you are attuned to conversational ability, you may find this episode a bit painful to imagine. It is from my notes on what I observed in a restaurant:

> There they sat in the restaurant, a man and woman in their mid fifties obviously married to one another. They finished eating, and each looked out the window in a different direction. During the next 10 minutes they exchanged about 10 words total. Every once in a while the woman would look quickly at the man, then pull away. She looked bored, resigned, and like she wanted to talk with him—somewhat. He looked just fine, watching the fire truck go by, chewing on his toothpick, catching a quick glance at various people in the restaurant. When it came time to leave, both got up without a word and started out in different directions. The woman looked over her shoulder and then turned and followed him out the front door.

The lack of conversational connection probably both reflects and creates a dampened relationship, at least if one judges a relationship based on quality of conversation.

Conversational ability, whether in a public context or in a private relationship, can be a bellwether for relationship quality. When we assume in our culture that the absence of talk means a lessened connection (since we see ourselves as disconnected, independent persons), talk becomes a "bridge" between people, allowing them to coordinate activities and continually reenergize the relationship. Imagine going to work and, for 8 hours not having a single conversation, not even a "hi" in the morning. This often reflects a work environment full of conflict and ill feelings—else we expect people to at least perform some "social niceties" such as greeting one another in the morning.

Of course, conversational ability does not exist in a vacuum; it comes bundled with a host of nonverbal acts. But for the sake of clarity, the rest of this chapter will focus exclusively on talk as an avenue for keeping a relationship going. Within contemporary western cultures, we often expect people in a relationship to talk to one another, and we assume that the lack of talk indicates conflict, distance, disgust, or a pending dissolution.

The role that conversations play in relationship enhancement has been subject to some gender research. We know, as mentioned above, that males experience intimacy by sharing activities, and females by talk, valuing talk for the sake of talk (Helgeson, 1987; Tannen, 1990). When males and females have different norms for conversations, the discrepancy creates deep schisms between them. For example, a man will most commonly be focused on what to do about a bad situation, whereas the woman will want sympathy. Then, we have "women feeling men don't hear them, men frustrated with women because they don't take advice to get rid of the distress" (Tannen, 1990, p. 291). As a result, "many men honestly do not know what women want, and women honestly do not know why men find what they want so hard to comprehend and deliver" (p. 167). As one author puts it, "though men may desperately want connection, they again become agents of disconnection" (Bergman, 1991, p. 9).

Conversations become our connective devices to reach each other and transcend the gulf between two separate humans. Increasing competence at talk can provide yet another important avenue for relational sustenance and enrichment. In intimate relations, for example, while lesbian couples do not differ from heterosexual couples on any personality traits, intelligence, or other factors, they do differ on their modal ability in talk. When there are two women who share a belief about the importance of relationships being maintained by talk, you have two people in a partnership attending to one another (Kurdek, 1989). As a result, lesbian couples consistently demonstrate more satisfaction, greater trust, and better decision making than male–female couplings (Kurdek, 1989). Any female–female pairing, even among strangers, will demonstrate more mutual and reciprocal communication styles than when a male is factored into the equation (Mulac, Studley, Wiemann, & Bradac, 1987).

The real issue is not whether males or females are better conversationalists, because large numbers of males are good talkers and large numbers of females are not. The issue is: Does this individual person possess conversational skills that can enhance the relationship? Especially in a culture that prizes independent selves, the connective thread of talk is crucial to creating and maintaining social harmony. In individualistic and pluralistic societies you simply have no idea about the values and orientation of the other—you basically can't assume anything about them. They may look like you but have been raised in a totally different context than you—and share only a few of your values. Therefore, relationships are literally created by our verbal communication and it sustains them.

CONVERSATIONAL QUALITY

Before we look at some of the details of conversational abilities, let's examine the willingness to engage conversations. Of course, no one index will give a complete picture, but for a cursory look, the "Willingness to Communicate" scale taps some of these diverse situations. Look at the items in Table 4-1, and put the percentage of time you would be willing to communicate (0=never, 100=always). This scale can give you a rough self-report index of your willingness to communicate in conversations (by excluding the public speaking situations).

Of more importance than your willingness to talk in a relationship is your content. Different topics, of course, are more or less difficult for us to talk about. Barnlund (1989, p. 190) lists eight topics, rank ordered for U.S. people, that reflect different degrees of "sensitivity." As one moves down the list, the items are seen in our culture as more sensitive and difficult to talk about:

1 General (the level and quality of my education; my family background and circumstances)

2 Tastes (my preferences in clothing, cars, housing; my preferences in plays, films, television)

TABLE 4-1

— 1. *Talk with a service station attendant.
— 2. *Talk with a physician.
— 3. Present a talk to a group of strangers.
— 4. Talk with an acquaintance while standing in line.
— 5. *Talk with a salesperson in a store.
— 6. Talk in a large meeting of friends.
— 7. *Talk with a policeman/policewoman.
— 8. Talk in a small group of strangers.
— 9. Talk with a friend while standing in line.
—10. *Talk with a waiter/waitress in a restaurant.
—11. Talk in a large meeting of acquaintances.
—12. Talk wit a stranger while standing in line.
—13. *Talk with a secretary.
—14. Present a talk to a group of friends.
—15. Talk in a small group of acquaintances.
—16. *Talk with a garbage collector.
—17. Talk in large meeting of strangers.
—18. *Talk with a spouse (or girl/boy friend).
—19. Talk in a small group of friends.
—20. Present a talk to a group of acquaintances.[3]

[3]Scoring is as follows: *items are filler items.
Public:3+14+20; divide by 3
Meeting:6+11+17; divide by 3
Group:8+15+19; divide by 3
Dyad:4+9+12; divide by 3
Stranger:3+8+12+17;divide by 4
Acquaintance:4+11+15+20;divide by 4
Friend:6+9+14+19;divide by 4
Total Willingness to Communicate=Stranger+Acquaintance+Friend

Source: Zahaki, W. R., & McCroskey, J. C. Willingness to communicate: A potential confounding variable in communication research. *Communication Reports, 2,* No. 2, 101, copyright © 1989. Reprinted by permission of the Western States Communication Association.

3 Feelings (my intensity of affection for this person; things about the person that annoy me)

4 Public (my views of the roles of men and women; my views on issues; what should be censored)

5 Work (my occupational goals and ambitions; my limitations and handicaps in my work)

6 Finance (how much money I earn or receive; pressing financial problems I have now)

7 Physical (what I like best about my face or by body; my history of diseases, injuries, operations)

8 Personality (the personal qualities I dislike in myself; my sexual inadequacy or problems in my sexual relations)

The topics are listed in the order U.S. students say they talk about with their acquaintances and friends. Different cultures, obviously, would supply different responses.

The overriding issue in ongoing relationships is one's *conversational sensitivity*. Daly, Vangelisti, and Daughton (1987) define it as:

1 Detecting meanings
2 Conversational meaning
3 Conversational alternatives
4 Conversational imagination
5 Conversational enjoyment
6 Interpretation
7 Perceiving affinity

In a broad sense, *conversational sensitivity* is the propensity to "attend to and interpret what occurs during conversations." It basically boils down to three dimensions: *perceptiveness, attentiveness,* and *responsiveness* (Daly et al., 1987). If you have a relationship that depends on overt recognition from the other, and he or she shows receptiveness, attentiveness, and is responsive to your concerns, you will be more satisfied with the relationship. When you are working hard to convey your message, understanding by the other gives you the confirmation you need (Hecht, Ribeau, & Alberts, 1989).

As you talk with another, there are nonverbal cues that are part of the conversational quality you show. For example, you show immediacy by direct body orientation, sitting closer, smiling, and head nods and more animated gesturing (Coker & Burgoon, 1987). Tannen (1990) found that women tend to anchor their gaze on the other's face, while men tend to anchor their gaze elsewhere in the room, only occasionally glancing at the other. Thus, women are seen as more perceptive, attentive, and responsive than men.

One difficulty with studying conversational ability is that we do not remember the conversations accurately after they have occurred. People typically recall only 10–15 percent of their conversations, with witty remarks, personal criticism, sarcasms, statements of intentions, and relationally significant utterances being better remembered (Kellermann, 1989). Even though people who are cognitively complex are better at conducting and recalling conversations than others (Daly, Bell, Glenn, & Lawrence,

1985; Neulip & Hazelton, 1986), people are not good at remembering conversations, whether they are inside the conversation or watching it from the outside (Stafford, Waldron, & Infield, 1988). As a result, self-report measures such as "sensitivity to feedback," which taps how well you performed in a conversation (Edwards, 1990), and a self-report on how well you remember what people say in conversations (Stacks & Murphy, 1993), are probably not very accurate.

We do know that there *are* certain types of conversational patterns that correlate with distressed and satisfied couples. Lewis and Spanier (1979) reviewed over 200 studies and found that satisfied couples experienced positive regard, emotional gratification, effective communication, and considerable interaction with one another. Similarly, it has been found that satisfied couples, compared to dissatisfied couples,

- Reward each other at equal rates
- Blame and threaten less
- Emphasize the importance of the relationship when they disagreed
- Resolve conflict more effectively
- Confirm each other
- Use more positive statements in response to the other
- Reciprocate pleasing behaviors
- Perceive their partners more accurately
- Agree more on the status of their relationship
- Disclose more to one another (Krueger, 1983; Jacobson, 1984).

Disclosure, you will note, keeps appearing on these lists of items associated with effective communication for certain types of relationships in mainstream U.S. culture. Disclosure, in these contexts, has been found to be positively related to (1) liking and loving romantic partners (Sprecher, 1987), (2) increased intimacy (Roloff et al., 1988), (3) level of marital satisfaction (Rosenfeld & Bowen, 1991; Kirchler, 1988), (4) romantic couples staying in relationships longer (Sprecher, 1987), (5) friendship satisfaction (Jones, 1991).

We have noted throughout that effective discourse in relationships is always tailored to the specific relationship—disclosing to someone you do not know is seen as inappropriate. I'll never forget Fred. Fred (who was studying Freudian psychology at the time) would go to the student union and see someone he didn't know, go to the table, and ask, "May I join you?" When he was invited to join, he would introduce himself, sit down, start eating, and ask, "Tell me about your sexual fantasies." He was often left sitting at the table by himself! Competent conversational communication involves (1) appropriateness and (2) effectiveness (Canary & Spitzberg, 1987), and in a culture that prizes openness, especially in friendship and romantic relationships, to be both appropriate and effective, self-disclosure becomes almost mandatory.

CONSTRUCTIVE CONFLICT

Part of how we manage discourse in our relationships is the management of conflict. In all relationships, especially those ones important to us, conflict will occur. Conflict erupts when people are interdependent, have a perception that something is in short supply (like money, esteem, power, space, computers), see the other as interfering with what they want, and see their goals as incompatible with the other's (Hocker & Wilmot, 1994). While the Hocker and Wilmot book is a comprehensive treatment of conflict, some salient issues are worth highlighting.

What determines the course of a relationship, whether at work or at home, is in a large measure determined by how successfully the participants move through conflict episodes. If you have conflict and productively manage it, the relationship emerges stronger and more vibrant than before. On the other hand, if the conflict is responded to in destructive ways (for that particular relationship) it starts sequences of episodes that detract from relational quality. Lloyd and Cate (1985) found that unresolved conflicts led to the dissolution of premarital romantic couples. And, Kelly, Huston, and Cate (1985) found that "conflict and maintenance" were the best predictors of how the partners felt about the marriage—more powerful than the feelings of love. Each unsuccessful resolution of the conflict (for either participant) sets the stage for lessened relationship quality.

The research on "productive conflict" shows an amazing similarity of findings (Hocker & Wilmot, 1994). Yet we must always keep in mind that the relationship culture will set the boundaries for successful conflict moves. In one family, maybe the most productive move is to "let it sit" for a week before discussing it; in another, jumping into the fray is the best policy. Similarly, in some organizational cultures it is "against the rules" to have open conflict; if you are verbally overt you cause even more problems.

Not all conflicts are alike. For example, Baxter, Wilmot, Simmons, and Swartz (1993) found 12 distinct types of conflict episodes mentioned by participants. Not only are conflicts not monolithic, our responses to them vary considerably. Hocker and Wilmot (1994) treat the different types of responses to conflict by examining avoidance, confrontation, and collaborative communication tactics. That classification corresponds well with the work of Sillars on conflict tactics.

Another way to conceptualize responses to conflict is to use Rusbult's (1987) typology. This typology fits well with indirect and direct notions we have been examining in this chapter. He orders communication in conflict according to dimension of active/passive and constructive/destructive. Table 4-2 displays how the four response modes—voice, loyalty, exit, and neglect—are ordered on the two dimensions.

During a conflict, if you exercise "voice," you act in a constructive, active way—telling the other what your concerns are, taking positions, and communicating about the issue. "Loyalty" is constructive but passive—you remain loyal to the person, do not bring up issues, but neither do you exit or overtly damage the relationship. "Exit" is

TABLE 4-2

	Active	Passive
Constructive	VOICE	LOYALTY
Destructive	EXIT	NEGLECT

destructive and active—you leave during the conflict. "Neglect" occurs when you let things ride, neglect to deal with them, and over time lose your investment to the relationship.

This framework is useful to pinpointing constructive responses to conflict, but all the work is done within the U.S. culture. And what do we find? Satisfaction in relationships is related to voice. Similarly, if you use exit and neglect, it will lower relational satisfaction (Metts & Cupach, 1990). The labeling of the responses as *constructive* and *destructive* is probably culture specific—useful information, but we must be careful about overgeneralizing. While we await more specific research on this model in other cultural settings, it would certainly appear that, in homogenous high-context cultures, exit and neglect would be seen more favorably than would voice, for we already know that direct communication is seen as rude and offensive.

Within U.S. dominant cultural groups, however, the findings on what types of conflict communication are productive are fairly conclusive across a variety of settings and relationship types. Canary and Cupach (1988), for instance, found that tactics that are integrative (using *voice* in Rusbult's terms) produce communication satisfaction and a perception of competence. Likewise, Sillars and Zietlow's (1993) work has demonstrated that, for young, expressive married couples, it is important to integrate with the other—to work with the other with verbal communication for a jointly acceptable solution. As they say, for young couples "a primary function of their communication is explicit negotiation of conflict" (p. 246). Married couples who can successfully work through conflict build a reservoir of resilience—they have a "sense of confidence that conflict can by successfully weathered" (Notarius & Vanzetti, 1983, p. 309). In sum, for many romantic and young married couples, available research shows that both (1) avoidance (exit or neglect) and (2) escalation are counterproductive, and that (3) voice is the path to successful management of conflict.

Avoidance, thinking about the conflict but not discussing it with the partner, clearly is not productive within our mainstream culture. Conflict, an interactive event, requires connection for its settlement. Cloven and Roloff (1991) found when you "mull" over a conflict, retreat from the other and think about it in isolation, you tend to get more polarized, see the conflict as more serious, and hold the partner responsible. Similarly, husbands and wives who both believe that conflict should be avoided report lower marital happiness in the first and third years of marriage than those who think conflicts should not be avoided (Crohan, 1992).

The *mid-range* responses between avoidance and escalation are the most productive (Hocker & Wilmot, 1994). Using tactics such as blaming, criticizing, or threatening the other is associated with less communication (and relationship) satisfaction (Newton & Burgoon, 1990). Using accusatory approaches ("it's your fault") is linked to less communication satisfaction (Newton & Burgoon, 1990). And when one manages to "control" the other, little satisfaction is gained from that either (Rubin, Perse, & Barbato, 1988). Couples who manage to interact in the mid-range, using more directness and involvement, repaired their relationships, while those who avoided, and used indirection and decreased involvement, were unable to keep their relationships together (Courtright, Millar, Rogers, & Bagarozzi, 1990). And when premarital couples tend to escalate and focus on the inadequacies of their partners, the prognosis is not good for their relationship (Kelly, Huston, & Cate, 1985). Finally, in Alberts and Driscoll's

(1992, p. 394) study, "satisfied couples were three times more likely to engage in passed, refocused, mitigated and responsive episodes," compared to dissatisfied couples, who were "twice as likely to engage in unresponsive or escalated episodes."

Within this cultural and relational frame, the research is amazingly consistent on which communication choices enhance a relationship and which ones damage it—don't forget that communication always is interactive. One move by someone ("I told you that it wouldn't work—it's all your fault") will not bring dissatisfaction. It is the *patterning* and sequencing of communication activity that leads to dissatisfaction or relationship enhancement. Individual-level styles do not tell us the complete picture (Baxter, Wilmot, Simmons, & Swartz, 1993); rather, since styles tend to be reciprocal (If I yell, so do you; if I avoid, so may you), the joint responses determine the outcome (Burggraf & Sillars, 1987; Alberts, 1989).

Clearly, within a culture based on individualism, we can transcend our differences by connecting collaboratively with the other—giving voice to the issues, negotiating with the other, and coming to a workable agreement. Either avoidance or escalation will suppress relational satisfaction rather than enhance it. The mid-range responses for young romantic partners are usually the most productive for improving their relationship, because of our cultural beliefs in the importance and efficacy of overt, open communication.

METACOMMUNICATION

We noted in the opening chapter of this book that communication occurs within a "frame" or context. Those frames guide us in our interpretation of communication cues. Anything that frames or contextualizes our communication serves the metacommunication function—providing communication about communication. Metacommunication is important to understand because of the role it can play in enhancing our relationships. If we can see how metacommunication functions, it gives us more options for how to enhance our relationships.

One of the unique properties of our language is its ability to "talk about itself" (Wilden, 1980). Basically, metacommunication provides information about the relationship between the parties; the content is always interpreted within the relationship parameters expressed metacommunicatively. If Kathy says to Bryan, "Darn it, Bryan, quit interrupting me," she is metacommunicating—commenting on their evolving relationship and letting him know that she expects to be treated as an equal. Similarly, if you are talking to your father and he scowls at you when you talk, he is sending a metacommunicative message—cueing you about how to interpret what he will say next.

The metacommunication function can be enacted in a variety of forms. It can occur on either the (1) episodic level or (2) relationship level (Wilmot, 1980). Episodic metacommunication is that which occurs when you are engaged in a conversational episode with someone. If you say, for example, "This is no joke," you are giving the other the "frame" for interpreting what you are saying. Whenever you make some comment about the ongoing transaction, you are engaging in episodic metacommunication. Episodic metacommunication can be directed to the other's acts, yourself, or the transactions between the two of *you* (Bernal & Baker, 1979). Saying, "You interrupt me a lot," or, "I'm sorry, I guess I wasn't clear," or, "That was an interesting talk—I enjoyed our give and take" is episodic metacommunication. If you are in the military and want to cue the other that you are no longer just talking, but want some action, you say, "And that is an order." Satir (1967) provides a more detailed listing of samples of episodic metacommunication. It occurs when someone:

- Labels what kind of message he sends and how serious he is
- Says why he sent the message
- Says why he sent the message by referring to the other's wishes
- Says why he sent the message by referring to a request of the other.
- Says why he sent the message by referring to the kind of response he was trying to elicit.
- Says what he was trying to get the other to do.

These episodic metacommunication expressions perform the "contexting" or framing functions. They are overt cues to signal the other how to interpret the communication messages, whether *you* say, "I was only kidding" or "You are not giving me eye contact."

Episodic metacommunication can, however, be conveyed implicitly without verbally labeling what is occurring. All the available nonverbal cues of our interaction—leaning close to another, talking in a hushed voice, making intense eye contact—provide information about the "framing" you intend for the episode. If you meet a good friend on campus, and he winks and calls you a nasty name, you both know it is not really an insult but a form of play. Dogs often get into mock fights with their owners, and the metacommunication cues sent by both the dog and the owner make it clear to all that the snarling and bared teeth are not really to be feared. These implicit metacommunicative cues are sent in almost all our communicative exchanges—we cue the other how to interpret what we are doing, even it we do not explicitly label it. All our "content" messages carry the implicit message, "This is how I see you in reference to me." Of course, many people send implicit metacommunication cues they are unaware of—being unfriendly or acting superior, for example—and then wonder why other people do not like them. Implicit metacommunication has one prominent feature—it occurs *all* the time you are in the presence of the other. If they are processing cues coming from you, you are letting them know by your nonverbal cues how to interpret the relationship. Just watch two people in conversation when you cannot hear any of the words. You will see those participants sending nonverbal messages all the time. Some will smile and nod their head as if to say "tell me more, I'm fascinated," while others will frown, turn away, and not make eye contact. In all cases, if the two people are processing one another, they are sending cues for how this conversation is to be framed.

In sum, on the conversational or episode level we have two types of metacommunication: (1) explicit (actually telling the other how to interpret your communication), and (2) implicit (the nonverbal cues).

Before we discuss the other types of metacommunication, an overall look at them might be helpful. Table 4-3 illustrates the types of metacommunication.

Relationship metacommunication is at a different level than episodic, yet it also occurs in explicit and implicit forms. Relationship metacommunication arises from our recurring episodes with another (Wilmot, 1980). As we have noted in Chapter 1, indi-

TABLE 4-3.
TYPES OF METACOMMUNICATION

	Implicit	Explicit
Episodic Level	1	2
Relationship Level	3	4

vidual episodes are clustered by the participants to provide an overall relational meaning or definition. Just as with episodic metacommunicative exchanges, relational-level metacommunication is exchanged both implicitly and explicitly.

The implicit relationship definitions or frames are built over time by having repetitive episodic events. (#3 in the figure) For example, if one person always interrupts, controls the topic flow, and generally "runs over" the other, this says that the first person has the right to control the interaction with the other. As described in Chapter 1, these repeated episodes build a relationship definition for the participants, and the more frequent the episodes, the more potent the relational frame. The content of discussions serves as the vehicle by which the relationship is constructed, defined, and maintained—while the content is expressed, the relationship is defined implicitly (Wilmot, 1980). Many times, these implicit relationship definitions are never shared or verbalized. Two people just "know" what their relationship is, and it is all done implicitly. Newman (1984) gives yet another example of how people implicitly define their relationships. She notes that talk about a past relationship partner can serve to clue the other about how you see the current relationship. As she says, "Talking about a past partner can be a means of implicitly communicating what is, or what would be, satisfying, dissatisfying, desirable, or undesirable, in the current relationship." If the person complains that his or her previous romantic partner was "stubborn," it might well be an implicit clue that he or she does not want you to act in a stubborn manner in this relationship.

Often, however, a change occurs in a relationship, where the frame or relationship definition is expressed verbally. When you say, "We are friends," you have provided an explicit metacommunication. (#4 in the figure) Calling someone your "bridge partner" or "best friend" or "live-in lover" tells the participants and others how to interpret the communication that is exchanged between the two of you. Any statement that overtly pertains to "this is how I see you and me in relation to one another" performs a contextualizing function for the communication acts (Wilmot, 1980). Obviously, a relationship-level definition arises from the recurring episodes, but once formed it exerts an interpretive function on all subsequent transactions. Owen (1984b) examined one of the most common forms of relationship metacommunication, the phrase "I love you." He found that it served as a "bid for the relationship," where the person who utters it is essentially asking, "Are we in love with one another?" After it is expressed, it exerts a pull on the other to reciprocate, and saying it too early in a relationship might frighten the partner into terminating the relationship. The relationship definition does bring with it obligations and assumptions about how the two of you will operate. As a result, many times there is a struggle over the overt definition. John says, "We are just friends," while Amy says, "We are beginning to move toward romance." They then get into an argument about whether they are developing a romantic relationship.

To what degree do people share their perceptions of their episodes and overall relationships with one another? Present research demonstrates that *explicit metacommunication* occurs *during turning points* or transitions in relationships (Baxter & Bullis, 1986; Cissna, Cox, & Bochner, 1990; Conville, 1988). In Baxter and Bullis's work, explicit metacommunication occurred at the turning points, which happened about every 2 months. In addition to romantic and friendship relations, stepfamilies who face the task of integrating two family systems into one explicitly define their relationship during the reorganization time. It may be that metacommunication serves usefully at turning points; for example, "perhaps relationship talk prevents disengagement events from turning into complete dissolution (Baxter & Bullis, 1986, p. 487).

Explicit metacommunication is seen by many to not be helpful. If you are being treated badly by a waiter, it is unlikely you will say, "I find you expressing a lot of negative nonverbal cues. Have I done something to offend you?" Similarly, many people resist explicitly talking to an important other about the status of the relationship. As one young man said, "Talking about a carefree relationship would ruin it" (Baxter & Wilmot, 1985). The exact conditions under which explicit metacommunication can serve to help rather than harm a relationship are not yet known, but we do know that people often actively avoid explicit metacommunication. Baxter and Wilmot (1985), for example, interviewed 90 people, asking them what topics were "taboo" in their relationships. All but three people stated that there were taboo topics; the four most frequent types involved explicit metacommunication. For example, people said it was a taboo to discuss (1) the state of the current relationship, (2) extrarelationship activity (other relationships, such as other friends or romantic partners), (3) relationship norms (the "rules" for the relationship), and (4) prior relationships. Other studies demonstrate that explicit metacommunication does occur, yet it may also be seen as threatening or conflict inducing (Hocker & Wilmot, 1994). Similarly, Weber and Vangelisti (1991) found the "state of the relationship was a taboo topic . . . something people, in this culture at least, find difficult or decline to discuss" (p. 91). And Duck (1988) writes, "it is not socially acceptable to comment either on non-verbal behavior or the state of a relationship" (p. 134). The key may lie in how one metacommunicates and the effect it has on the other and the relationship, rather than in whether one should metacommunicate explicitly or not.

The key may lie in *how* one metacommunicates. Clearly, cross-complaining on the metacommunicative level does not enhance relationship quality. Gottman (1982) provides an example of explicit metacommunication from a happy couple:

Person A	Person B
You're interrupting me. I was saying we should take a vacation alone.	Sorry, what were you saying?

Now the dissatisfied couple:

Person A	Person B
You're interrupting me.	
	I wouldn't have to if I could get a word in edgewise.
Oh, now I talk too much. Maybe you'd like me never to say anything.	
	Be nice for a change.
Then you'd never have to listen to me, which you never do anyway.	
	If you'd say something instead of jibber-jabbering all the time, maybe I'd listen.

The cross-complaining, and linking of metacommunicative comments, are clear in this example. It is examples such as these that probably led Watzlawick, Beavin, and Jackson (1967), the first people to write about metacommunication, to feel that it was destructive to relationships.

Recent research linking metacommunication to the enhancement of relationships tends to show the opposite effect—that metacommunication can be an effective way to enhance relationships. Dindia and Canary (1993) found that talking about the relationship and problems in the relationship was reported frequently when the goal was to enhance the relationship. Similarly, Gottman's (1982) research on the happy married couples listed above showed that they used metacommunication in a way that brought issues out without setting off a sequence of negative complaints.

Because of the difficulty of capturing real-life metacommunication for research purposes, we may never know the full impact of metacommunication. When people are asked retrospectively, for example, given that they cannot accurately recall conversations, it is sometimes found that metacommunication is not related to couple adjustment (Baxter & Bullis, 1986). Yet Gottman's work is rather compelling—that different types of metacommunication seem to be linked with distressed and nondistressed spouses. In a sense, though, explicit metacommunication is the natural extension of beliefs that one should be open in communication. And handled with skill, metacommunication in relationships may yet be found to be a powerful force for the enhancement of relationships when the partners believe in open and direct communication.

A context-sensitive approach to relationship enhancement demands we be sensitive to a variety of ways to improve relationships. Indirect and symbolic communication are often more important and powerful than direct verbal expression, depending on the particular relationship culture one is in. Many times, of course, one uses a combination of (1) indirect and (2) overt communication moves to revitalize and enhance a relationship. If you automatically assume, however, that one approach is superior to the other, you will probably neglect the very choice that can enhance a relationship that is important to you, whether on the job, in the family, between friends, or with your romantic partner.

5

THE DARK SIDE: RELATIONSHIP-CONSTRICTING COMMUNICATION

Sometimes, in spite of their best efforts, partners in a relational dance hurt one another—they step on toes, shove and push the partner, force the other to do a dance they don't want, and storm off the dance floor. Similarly, our communication behavior often restrains, damages, and injures our relationships—communication becomes the mechanism of damage rather than enhancement. Our communication connections *do* cause pain and suffering, both in the private relationships and in the world at large. Most of us do not think relationships will be damaging; we enter into jobs, families, love relations, and friendships, usually assuming they will work—we often have an "optimism bias." Much like thinking, I am not the one who will be hurt in a car accident, the relational parallel is, Now *this* relationship will be far better than the last two, or, At *this* job I will not have tangles with the supervisor like I did the last time.

All important relationships have their dark side, even families. While acknowledging that most of us "have survived and flourished thanks to (or despite) our families" Stafford and Dainton (1994, p. 276) note this for us:

> Members of normal families routinely fight with each other, ignore each other, disconfirm each other, criticize each other, are rude to each other, and generally treat each other in a manner as heartless as anything experienced in the outside world. (p. 275)

The framework for examining damaging communication patterns brings us back to the self–other dialectic of the first chapter. One way to view dysfunctional communication patterns is to look for excesses in either (1) an overemphasis on the self at the expense of the other, or (2) an overemphasis on the other and relationships at the expense of the self. Both extremes of independence and dependence "are inherently and precariously imbalanced and consequently preclude the healthiness and rewards of loving relations" (Pingelton, 1984, p. 65).

The conceptual difficulty with looking at the overemphasis on self and other is that the same communication event can be interpreted differently. For example, if you deceive your best friend, do you do it because (1) you want to protect her, (2) you want to protect yourself, or (3) you want to protect the relationship—or some combination of these three? As with all the other examples noted in this chapter, it may be impossible to actually know "why" someone deceives someone else. Further, since we noted the dialectic between protectiveness and expressiveness, the decision to withhold or express is a continual one, and there may be good reasons for deception—and it can bring positive results. Wouldn't it be something if, everytime we met a potential romantic partner, his or her entire relational history, complete with scenes from his or her life, were flashed on a screen behind them? You would enter into a relationship with absolute, total honesty—you would know everything about that person's relational past (and, they would also see yours!).

The perspective of this chapter is that an overemphasis on the self and an overemphasis on the other share something—both bring about the constriction of relationships. Over time, repeated patterns of self/other overemphasis can distort and limit the positive features of a relationship, leaving only pain and disappointment.

STRETCHING THE THREAD TOO THIN: OVEREMPHASIS ON SELF

Successful, integrated, balanced living requires "a stable, realistic, essentially positive sense of self as effective and competent, as well as a capacity for relatedness characterized by mutuality, reciprocity and intimacy" (Guisinger & Blatt, in press). One major type of relationship constricting communication is that which errs with too much one-self-sidedness, overemphasizing the self at the expense of the other and the relationship. Some folks argue in favor of an underdeveloped sense of relatedness—saying it is necessary to "get ahead," and saying people are constitutionally unable to relate (men, you know, can never become relational). Whether condoned or not, if your sense of relatedness is underdeveloped, it has consequences for your entire relational web.

The overemphasis on the self comes in two major forms: (1) being bound up and ineffective at relating with others, and (2) being effective with others but misusing them. We will first examine communication associated with people who have skill deficits and, as a result, are not able to effectively get out of the self and into effective relationships.

The Bound-Up Self: Communication Skill Deficits

When one is unable to carry on a back-and-forth dialogue by responding appropriately to the other, it undermines the relationship. When we change topics to always bring them back to our concerns rather than the other's, it is an act of control, trying to bring the focus back to the self (Palmer, 1989). In distressed marriages, there is often a communication skills deficit on the husband's part, so while he performs adequately in the world of work, he decodes his spouse less accurately than they do strangers (Noller &

Ruzzene, 1991). Surprisingly, in general, males rate their communicative performance more positively than females rate themselves (Andrews, 1987).

Communication skills deficits are not limited to marital situations—many people also cannot perform adequately on the job or in public situations. Communication apprehension, the fear or anxiety of real or anticipated communication with another person, afflicts many people. It arises from poor skills, past negative experiences, and reinforcement of the poor skills. For example, Ned was often quiet, and eventually it became so that teachers and others would not even attempt to include him, creating a spiral of apprehension. The consequences of communication apprehension are well documented. For example, students with higher communication apprehension earn lower grade point averages and are less likely to persist in a university (McCroskey, Booth-Butterfield, & Payne, 1989). There are, of course, cultural differences; for example, Swedish nationals were more apprehensive than Americans (Watson, Monroe & Atterstrom, 1989). People with communication apprehension are less socially relaxed and have more problems of articulation and fewer social experiences (Duran & Kelly, 1989). Whether one's apprehension is general or limited to a specific type of communication event (Parks, 1980), when one faces a situation that provokes anxiety or possible poor performance, it can be quite devastating. People with communication apprehension are perceived as likely to:

- Be less socially attractive
- Be less competent
- Be less sexually attractive
- Be less attractive as a communication partner
- Be less sociable
- Be less composed
- Be less extroverted but of higher character
- Drop classes more
- Talk less in small groups
- Avoid communication that is threatening to them (e.g., giving a speech)
- Prefer large classes
- Choose classroom seats at the periphery
- Prefer occupations that require less communication
- Have lower overall college grade point averages
- Have lower scores on standardized tests given upon high school graduation
- Develop negative attitudes toward school in both junior high school and college

(McCroskey, 1977).

Communication apprehension has an indirect effect on the lives of a wide range of people. Because those with high apprehension avoid or withdraw from communication, they are perceived less positively than others, and the withdrawal plus the negative perceptions of others leads to negative impacts on their "economic, academic, political, and social lives" (McCroskey, 1977). For example, people who have high apprehension are more likely to be lonely than others (Zakahi & Duran, 1982, 1985) and to feel alienated from others (Parks, 1977). Although people with low apprehension may sometimes find themselves in difficulty too, it is clear that high apprehension has demonstrably negative results. There are some training programs for apprehensive individuals to help them with fear and anxiety, and the communication patterns of apprehensives can be altered.

Quite clearly, communication competence in individual episodes is important to our lives. Moreover, Zimbardo (1977) has stated that fully 40 percent of his respondents considered themselves shy and had difficulties in communication situations. Phillips (1977) conducted a detailed analysis of the fears and difficulties college students face. The following items consistently emerged from the students' reports:

1 Inability to open conversation with strangers or to make small talk

2 Inability to extend conversations or to initiate friendships

3 Inability to follow the thread of discussion or to make pertinent remarks in discussions

4 Inability to answer questions asked in a normal classroom or job situation

5 Incompetence at answering questions that arise on the job or in the classroom, not through lack of knowledge but through an inability to phrase or time answers

6 Inability to deliver a complete message even though it is planned and organized

7 General inaptitude in communication situations characterized by avoidance of participants

Finally, Wiemann (1977), who studied the perceptions that members of a sorority had of the other women in the house, discovered that the moment-to-moment conversational behaviors of each woman distinguished whether she was judged as a competent or incompetent communicator by the others. The small bits of conversational communication had large impacts on the judgments made by others of their competence.

The good news is that "even relatively small changes in conversational management result in large variations in how others see our competence" (Wiemann, 1977). Why is this ability to manage transactions successfully so central to how we are seen in terms of our social competence? Rushing (1976) says it best:

> Ordinary, basically honest people give much thought to, and develop a considerable degree of skill in presenting themselves in front of other people. The self is everyone's most valuable possession; one does not present it to the world without protection.

In the course of our transactions with others, we confirm both our own and others' selfhood. Goffman states that competence at managing transactions is inextricably linked to the ability to "maintain face" (Goffman, 1959). The need to be a competent transactor is so pervasive that, when someone is a *faulty interactant* (to use Goffman's term), that person is called a "cold fish," a "wet blanket," a "weirdo," or some other negative term. To make a transaction flow smoothly, one has to work to accept the other's moves and to structure responses that build on what has come before.

Effective transaction management involves being able to (1) initiate a conversation, (2) maintain that conversation, and (3) bring it to a smooth close. Whether your dyadic partner is your business associate, teacher, friend, lover, relative, or acquaintance, the management of the separate transactions is the single most important determinant of the quality of the relationship.

The Self Who Misuses Others

The greatest difficulty is that many people raised in a democratic society are not well enough trained, in social and personal relationships, to honor its principles. They interpret the democratic system as the freedom to do what they like, even when their behavior violates the rights of others. (Mace, 1985, p. 85)

Self-centered rather than relation-centered communication takes many forms. At the first level is just a lack of ability to see the other's point of view—how you see things is how they *are!* It also is reflected in the ability to "hold the relational moment"; men, for example, often joke, shift their attention, physicalize it, and break the tension of connection, fragmenting the process" (Bergman, 1991, p. 7). When you (as either male or female) put the emphasis on "being someone special" (Bergman, 1991), you inevitably compare yourself to others rather than identify with them. You become a self-in-spite-of-relationship, stretching the connective threads until they have no resilience and atrophy.

An overemphasis on the self brings disconnection, disregard, and devaluing others. Crises are resolved "through separation and detachment of the self from others" (Mellor, 1989, p. 363). They become, not partners in a dance with you, but an object to be manipulated. You can't see them because your self is so enlarged; it blocks your view of the other. Such an overemphasized self reflects a society where self-interest is the most important thing in life; all gets sacrificed to the individualistic interpretations, including marriages. If you happen to be male, you limit what you give your partner, or as Bergman (1991) says, "men don't give women enough information to keep them from going crazy." You have a wish to be alone and at the top and fear letting others get close, because they will "drag you down." You want to be the center of the connection, all the while stretching the relational thread until it is misshapen or breaks. Such extreme independence moves reflect a "counter-dependent" approach, being relationally immature and denying your true need for relationship (Pingelton, 1984).

One handy way to understand this classic overemphasis on self is the work on narcissism. Narcissists, who see themselves as the center of the world, are "determined to manipulate the emotions of others while protecting themselves against emotional injury" (Lasch, 1978, p. 78). The narcissist has a "grandiose self" reflected in the attentions of others; others are just there for the narcissist to manipulate and use. In sexual terms, the narcissist escapes from emotional complexity by promiscuity, making an ideology out of "nonbinding commitments" and "cool sex" (Lasch, 1978, p. 200). All forms of communicative encounters, including intimacy, become ways to exploit others. Just as, centuries ago, we thought all the planets and sun revolved around the earth, the narcissist sees all people revolving around himself or herself. Narcissism is, first and foremost, an overemphasis on the self, not factoring in the personhood or needs of the other person. On the lighter side, I have a friend who, while holding up a copy of *Self* magazine, said with a sly grin, "Ah, the quarterly journal of narcissism."

The communicative representations of an overemphasis on the self come, of course, in many forms—breaking relational rules, relational skill deficits, deception, and domination of the other.

Breaking Relational Rules   When you break relational rules, you are expressing an overemphasis on the self—you do what you want regardless of the impacts on the partner. For example, partners create public embarrassment for one another, engage in affairs, and do other forms of "relational transgressions," all of which break the rules of the relationship (Metts, 1993; Petronio, Olson, & Dollar, 1988; Prins et al., 1993). Here are some of the more common forms of breaking the relational rules.

- violating a confidence
- violating privacy of relationship to network of people
- forgetting plans and special occasions
- emotional attachment to a former partner
- sex with a former partner
- failure to reciprocate affection/love/commitment
- not trusting/being jealous
- breaking a significant promise
- changing important plans
- being physically abusive
- not there during a time of need
- not fighting fair (bringing up past mistakes in an argument)
- unfair comparisons (to current relationship or past partner) (Metts, 1993)

In Metts's (1993) research, these items were identified by the recipients of the rule breaking. They were reporting on actual things that had happened in their relationships. It is a good overview of some of the communication manifestations of an overemphasis on the self.

Deception   Whether in business relations, friendship arrangements, or romantic entanglements, deception occurs in many forms. As we noted at the outset of this chapter, there are many ways to interpret deception—one can even argue that it helps a relationship.

Deception may arise as a form of omission. In one study with dating and married persons, most of the deception was through omissions (not telling the romantic partner something) rather than outright lies (Metts, 1989). Dating individuals in this study used deception in order to avoid relational trauma or termination—they felt the deception allowed the relationship to continue. Married respondents, on the other hand, focused more on deceiving in order to avoid threats to the partner's self-esteem; e.g., "if she knew, it would really hurt her" (Metts, 1989). Note that, in both types of relationships, the ones reporting the deception (the partner didn't know about it, or else it wouldn't have been deceptive!), the respondents, felt they were engaging in deception in order to avoid impacts on (1) the relationship or (2) the other. Some recent research notes that the most frequent reason to withhold information was the "anticipation of a negative reaction" from the relational partner (Baxter & Widenmann, 1993). To an outsider, such omissions appear to serve the function of protecting the self, but since the self/other/relationship are all intertwined, the one doing the omission can certainly argue that it was designed to protect the other or the relationship. Of course, the other side of the equation is that the *recipient* of deception has no hand in deciding if it is "good" for the relationship or not—he or she is out of the loop. From the perspective of this chapter, deception, even in its most benign forms, is a form of information control that one exercises; you want to be the one determining the course of the relationship, so you withhold information from the partner. Deception, whether cloaked in "I want to protect him/her" or not, is a form of self-emphasis—you are leaving the partner out of a decision-making role and making the decisions by yourself.

Withholding information, whether to keep an intimate romantic partner from knowing something about your past, or just "putting your best foot forward" when interviewing for a job, serves the function of protection of the self. When you apply for a job but don't tell them you were fired 5 years ago from another job, it certainly seems you are protecting yourself. For most of us, when we are confronted about withholding information, the immediate reaction is a defensive one—"I had to, because they wouldn't have hired me if they knew." Clearly, such automatic responses make it clear that we are in this case trying to protect the "self" that we don't want damaged.

One of the ironies of withholding information, or of telling falsehoods, is that it tends to become self-reinforcing. For example, if one engages in behaviors that are unacceptable to their marriage partner, such as sex with multiple partners, the deception can become ingrained as a way of life. If a married couple has an explicit agreement regarding no outside sexual involvements, then one must keep the activities hidden, which reinforces further deception. And the longer the behavior continues, the more deception is called for, and the person may think, Well, I could have told him/her about the first one, but now that there are seven, there is no way he/she can stick with me if they are revealed. If, on the other hand, one reveals to one's partner before too many transgressions are activated, and the partner gives positive feedback for revealing untruths, then the individual is more predisposed to reveal (Stiff & Miller, 1986). The central key to revealing to a partner is that, if the partner can "stick with you," it may lead the withholder to begin both changing behavior and opening up to the partner. Basically, one enters a spiral of (1) deception or (2) truth telling, where each experience predisposes one to continue either deceiving or staying open.

What about our partners; do they know it when we deceive them? Many outsiders to a relationship will say, "I can't believe she/he didn't know it was going on; everyone was talking about it." For the one in the relationship, however, the degree of intimacy with the partner does not help one see deception (McCornack & Parks, 1990). Most of us believe intimates are better at detecting deception because they "know" the other, yet involvement in a relationship does not assist one in seeing deception.

The very nature of the deepest secrets, behavior that is unacceptable to wide groups of people, means you need to keep them hidden from the partner; you protect yourself at the expense of the partner. Thus, withholding information (omission), or outright lying (commission), is a relational event—it is always within a relational context, designed to protect yourself from negative reactions from the other (Gergen, 1991).

Domination of Others   Relationships continually reflect how individuals balance their individual needs against the needs of the other; the tension is always between self-assertion and recognition of the other's needs. When it is lopsided, we have domination—disregard of the other in order to force your will upon him or her.

Domination of others appears in many communicative forms, ranging from simply controlling conversations all the way to physical violence. Conversational control, while not bothersome to many, is certainly one form of serving our needs without factoring in the other person. The "controller" makes sure the conversation stays focused on him or her, taking every opportunity to stay in the conversational limelight. Conversational control is shown by interrupting the other, talking longer than the other, taking the other's speech as just an opening for your talk and not responding to the other or asking questions about what he or she thinks or feels. Interestingly, conversational control of another does not bring communication satisfaction (Rubin, Perse, & Barbato, 1988), or success in the workplace (Camden & Kennedy, 1986). If you are out of balance with others, they will shy away from you or engage in open struggles for conversational dominance with you. Ever spend time with someone who talks unendingly about himself or herself? As the recipient, you soon come to feel just how unimportant you are—you are just a set of ears so he or she can keep talking.

Conversational control, of course, is not as extreme as other forms of putting self before others. When one goes another notch on the "self before others" scale, one moves into overtly harming the other person by using verbal aggressiveness and harassment.

Verbal Aggressiveness and Harassment   Verbal aggressiveness is making overt comments about the other by verbally attacking him or her (Infante & Wigley, 1986). The following examples should make verbal aggressiveness clear:

"You are a rotten wife (husband)."
"You are just so stupid."
"Any lamebrain knows that."
"Oh, you kids are just delinquents."
"I could just kill you; you are so aggravating."
"You are the worst cook in the universe."
"You don't even know how to think logically."
"You are the worst communicator I have ever dated."
"God, can't you do anything right?"

Verbal aggressiveness serves basically to say, "I'm right," and "It's all your fault," when things go wrong. It serves to demean and diminish the other and, simultaneously, elevate the self over the other.

Recently, our society is recognizing that sexual harassment, sexually offensive or threatening actions against another, occurs in the workplace with alarming frequency, and it takes many forms. (Booth-Butterfield, 1989) A typical university handout on sexual harassment defines it as "any unwanted and repeated attention," which takes many forms and may include:

• sexual propositions with implied or overt threat of reprisal or promise of reward
• unwelcome attention of a sexually oriented nature (patting, pinching, fondling, touching, etc.) by a person who knows or ought to know that such attention is unwanted

• sexually oriented remarks (jokes, innuendoes, etc.) and/or behavior (gestures, staring, display of pornographic materials) that can reasonably be considered to create a negative environment for work or study (EEO, 1989)

Or, alternatively, you could say that if it *offends,* then it's sexual harassment (Elgin, 1993, p. 207).

How often does sexual harassment occur? This varies depending on the study, from a 1976 *Redbook* survey showing 92% of 9,000 clerical and professional women experiencing sexual harassment, to 70% of women in military service (Wood, 1992).

Harassment is forcing your will and interpretation onto another in a way that is offensive to him or her. For example, I once did work at a job site with a brunette male and blond female supervisors who were at the same level in the organization. The male often made statements in her presence such as "saying dumb blond is redundant." She rightfully interpreted the remarks as harassing; he interpreted them as "just jokes." As Booth-Butterfield notes, the harasser and victim do *not* necessarily have the same perception of the intention or harm from such statements—he saw her as "too sensitive," and she saw him as harassing her. In fact, this follows the same pattern as what we noted above about deception—the two participants will have widely divergent views about its effects. The one doing the harassing will usually not see it as offensive and often goes on the attack against the one complaining about it. For, you see, if I am verbally harassing you, if I admit it as "harassment," then I have to somehow adjust or stop. But on the other hand, if "you had it coming" (in my eyes), then I can continue with the destructive patterns.

It should also be noted that sometimes it is also the case the harasser knows that the remarks or moves are distasteful and unwanted, but continues anyway. Some people apparently feel justified in anything they choose to do. I know of one case of a doctor who got into trouble because of inappropriate, offensive touching behavior with patients. When confronted by his partners and an outsider, he said with great emotion, "They were asking for it—you should have seen their breasts."

Some excellent techniques for responding to harassing situations can be found in Elgin (1993). She suggests these four principles:

1 Know that you are under attack.
2 Know what kind of attack you are facing.
3 Know how to make your defense fit the attack.
4 Know how to follow through.

If you are being touched inappropriately, as when a patient in a chair, saying *"stop"* and moving the doctor's hand would be an appropriate response. And following through would involve reporting the harassment, because you can bet that, if the doctor violated you, others have been or are in similar situations. Elgin (1993) provides an example of a dialogue that is unmistakable sexual harassment, and an appropriate response:

Male: "I thought I'd let you know I'm in Room 615."
Female: "Thank you; if I have any news after the meeting, I'll call you on the house phone."

Male: "That won't be necessary . . . you just come on up. If you want to go on *work*ing for *me.*"
Female: "That's not funny!"
Male: "It wasn't intended to be. I'll have the bed turned down and the champagne waiting."
Female: "Mr. Smith, I'm surprised. I thought better of you. But let's get this straight right now: There will never be any relationship between us except the business one. If you feel that the only choice available to you under these circumstances is to fire me, so be it. Now—I'm going to the meeting." (Elgin, 1993, pp. 225–226)

Don't forget that both verbal and physical harassment are inappropriate and illegal. One of the sad aspects of harassment is that, like other forms of victimizing people, it is rarely reported. Only 2.5 percent of those harassed reported it to formal channels, and it is reported, regardless of the settings, with similar low rates in both corporations and universities (Livingston, 1982; Rubin & Borgers, 1990). One can read, however, first person accounts of sexual harassment in the academic world. I recommend the November 1992 issue of *Journal of Applied Communication Research,* both the articles and the section entitled "Our Stories: Communication Professionals' Narratives of Sexual Harassment."

Sexual victimization is yet another form of behavior that is damaging to the recipient. At my university, a survey in 1992 found that, in the previous academic year, 6.6 percent of female students experienced at least one case of forced sexual intercourse. In the vast majority of incidents (83 percent), the victim was acquainted with the assailant, and 51 percent of the victims reported they were held down, hit, choked, or beaten by the assailant. And only 5 percent reported the incident of sexual assault to the police, preferring instead to forget about it, thinking a crime had not occurred, feeling they were partially to blame, and not wanting others to know it had happened to them or that they felt shame or embarrassment (Burfeind et al., 1992).

What allows one to commit such acts? It has been found that holding adversarial (us against them) sexual beliefs was predictive of using threats of force, use of force, ridicule, and guilt to gain sexual wishes (Christopher, 1987). Further, sexual aggression is best predicted by past aggression and beliefs in rape myths. For example, believing that women are in control of their fate, and that any healthy woman can resist a rapist if she really wants to, helps justify in the aggressor's mind not being responsible for the act (Christopher, 1987).

Physical Violence   Sexual victimization is just one form of physical abuse; physical violence occurs with alarming frequency. Violence is prevalent, occurs across many private relationships (especially in the family), and has a strong negative impact on the victim. As Miller says, "to beat a child, to humiliate him or sexually abuse him is a crime because it damages a human being for life" (1992, p. 30). Some parents, of course, argue that they hit the child out of love and/or discipline, to which Miller responds, "No one ever slaps a child out of love" (p. 28). Violence in personal relationships is usually not an isolated experience; it occurs repeatedly over time but is firmly embedded in the mode of communicating with one another (Infante, Chandler, & Rudd, 1989). As Miller says, "something is wrong when they vent their rage or satisfy their sexual urges on their defenseless child" (1992, p. 29). Similarly, anyone who forces others to have sex is committing a heinous act. There are good reasons for the laws against forcing yourself on others—such behavior violates all our standards of decency and wreaks incredible psychological damage on the victim.

Within dating relationships, violence is more commonplace than we used to believe. Marshall and Rose (1987), for example, found that 62 percent of their sample reported expressing violence and 53 reported receiving violence. There are lots of complicated issues regarding violence within families and dating situations, such as the "transmission" theory—that abusers come from people who were abused themselves (Gelles & Cornell, 1990). Further questions, such as what precise communication sequences lead to physical violence, are just beginning to be investigated. For example, it appears that both the aggressor and victim are engaging in some form of physical violence during episodes, though someone ends up a clear loser (Marshall & Rose, 1987). Violence is putting your will above the other, forcing them into compliance. Deal and Wampler (1986) give a list of forms of violence:

- throwing something at the other
- pushing, grabbing, or shoving the other
- slapping the other
- kicking, biting, or hitting with a fist
- hitting or trying to hit with something
- beating up the other
- threatening with a knife or gun

Many people in our culture feel spanking a child is not physical violence (Gelles & Cornell, 1990), yet it too is a case of asserting your own will over another, using force or threat to get what you want.

A final comment regarding all these types of aggression, verbal as well as physical: One common thread underlying them is that the harasser/aggressor does not see the behavior the same as does the victim. The one in "command" of the situation may label potentially threatening cues as innocuous. The person who is controlled by others, however, will be more attuned to the intimidation and coercion involved (Booth-Butterfield, 1989). In terms of defining "what happened," the law has stated clearly that the victim's interpretation will be used. The verbal or physical abuser will not be attuned to the negative effects of his or her actions, for, after all, *not* seeing the negative effects allows one to continue exploiting others. The one in control of the situation hasn't in the past "named" the event as harmful, yet now that we see the patterns of abuse, the victim also can have a hand in "naming" what has happened (Wood, 1992).

Now we will switch to the other end of the self–other continuum and examine situations where the self is submerged to such a degree that it too constricts the relationship.

BEING TRAPPED BY THE WEBS YOU SPIN: EXCESSIVE DEPENDENCE

As Cermack sums it up—when codependents die, they see someone else's life flash before their eyes. (Blau, 1990, p. 58)

When, instead of too much self-concern, there is *too little self-assertion,* the vitality and health of a relationship can be constricted. Imagine two people in a relationship on a teeter-totter; when you overemphasize the other, you don't have enough "weight" to balance; you are in the air with feet flailing, while the other has her or his feet on the ground. You are tied to the other, but the other is determining the movement of the relationship.

Being *too relationally involved* causes relationship constriction because of the entrapment of the individual. For example, family caregivers of the elderly tend to "complain most frequently of feeling physically worn out, being emotionally exhausted and perceiving that the parent was not satisfied no matter what one did" (LaGaipa, 1990, p. 133). In terms of family system theorists, one is "enmeshed" in relationships, not able to forge boundaries between the self and others (Minuchin, 1974; Olson & McCubbin, 1983). For caregivers and others enmeshed in webs of relationships, there is "role overload"—family and friends become a source of stress because of your obligations (Leslie, 1989). There is, for example, a tendency for caregivers to suffer from depressive symptoms as a result of the relational burdens (LaGaipa, 1990).

Just as it is more typical for men to overemphasize the self, women are especially prone to overemphasize the other, caretake the relationship, and take responsibility for others. And women are more vulnerable to the husband's distress than vice versa (Whiffen & Gotlib, 1989); women are more likely to "pick up" the distress of others and take it onto themselves. Unfortunately, just as an overemphasis on the self often brings relational disaster, those who lose themselves in relationships tend to be exploited and abandoned by the one they love (Bellah et al., 1985). Here is how Bobbie, a 50-year-old mother of six children, says it:

> For much of my life, I invested myself so completely into my relationships it became impossible to imagine myself living alone. When my marriage became abusive, the decision to move out always brought a sense of terror. . . . I've always formed "close" relationships quite easily. I now know these skills developed as a result of my need to feel wanted, acceptable, and "having value"; needs I was able to meet through relationships . . . but needs that trapped me into unsatisfactory interactions with my spouse. I had spoon fed my children for 23 years, served my church, and poured out my energy at school for my students. I felt as if my glass was drained and my plate empty. Instead of drawing my life from enmeshed relationships, always doing for others and giving out, I began experiencing learning by confrontation, helping by *not* doing for others.

Bobbie suffocated via her responsibility for, and enmeshment in, relationships. She continues with an observation on more typical male styles of relating:

> During this time I began to envy men and their ability to view relationships more objectively. They have the ability to remain more autonomous, because they do not invest themselves so completely in their relationships. Previously, I had viewed this as being cold; I now know this to be a much more functional way to live than my "warmer," clinging, suffocating way.

When people anesthetize themselves with relationship overinvolvement, they build webs that entrap them. They often are unable to separate, be alone, stand apart, or even take a firm stand against an important partner. Individual success is avoided (Mellor, 1989). They get their power through self-sacrifice (Cermack, 1987).

In its strictest sense, a codependent is someone bound to others who are addicts. For example, if you are married to an alcoholic or drug addict, the addict is trapped by alcohol, and you are the partner of the dependent one, thus codependent. Codependence is essentially a "disease of relationship" (Cermak, 1987), where the person is trapped in his or her own relational web. Technically, a "codependent" is, just like the alcoholic, hooked; the "drug" is the other person. For example, a codependent will drop dinner plans with a friend in favor of being with the addict. And "in the end, the co-dependent's world becomes smaller and smaller as finally everything revolves around the addict" (Blau, 1990, p. 58). And, when everything revolves around the addict, the partner is concentrating so much on the addict that his or her own problems do not get examined (LaGaipa, 1990). Just as the addict is "dependent" on the chemical substance, the "codependent" is addicted to the relationship.

The following checklist gives some insight into the specific communication behaviors of the codependent:

1 I find myself "covering" for another person's alcohol or drug use, eating or work habits, gambling, sexual escapades, or general behavior.

2 I spend a great deal of time talking about—and worrying about—other people's behavior/problems/future, instead of living my own life.

3 I have marked or counted bottles, searched for a hidden "stash," or in other ways monitored someone else's behavior.

4 I find myself taking on more responsibility at home or in a relationship—even when I resent it.

5 I ignore my needs in favor of meeting someone else's.

6 I'm afraid that, if I get angry, the other person will leave or not love me.

7 I worry that, if I leave a relationship or stop controlling the other person, that person will fall apart.

8 I spend less time with friends and more with my partner/child in activities I wouldn't normally choose.

9 My self-esteem depends on what others say and think of me, or on my possessions or job.

10 I grew up in a family where there was little communication, where expressing feelings was not acceptable, and where there were either rigid rules or none at all. (Blau, 1990).

The degree to which you find yourself identifying with these statements means you have a proclivity to be trapped into relationships with others. There are, of course, more specific definitions of codependency worth reading; Cermack, in *Diagnosing and Treating Co-Dependence* (1987), discusses this overinvolvement with others that causes difficulties.

Whether one is overly dependent on others who are chemically addicted, or just overinvolved as a lifestyle, swinging too far on the "defining myself through others" causes difficulties just as overinvolvement with the self does. One of the problems of concepts such as codependence working their way into the popular literature is that they lose their meaning. For example, many people now talk about "codependents" as anyone who feels a need for a relationship. Stretching the definition to such a degree can make even a healthy response to a relationship seem to be "out of range." More work needs to be done on the precise communication indicators of degrees of overdependence on the other for one's sense of worth. We simply have not systematically examined all the forms of too much "we-ness" (Neimeyer & Neimeyer, 1985).

Many people *move from service to separation.* Anecdotally, we see lots of examples of people who suddenly move out of overresponsibility into self-assertion. Gray-haired women and men who have separated from their spouses and go to schools are one such outflow of this dynamic. They are trying to "balance" their lives, and often swing from total responsibility for others to (for the first time in their lives) "doing my own thing."

Of course, overinvolvement isn't restricted to women. One woman I know, Andie, was in a romantic relationship with a recently divorced man. His ex-wife, who lived out of town, kept calling him and leaving long messages on his answering machine. One day Andie happened to overhear one of the messages on the telephone answering machine; her boyfriend had agreed to father a child for his ex-spouse. Andie, enraged, later read all the letters that the ex-spouse had sent to him. They were full of endearing, intimate, and seductive talk, all the while the man denied his closeness to his ex-wife. Andie finally got clear that he (1) had not, and could not "separate" from the ex-wife; and (2) was lying to Andie about the extent of his involvement with his former wife. With much pain, Andie broke off the relationship, and reestablished her own set of boundaries.

RELATIONAL DECLINE OVER TIME

We noted in the chapter on relational enhancement that long-term maintenance and enhancement of relationships seem to be key issues of our time. In many contexts, such as work relationships, research does not track people over time to see the course of relationships. Similarly, the ebbs and flows of relationships within families of origin are not precisely known. We *do* know, however, the predominant mode of satisfaction in long-term marriages, and it is not a happy picture. Guggenbuhl-Craig (1977) captures it well:

> If, using great psychological acuity, one were to dream up a social institution which would be unable to function in every single case and which was meant to torment its members, one would certainly invent the contemporary marriage and the institution of today's family. Two different people of different sex, usually with extremely different images, fantasies and myths, with differing strength and vitality promise one another to be with each other night and day, so to speak, for a whole lifetime. Neither of them is supposed to spoil the other's existence, neither is supposed to control the other, both of them should develop all their potentials fully. This mighty oath is often declared, however, only because of an overwhelming sexual intoxication. Such an intoxication is wonderful, but is it a solid groundwork for a lifetime together?" (p. 10)

At any one point in time, about 20% of all married couples are experiencing marital discord (Beach, 1991). In spite of the rather resilient belief that good relationships won't (or shouldn't) change, and that they can bring us lasting happiness, most marriages and other romantic couplings do not (Chodron, 1990). Of course, it is a sizable order to have a relationship last 10, 20, 30, or more years. If you are in a long-term relationship, how would you answer these questions?

---

1. How well does your partner meet your needs?
2. In general, how satisfied are you with your relationship?
3. How good is your relationship?
4. How often do you wish you hadn't gotten into this relationship?
5. To what extent has your relationship met your original expectations?
6. How much do you love your partner?
7. How many problems are there in your relationship? (Hendrick, 1988)

It is a common observation that there is a decline in marital satisfaction over time (Swensen et al., 1981). The pressures of jobs, children, and other concerns external to the marriage relationship "prevent a husband and wife from maintaining intimate contact with each other (Swensen, Eskew & Kohlhepp, 1981). Even arranged marriages in other cultures suffer the same fate, because love matches are superior to arranged marriages in terms of satisfaction expressed by the wives (Xiaohe & Whyte, 1990).

For many people, because of the constriction of the relationship, the relationship undergoes imperceptible decline over time. On a day-to-day, week-to-week basis, we don't notice any large changes, but over time there is a slow, not-noticed decline in satisfaction. This change in satisfaction is correlated with constricting communication behavior.

Here are some of the communication behaviors associated with a constricted, unsatisfying personal relationship.

- cross-complaining
- insults
- put-downs
- blaming the other with high levels of certainty
- fewer strategies for maintenance and repair
- giving negative information more weight than positive (Hays, 1989; Fincham & Bradbury, 1989; Dindia & Baxter, 1987; Beach, 1991; Noller & Ruzzene, 1991)

Along with such changes in communication behavior are negative attributions—how you process and make sense of the other. Dissatisfied spouses produce "attributions that maintain their current level of distress" (Kurdek, 1989). The participants make "sense" of the relationship and communication in ways that emphasize the unpleasant implications of negative behaviors (Fletcher & Fincham, 1991b). Two authors suggest that the mental frames of dissatisfied spouses come from these beliefs:

1 Disagreement is destructive
2 Partners cannot change
3 Mindreading is expected
4 Sexual perfectionism
5 The sexes are different (Eidelson & Epstein, 1982).

The notion is that such a set of beliefs sets one up for experiencing a decline in satisfaction over time. If you believe that disagreement is destructive, that your partner cannot change, and that the sexes are different, it is no wonder that decline in relational satisfaction is correlated with these. Add mind reading (you think you know what he or she is thinking) and sexual perfectionism to the list, and you have set up an impossible situation. Then, of course, there is no avenue for improvement—all is fixed and immovable; you are locked in by your own beliefs.

Sometimes, the relational thread gets too brittle, loses its elasticity, and the tie between two people breaks. It can happen in romance, friendship, work relationships, and in extreme cases, family relations. Dissolution of the relationship can be seen as yet another form of "relational constriction," this time all the way to a termination of the relationship.

BREAKING THE THREAD: DISSOLUTION

> Marriage . . . can undermine well-being and escape may lead to an expansion of self and life. (Spanier & Tompson, 1984, p. 216)

Regardless of the particular communication of a given dissolution, two features become prominent: (1) at least one partner reaches the "point of no return," and (2) disengagement from the other is a self-reinforcing event. One crucial "turning point" in a relationship comes when one person begins to think, Maybe I should divorce her, or I wonder what would happen if I quit that job? Although it often happens that people have such thoughts, if they become one's prime way of thinking they will bring cracks into the relationship foundation that eventually may be acted upon. Sometimes the person resists the internal thoughts for years, stays in an unhappy marriage or unfulfilling job, and refuses to let himself or herself think about leaving. Then, when the thoughts begin to come, the person starts to envision life without the partner or freedom from the job.

Duck (1982) suggests this list of stages in the dissolution process. Note that the first stage is the "intrapsychic" stage—where you are thinking to yourself about the relationship:

Intrapsychic Phase
Dyadic Phase
Social Phase
Grave-Dressing Phase

During the Intrapsychic stage, you focus on the partner's behavior, evaluate negative aspects of leaving the relationship, look at the costs involved in leaving or withdrawing, and face the dilemma of expressing or repressing your feelings.

If you proceed on to the Dyadic Phase, you begin confronting the partner, negotiate with him or her, attempt to repair or reconcile with the other, and jointly assess the costs of withdrawing. If the progression continues (which it doesn't necessarily do), then you get into the social phase, where you talk to your social network, create public moves to "save face" for yourself by telling your side of the story, and face up to the effects of a dissolution on your social network. If the termination continues, you go into "grave dressing"—healing your wounds, creating your own version of the breakup and doing "postmortems" (well, what happened was, we. . . .).

You may recall Knapp and Vangelisti's stages of coming apart—differentiating, circumscribing, stagnating, avoiding, and finally, terminating (see Chapter 3 on ebbs and flows).

Regardless of what particular set of "stages" you favor to explain moving to dissolution, it is important to note that disengagement moves tend to be self-sealing and reinforcing. As one engages in communication that constricts the relationship, each distancing move tends to be reciprocated by the partner, and a degenerative spiral is set in motion. The degenerative spirals can be in the form of gradual withdrawal of interaction, the "reduction hypothesis," where you slowly reduce the communication with the other (Wilmot & Shellen, 1990). Other times a degenerative spiral is subtle and unseen; then, all of a sudden, a dramatic event occurs. Murray Davis (1973) calls them "passing away" and "sudden death."

In *passing away,* the intimacy declines by almost imperceptible degrees until the relationship can no longer endure. This is typically brought about by the intrusion of a new intimate, by the physical separation of the two, or by the aging of the participants over time. One of the most common experiences of modern life is moving and leaving friends behind, then having to establish new friendships. The previous relationship slowly passes away, as if it were eroded by time. Those people who endure the long separations brought on by military assignments or jobs overseas experience tremendous change and readjustment when the missing one returns home once again. Some relationships endure the separations well—in fact, the two people can often thrive on the separation. Sometimes this happens when a relationship is in the building stages and the two people become so aware of the pain of missing the other that they engage in extraordinary effort to fan the flames. Or they may simply be used to it after many years. Two long-distance lovers talked to each other three times a day and spent over $250 a month on phone calls. If the persons are not able to garner the resources to overcome the spatial separation by phone calls, letters, or other forms of frequent contact, they slowly drift apart.

Some of the literature on relationships between fathers and children who live in different cities demonstrates that the most important variable in maintaining a close relationship over the months of separation is the father's income. (In years to come, if more fathers gain custody of their children, the same will apply to mothers.) If the parent can afford to make frequent calls and go for visits, the relationship with the children will endure. If the parent stops having contact with the children, the relationship is likely to fade away (Weiss, 1975).

Separation is often consciously used by a person in order to let the relationship die slowly. The surest death to romantic or other intimate relationships is to let the energy ooze out of them; they do not have a life of their own independent of the two people. Letting a relationship die by increasing distance takes many forms. A college student, for instance, will increase the psychological distance between herself and another person simply by making herself unavailable. The typical maneuver is to let the roommate answer the phone and "tell him that I am not here." Similarly, people will change the routes they take to their classes or work in order not to encounter the other—knowing that the lack of contact lets the relationship die. People may just let the life slowly fade out of long-term relationships, often without being aware of the choices they are making—but the effects are the same. In the first stanza of the song "Isn't It Enough?" a young man is becoming aware of the slow passing of his marriage.

> Isn't It Enough?
> Monday night and you're out somewhere dancing
> And I'm waiting here for *you* at home.
> You said you'd be at your office working,
> But no one seems to answer when I phone.
> Working late is just your way to say we're on the skids, I know,
> I can see it in your eyes, I can feel it in your touch. And all I've ever
> wanted is to be your lovin' man,
> Is that too much,
> Or isn't it enough?[1]

In this case, the passing away is one-sided; one person vetoed the relationship. It has one element common to many one-sided dissolutions: one of the persons engages in relational sabotage. A person can let a relationship pass away by refusing to make choices that would arrest its decline. He or she may partially want the relationship to dissolve, and while protesting that the relationship is important, all effort is directed to producing its failure. The sabotage can also come from both people as they mutually work to let the relationship fade away.

Sudden death has the same effect as passing away, but the tactics are more obvious. In sudden death endings, the end is announced or made apparent with the swift stroke of death. While passing away is akin to starving, sudden death is similar to execution. Davis (1973) maintains that sudden death is caused by (1) both people, (2) one person, or (3) neither person, with outside forces responsible. The most common form is when one person terminates the relationship and the other is not expecting it. Ted was a student who had an ongoing war with his roommate Marc for over a year. One day he came home to find that Marc had changed the lock on the door and moved all of Ted's belongings into the hall. People sometimes just disappear, without any warning or indication of their discomfort in the relationship. Similarly, a person may pass the word that "it is over" to an ex-intimate via a mutual friend. One man had his oldest daughter inform his spouse that he had left (Weiss, 1975). Or maybe the phone just won't ring anymore. The various tactics are as unique as the individual. One married man with two small children asked his wife if she would like to go to Hawaii. They busied themselves with the preparations and worked out all the details. Then, when sitting on the plane just before takeoff, the man turned to his wife, said, "Have a nice trip," and quickly disappeared. She returned from her traumatic vacation to a set of divorce papers and an empty house.

Why might a person engage in the "sudden death" tactic for dissolving a relation-

[1]Copyright Robert Geis (1977).

ship? Two probable reasons are: (1) some external event moves one to sudden action, and (2) it serves to balance out previous patterns in a relationship. Just as the elements of a conflict can stay underground until some "minor" event brings them to the surface, most relationships end with a triggering event (Hocker & Wilmot, 1994). Often the discovery of an extramarital relationship, a new job opportunity, a chance for a new career, or some other external event moves the people to action. It is precisely because the prospect of termination is so troubling to people that the tactics they use to end a relationship are often destructive and inhumane. How do you, after all, tell a person who still loves you that you want the relationship to end? Especially in relationships characterized by small amounts of metacommunication, the burden of talking about the ending is just too painful to bear. As a result, tactics are used that appear nonsensical to an outsider.

The second reason for quickly killing a relationship is a reaction to long-term patterns that the person feels he or she cannot alter. For instance, if a person feels less powerful than the partner, undergoes years of frustration, and feels that "talking about it" will only rob him or her of personal power, a sudden death might be the chosen alternative. In more extreme forms, a person who has suffered abuse from another may find that the pattern of making up, abuse, making up, and abuse seems to occur regardless of what is done. Then, in an attempt to alter such patterns, one might make a final decision about the relationship, move to a new city, and try to avoid all contact with the former partner. Sudden unexpected moves to dissolve a relationship can be seen as the ultimate power-balancing act, with the one who feels less powerful finally bringing balance by one dramatic act (Hocker & Wilmot, 1994). Similarly, such overt, unexpected moves keep one from being vulnerable to the other's countermoves; if you intend to dissolve the relationship, you might not want the other to initiate the final actions (Baxter, 1979).

Communication Choices During Dissolution

One of the central factors influencing communicative tactics of dissolution is the fact that *it requires two persons to build a relationship but only one to destroy it.* Each participant can make choices to move the relationship toward dissolution, with or without the cooperation of the other person.

Baxter and Philpott (1982) noted for us that the strategies used in termination show less variation than those used at the initiation stage of relationships. Such constriction of options is also present in the actual communicative choices of those moving toward dissolution. For example, friends in the process of dissolution most often do not self-disclose about the decline in the relationship. As Baxter (1979) notes, their disengagements were indirect. Disengagers seem to hint at a "desire to disengage by conversing only on superficial topics, hoping the other is socially perceptive."

Overall, the tactics used by disengagers seem to reflect two basic dimensions: directness–indirectness and other–self orientation. A direct tactic would be using open confrontation, telling the other directly that the relationship is in trouble or that you wish it to be over. Indirectness, as noted earlier, gives subtle clues about the deterioration of the relationship and any other type of withdrawal or avoidance. A self-oriented tactical move would be manipulating the other to accomplish the dissolution, whereas an other-oriented move would help the other by "letting him down gently."

Not only do the tactics you use affect how the termination is experienced, but the way you make sense of the failure of the relationship has an impact. Newman and Langer (1981) surveyed divorced women and discovered that those who blamed their ex-spouse for the dissolution (he was selfish, lacked emotional maturity, had behavior problems, and others) adjusted less well to the divorce than those who made "interactive attributions." An "interactive attribution" would be attributing the cause for failure of the relationship to incompatibility, changing lifestyles, lack of cohesiveness or love, money problems, or lack of communication. A related finding by Wilmot, Carbaugh, and Baxter (1985), surveying long-distance romantic partners who broke up, found a similar result. In this case, unilateral terminations yielded more dissolution pain than did mutual dissolutions. Clearly, how one goes about terminating a relationship affects the long-range outcome for both yourself and feelings about the prior relationship.

One final note about the communication behaviors during deescalation and dissolution. The "reversal hypothesis" holds that communication behavior during dissolution is the opposite of that during initiation and moves toward intimacy. Some research shows reversal occurring in some behaviors like self-disclosure, but not in those linked to one's knowing of the other (Baxter, 1982, 1983). Put simply, if we know things about the other, they are often used in the dissolution process to harm the other.

Vacillation

It is easy to assume that the process of dissolution is straightforward and moves step by step toward a predetermined goal. For example, talking of "stages" or "tactics" suggests that disengaging is without attendant difficulties. But most of us know that the process is not linear and step by step. Rather, it more often reflects the dialectical tensions in relationships—as we try to get farther away from the other, we occasionally move closer. The relationship partners *vacillate* between closeness and distance, with the participants moving farther and farther away. The "now-close, now-far" of the partners between closeness and apartness can sometimes cause distress for others involved in a dissolution. For example, if Phil has filed for divorce and has another romantic partner, she will probably be distressed if he engages in lovemaking with his soon-to-be ex-wife. Yet such patterns of vacillation are very common. One young college male, in his words, "terminated 17 times." After a few turns, the "on again off again arrangement is too painful to be sustained" (Weiss, 1969). Given all the swings, the repetitive moves toward distance have a cumulative effect, with the discord feeding back into the relationship. The partners move farther apart over time, until the relationship can be dissolved. The relationship tends to get into "autodisintegration," where the regressive spiral picks up speed until a dissolution is achieved.

The "lingering lover" syndrome, where the movement toward dissolution is less rational, straightforward, and sequential than many think it should be, occurs for many reasons. For one, the pain of dissolution does not hit many people ahead of time. But moving farther away makes them understand the positive features of the relationship, so they move closer. Upon moving closer together they are reminded of their dissatisfactions, and they move away again.

A second reason for vacillation is that people often discover their goals after they act. One may move away from a friend, lover, or family member without consciously realizing it, then discover that one really *does* want to see the relationship end.

Such back-and-forth movement is, in fact, the most common of termination trajectories. As Baxter says, "The most frequent dissolution trajectory was unilateral and indirect, requiring multiple 'passes' through the model, with no attempted repairs, and with an outcome of relationship termination" (1982). Yet when asked what they regretted about their process of disengagement, the most frequently mentioned regret was the "overreliance" on indirectness.

6

MOVING THROUGH THE LABYRINTH

This final chapter addresses questions about moving through time—what we do when an important relationship ends, how the challenges of our relationships change as we move through our life span, what types of paradoxes crop up during this movement, and how we go about moving into a wider view of communication, one infused with a community value. The two large issues of "moving through time" are (1) what we do after the demise of an important relationship, and (2) age-specific challenges and opportunities.

MOVING THROUGH TIME

Reconnecting and Rebuilding

Debra, during her divorce, said:

> I'm on a raft in white water. I'm wet and cold. My knuckles are white from hanging on, and I don't know what is coming next.

Yet Debra's raft trip did end. She moved on to calmer waters. Some of us go through more rapids and whitewater than others, often forcing us to abandon the raft and hike. Regardless of the particular relational configuration, we *do* move on through life. As we get fired, lose important romantic relationships, watch our best friend move out of town, and experience ongoing changes in our families, the degree of "recovery" from life's sometimes unexpected turns depends on lots of factors: inner resources such as self-esteem and spiritual strength, the networks of supporters, and the available options for the next phase of life.

Most romantic breakups are stressful, but individuals with good social support recover more quickly (Frazier & Cook, 1993). Our existing constellation of relationships helps us adjust as we begin shaping a slightly different future network. In romantic breakups we typically will have less communication and receive less support from the partner's network (Parks & Eggert, 1991), yet we move out to expanded or new networks. Family and friends help us weather times of transition and changes in jobs and romantic partners (Spanier & Thompson, 1984). And for some, counselors and therapists provide a bridge to a changing life, even if those relationships that you pay for do not give you true reciprocal closeness and honesty (Bellah et al., 1985).

When a dramatic change occurs—being fired from a job, losing your lover—it forces a complete reexamination and definition of the self. You literally "relationally redefine" yourself, moving into other activities and networks, orienting yourself to the new job or new romantic partner. For most people in our culture there is an attempt to *default to the self,* to say, "now its *my* turn" or "I really want a new car that my spouse disapproved of all these years." There often is an overemphasis on the self, an intense focus on what *you* want!

The relationship implications of a self-focus are diverse. For some people, it becomes a time of *relational fasting*—not getting involved in a new love relationship. For others, the hunger is so intense they begin another relationship even before the former has begun to untangle. Figure 6-1 illustrates some of the diversity in how individuals handle such events as a dissolution of an important romantic relationship. Relationship #1 ends at the X; relationship #2 is another romantic relationship. Basically, people range from having overlapping relationships to having no relationship.

What are the recovery routes? For many, especially if it is an important romantic breakup, there is an immediate replacement with someone else; the relationships overlap. Others only initiate a new relationship once the other is recognized as "dead." A delayed relationship is when you wait a few months or even years before beginning another romantic relationship. And, finally, one feature of our modern age is that people are choosing to remain celibate and single—to not replace a dissolved romantic bond with another.

We don't know how often people take these different paths, what the consequences

Relationship #1   Relationship #2   **FIGURE 6-1.**
                                                         Choices after dissolution.

--------------X
               --------------------- Overlapping relationship

--------------X-------------- Sequential relationship

--------------X   ---- Delayed relationship

--------------X   No relationship

are, or the impact on subsequent relationships. Most counselors and therapists caution people to at least delay beginning another relationship, feeling that the personal adjust-ment issues are shoved underground by rushing into another relationship. Yet most people who experience the termination of an important romantic relationship neither delay very long nor decide to forgo relationships. For many, facing the void alone with-out a partner is terrifying, so they begin another relationship, merge into other net-works, and begin again. Such people cannot agree with this statement:

Preferring to be together but able to stand alone.
                                        Pingelton (1984, p. 61)

We also know that men more often respond to relational crises by constricting their self-definition, defining the self as separated from the other, while women more often do their dissolution recovery through connectedness (Mellor, 1989).

One crucial question is our cross-relational impact on others. We all know about "relational baggage," the residual influence of the past relationship on your current one. One foreign-born person I know said to her husband during divorce mediation, "You brought your luggage from your first marriage into ours," and she didn't mean his Samsonite! There is relational spillover and surprisingly, it has not been studied. Since we tend to disregard the overall relational life span of people, we tend to see relation-ships across time disconnected from one another. Yet we all know there is potentially some impact. When folks speak of "on the rebound," they mean you rush from one relationship to another and your love for the new other is contaminated by your hurt from the first—hardly a recommended route, yet a very common one nevertheless.

As a starting point, we might gauge "relational recovery" by the following indexes:

1 Can you effectively engage in a new relationship?
2 Can you return to places (house, waterfalls, hometown) that were special for you and the other and feel appreciative of the experience rather than lonely or angry?
3 Can you have contact with the old partner without emotional disruptions?
4 Can you feel genuine compassion for the old partner?

This is, admittedly, just a starter list. We need some systematic research on postrela-tional adjustment, tracing the continuing reactions we have to our pasts. Ambert (1988) found, for example, that postmarital harmony (#3 above) between ex-spouses was rare, and that lessened contact brought more individual adjustment to a divorce.

In a sense, we are all "survivors"—we are touched by death, either literally or figu-ratively, and remain alive and move on (Lifton, 1993). But "rather than collapse under these threats and pulls, the self turns out to be surprisingly resilient" (Lifton, 1993, p. 2). People *do* recover from losing the love of their life, from the death of their par-ents, and from losing their lifelong friend. Jordan says it like this:

Given that life subjects all of us to tensions and suffering and that relationships as well as individuals are buffeted by forces which create pain, disconnection, and the threat of dissolution, the capacity for relational resilience, or transformation, is essential. (Jordan, 1992, p. 1)

And the more we look, the more we see examples of recovery and moving on. What makes the crucial difference in our adjustments? Jordan suggests this list:

1 from individual "control over" to a model of supported vulnerability
2 from a one-directional need for support from others to mutual empathic involvement in the well-being of each person and of the relationship itself
3 from separate self-esteem to a relational confidence
4 from exercise of "power over" to empowerment, by encouraging mutual growth and constructive conflict
5 from finding meaning in self-centered self-consciousness to creating meaning in a more expansive relational awareness. (Jordan, 1992, p. 3)

If we use "trauma for transformation," we can move in and out of connection as a "journey of discovery about self, other and relationship—about 'being in relation' " (Jordan, 1992, p. 9). When we have relational trauma, we (1) learn from the experience and (2) transcend it. If your most important romantic partner creates deep pain for you, the real question is, "What can I learn from this?" Moving past blame to a new level of self-in-relation discovery can provide the path to transformation and propel us into another relationship (if that is what we do) as a stronger, more complex, and adaptable "self." As Lifton says, "we have been evolving a sense of self appropriate to the restlessness and flux of our time" (1993, p. 1).

Looking at Jordan's list above, you can sense the always-in-relationship thread running through it. While we have been discussing the "self" moving on, that is always the embedded, contextualized self located within a constellation of networks. Two points need to be made: (1) we do not accomplish the adjustment by ourselves—there are always others who help us negotiate the passage between life events such as relationship terminations, and (2) true transcendence is not establishing an "independent" self, it is working on a self-in-relation that fully recognizes our need of others while we are increasing our resilience. We strive for "individual identity and shared intimacy . . . intact in a constantly shifting balance (Mace, 1985, p. 85). As noted in Chapter 1, we do not set sail alone—others help us negotiate our passages. The support from our network enables us to move through each situation and emerge, not as a stronger, separate, self, but a more resilient self-in-relation. For example, cancer patients' adjustment is better when there is emotional support from others—in fact the presence of support is the best predictor of adjustment (Gotcher, 1993). And children's adjustment in divorce is the continuity in the relational bond with an absentee father (Petronio & Bradford, 1993). The impact on the constellation of relationships, in fact, is one of the reasons that romantic relationships are so difficult for many individuals. Friends shift alliances, in-laws get angry and refuse to speak to you, and members of your own family may "side" with your former partner—and these ripples in our constellations contribute significantly to the pain of dissolution (Vaughan, 1990). The key to successful transitioning seems to be the quality of the connections with others in your network (Jordan, 1992).

While most research and discussion of "moving on" focuses on romantic relation-ships (because of the deep emotional impact), the same issues surface at different inten-sities for friendship and less intimate acquaintances. When you move, all the less-than-intimate relationships also require some adjustment. We need to become more sensitized to the effects and transformations of all our relationships. For exam-ple, when you change work locations—going to a new plant across town, working for a different division of the same company, or changing jobs even within the same building—you will face transformational issues, too. We need to pay much closer attention to the changing of all our connections as we adjust to life changes.

Relationship Changes Across the Life Span

Given the individualistic focus in the mainstream U.S. culture, we find contributions to our understanding of our "selves" in many areas. Recently, there has been an empha sis on the individual life structure, sensitizing us to some of the individual changes across the life span (Levinson, 1986). And each "season" of a person's life has its "own purpose, not more noble or useful than the next or more "advanced" than the next" (Levinson, 1986, p. 10).

We could profit from refocusing our research efforts and, instead of taking the indi-vidual self as the primary unit of interest, begin to value relationships per se, noting how they evolve and create the very "selves" we usually conceptualize as moving across time. Current research treats relationships as just one small feature of the move-ment of a person across his or her life. If we valued relationships enough to make them the focus, we could answer questions such as these:

1 What changes are there within specific relationships across time?

2 How do the constellations within which an individual relationship (and individ-ual self) are embedded alter, change, and flow across the life span?

3 How do relational events that look similar (the ending of an important romantic relationship, for instance) have differential impact depending on their embeddedness in other relationships? For example, how differently does someone respond to a romantic termination depending on whether he or she has children, family networks, and job connections?

4 What are the impacts of the relationship constellations changing across the life span?

5 Do individuals learn new communication patterns of initiating, maintaining, and terminating relationships?

6 Do the same relationships serve vastly different functions across the life span? For example, do friendships serve markedly different functions before and after the exit of children from the home?

7 With half the population going through divorce, how does the "blended family" communication impact on all other relationships in the constellations?

What are the primary themes in given types of relationships? Do we "recycle" those themes, rediscover our "selves" many times over? What are the elements that produce our response to *change* in relational configurations over time?

While the above suggests making *relationships per se* the context for our research and theorizing, even with our individualized focus, we have learned much about relationships across the life span. We know that friendships for kids change as the kids grow older, with their views of friends becoming more complex and less egocentric (McAdams & Losoff, 1984; see Schofield & Kafer, 1985). And Dickson-Markman (1986) notes that the functions of friendship change with aging, with the elderly having specific needs for friends. And there are some notions that friendship for the elderly provides a compensatory mechanism for "family-less elderly" (Adelman, Parks, & Albrecht, 1987a). Friendship has not been studied systematically across the life span, with longitudinal research; rather, much research has been cross-sectional (looking at friendship at one point in time), at best contrasting friends at one age to friends of folks at other ages.

Of all relationships garnering attention from a life span perspective, marriage has been the chosen topic of interest. As we noted in Chapter 5, most long-term relationships tend to decline in time. One of the changes is moving from the prototypes of friendship and romance to a partnership (Belsky, Lang, & Rovine, 1985). And many of our beliefs about marriage, for example, that the partners are more similar across time, are coming in for reexamination. Viewing marriage within the constellation of other relationships, like extended family or the presence of children, can add important understandings to the experience people have. There is evidence, for example, that when children are in the home they compete for the amount of time spouses are able to communicate with one another, and when adults are accompanied in public by children, they touch, talk, and smile less than couples unaccompanied by children (Anderson, Russell, & Schrumm, 1983). Furthermore, when the children leave home, "if the children are the focal point of the marriage and the main catalyst for fun, then maturation of the children will be experienced as a loss. Individuals who focus intensely on their role as parents are prone to midlife crises when the children leave" (Sillars & Wilmot, 1989).

The aged are receiving more research attention, and with the aging of the overall U.S. culture we can expect to see more work on this era. Nussbaum has led the way in the communication discipline, continuing to focus on communication needs and characteristics of the elderly (Nussbaum, 1989). Retirement communities provide for homogenous contact within "security of a fixed social order" (Bellah et al., 1985). And some work shows that, when an elderly person becomes frail, too many people in his or her network can foster competition and undermine one another. It does happen that relatives, friends, and professionals can find it difficult to work in unison (LaGaipa, 1990). And the elderly often find that the very topics they need to discuss are ones that threaten and upset others, such as talking about past conflicts or present distress (LaGaipa, 1990).

The current research approaches to family life cycle have serious limitations. For example, most of the work is cross-sectional—viewing a given relationship within only one time frame then comparing it to other relationships (Swensen, Eskew & Kohlhepp, 1981). It is a bit like trying to understand your relational life by taking a snapshot of you and your parents today and again in 10 years, then trying to say "this is how people change across time." The snapshot cannot be accurately translated into a movie of your life but, rather, tells us more about where we are culturally or with each cohort (age group). Most of what we know about differences between, say, married couples at different age categories, is confounded by three influences: (1) intrinsic developmental processes, (2) cohort, and (3) life stage (Sillars & Wilmot, 1989). *Intrinsic developmental processes* are what happens as a result of, say, being married or being friends for 20 years. *Cohort* effects are influences due to the particular culture and time you were born. If you were born in 1943, you have a different set of experiences than someone born in 1975. Finally, there may be differences in communication due to the *life stage,* with older people having different communication patterns than younger persons. When older married persons are noted for less explicit conflict, for example, is that due to (1) changes they have experienced being married for 25 years, (2) the general norms about expressiveness in marriage identified with their age group (most people of that cohort rarely engage in open conflict), or (3) something due to where they are in the family life cycle, such as having grown children who have left the home (Sillars & Wilmot, 1989)?

Much remains to be done in tracking communication across the life span. For example, we know that, during retirement, the former connections with work colleagues change dramatically (van Tilburg, 1992). But we do not know, for example, about how individuals handle the changes in constellations that emerge during such life transitions. We know, for example, that the elderly are more discriminating in their friendships than previously thought (Patterson, Bettini, & Nussbaum, 1993), but no one has looked at the changes in "relational knowledge" or views of relationships per se as we move to more advanced ages. There are some fascinating elements of the elderly that will inform our understanding of relationships. For example, elderly narratives about their relationships, their reminiscence about relationships (their family, friends, romantic partners), would be interesting (Buchanan & Middleton, 1993). Much of what the elderly would talk about would be relationships—struggles, choices, celebrations, and observations formed through the entire life span.

TANGLES IN THE WEB: PARADOXES AND CONUNDRUMS

As you go through life, whether you are 18 or 80, the experience and understanding of your relationships is not a linear, step-by-step process. Like relationships themselves, our understanding is imperfect, and it is easy to overestimate how much we know. Relationships are elusive.

There are some relational paradoxes (statements that are both true but contradict one another) (Wilmot, 1987) and conundrums—puzzlements and elements that are inherently unsolvable. Here are a few of them.

1 We want contradictory things in relationships: freedom and closeness, openness to talk yet protection, stability and excitement. These dialectic tensions seem to be present in all relationships.

In many romantic relationships we want both freedom and connection, excitement and stability. In the family context we often want the others to accept who we are, yet we spend inordinate amounts of time centering on how we can change them. We talk openly about the importance of "communication" in relationships, but it appears to be more of a cultural belief than an actual fact (Wilmot & Stevens, 1994; Parks, 1982). Maybe we can begin to celebrate the tension inherent in all relationships rather than trying to solve the contradictory needs, flowing with the needs as they change back and forth.

2 Both insider and outsider views of relationships are fraught with errors.

Outsiders to relationships can more accurately observe our actual communication behavior but are less accurate than we are at specifying the *meaning* of those behaviors within this particular relationship. When you, as an outsider, look at someone else's relationship, your judgments can be a good projective test for what you personally believe is the "key" to success. Think of a marriage you know that you would describe as high quality. To what would you attribute it?

- hard work
- good match on background characteristics
- being raised in non-dysfunctional families
- luck
- how well they communicate with one another
- a fine match on introversion/extroversion
- similar religious affiliations
- the support of their networks of family and friends
- both being raised in the same part of the country
- the length of time they have been together
- their ability to raise children successfully
- their mutual respect and compassion
- their intelligence
- their warmth and expressiveness
- their similar life struggles
- their commitment to one another
- their clarity about how to perform their roles
- their overriding love of one another
- their supportive friends
- similar hobbies and pastimes
- being at the same level of attractiveness

Outsiders, looking at someone else's relationship, tend to rely on external or situational factors in making their guesses (Burgoon & Newton, 1991). And we tend to evaluate others a bit more harshly than they do themselves, with us seeing the limitations of one or both of the partners: "I can't believe she stays married to him—he is so boring in public." When looking at someone's communication behavior, outsiders judge conversations less favorably than do those on the inside (Street, Mulac, & Wiemann, 1988). Outsiders generate faulty hypotheses about the intentions of the communicators—"she did that because she wants to control him" (Stafford, Waldron, & Infield, 1989). When we observe others' communication, we compensate for lack of information about their internal states by using our own personal theories—our "implicit personality theories"

(Stafford, Waldron, & Infield, 1989). As an outsider, our observations are fraught with errors and overinterpretations, sort of "what we get is what we see," with most of it coming from us.

As insiders, our views aren't any less biased; we just tend to focus on different aspects (Dillard, 1987; Sillars & Scott, 1983). For example, insiders to marital relationships tend to overestimate their similarity and act with confidence on their views of the other. Yet the perceptions are not objectively accurate. Therefore, *all* views of relationships are inherently distorted—outsiders and insiders alike. Researchers and book writers (including this one) are themselves influenced by their own needs and perspectives, often looking for some order in the midst of considerable chaos.

3 Relationships are problematic—if we don't do anything about their natural dynamic, they may atrophy. If we try to force them, to "make them happen," we may destroy their essential nature.

The natural forces on relationships, marriage partners having to earn a living and nurture children, friends moving away from one another, tend to move most in the direction of decreased quality over time. In a sense, it is as if there is an energy in relationships that, if you don't continually reinvest in it, will cause the relationship to atrophy. Yet, on the other hand, we need to not try to "force" relationships. It is a rare individual in this culture who can command himself or herself to "love" someone else. The question of how to enhance a long-term relationship—whether family, romantic, or friend—looms large for all of us. In the chapter on relationship enhancement, some suggestions are offered, but it is clear that, so far, there are no guarantees in relationships.

4 Committed relationships, such as marriage, may bring us much unhappiness because we think their purpose is happiness generation. Maybe their purpose is wholeness, grounded in the dialectical encounter between mates. (Guggenbuhl-Craig, 1977)

In North America and most western cultures, people choose marriage partners and friends for what they do for us—make us happy, excite us sexually, provide a sense of fun and connection. Yet as we discussed in Paradigm III in the second chapter, maybe this "what does it do for me" sets us up for disappointment and failure. From a spiritual perspective, one could say that our relationships, while started to "make us happy," have a more difficult and nobler purpose—to allow us to be challenged, to grow, and to change. Lifetime friends, for example, may serve the function of helping us correct ourselves when we get out of line in public. Romantic partners will set the stage for our unresolved issues of life and eccentricity to flourish, and see their downside. Family members will test our commitment, resilience and love, and if we move through that test we can emerge on a higher plane of relatedness.

5 The more intimacy and closeness we want, the more risk we face in the relationship. The greatest pleasure *and* pain come from those to whom we are the closest. Relationships bring both joy and suffering.

The very relationships people spend so much time processing—romantic, family, and friendships—are the ones to bring both the extremes of joy and pain. The less close relationships, while they can bring stability and meaning into life, may not address some of our deepest needs. Risk and reward seem to be opposite sides of the same coin.

6 We often see the "self" as concrete and findable. Yet relationships are no less "real" than an individual self is.

In our culture, we take, as has been noted many times, the "self" as individual, disconnected, separate, and findable. We put the locus of most things into the self—discussing "self-esteem" and "personality" as if they were real things and not abstract concepts. Relationships are neither more nor less figments of our concepts than are our selves—but we don't tend to see it that way in this culture. It is important to note that our selves do have a conventional reality—there is a person standing there. Yet upon close examination, the "self" cannot be found. Is your brain yourself? Your torso? Your legs? Your emotions? We impose the concept of "self" onto the physical and emotional aspects and stop our analysis. Relationships, while not physically represented, are no less real than are our selves. We talk about relationships, and their "reality," upon examination, is just as findable (and no less so) than that of the self.

7 Self is produced in relationship to others; relationships are produced from two selves.

All through this book, it has been argued that we originate and live in-relation; we co-create our selves in relation to one another. And relationships are produced from the two persons who have a communication connection. Self and other produce, and are produced by, relationship. And self is more fruitfully viewed as "with the ecological system" rather than as the center of one's world (Broome, 1991, p. 375).

8 The greatest individual growth, and the greatest derailment of individual growth, come from the hurt and disappointment of relationships gone awry. Relationships can serve as springboards for growth or just toss you higher so you land harder.

When we face the natural traumas of life, our response determines the outcome. Trauma can bring transformation or derailment. Some people are broken when a relationship terminates, for example, or when an important person dies. Others, through grieving and slowly transforming themselves, reopen to relationships and life, reconnecting anew and building better relationships in the future.

9 We can solve problems in relationships by (1) internal, personal change; and (2) changing the external, communication connection between the two. Change at any one level reverberates to the other level, for both us and the other person.

Like the chicken and the egg, which comes first—you or relationship? And if you have difficulties, do you "get your stuff together" and then reenter other relationships, or do you begin other relationships so you can become stronger? Both routes are used, and both can work. If you undergo change, it will reverberate in all your relationships: the boundaries are permeable. If your relationship changes, it will alter you; the influence always flows both ways.

10 We can't fully understand our relationships without concepts, and as soon as we use an abstract notion we impose its limitations on what we are seeing. Labels are essential and limiting, and cannot capture an ever-changing reality. As Wilden says, "all theories of relationship require a certain artificial closure" (Wilden, 1980, p. 114).

We can't really proceed with understanding without labels, and when you introduce your "boyfriend" to your family, it gives them a clue about the relationship. Yet when you use the label, it restricts both your and the other's views of that relationship. Each relationship contains many complex and contradictory elements, and it cannot be accurately captured by "boyfriend." Further, there is always "label lag"—the relationship changes, and the label stays the same. A "married couple" of 6 months will be very different than that very same couple at 6 years or 6 decades, yet they are still referred to as married. All concepts and labels are limiting and constricting—and essential.

11 General conclusions about gender, culture, and relationships may not apply at all to your particular relationships.

One of the problems in talking about "gender" or "cultural" effects is that we are always talking about groupings that help us "understand" on an abstract level. But your particular relationship may not reflect the general norms at all. Just like a theory of gravity cannot tell you about when a particular apple will fall from a tree, studying relational dynamics will not tell you about what will happen in your relationship. When studies on gender, for example, show that females are more expressive than males, what do you do if the woman in a cross-sex romantic relationship is the less expressive of the two? It is probably better to focus on the central issue—expressiveness, and the match or mismatch between the partners—rather than trying to reflect the general norm. Similarly, the finding that gay males have more partners than lesbians or heterosexuals does not mean that a gay man cannot live a life of commitment to another.

12. Learning about relationships occurs before, during, and after the relationship is a findable event.

Our perspectives on our relationships do not end—they only change. Just think for a moment about how you interpret events that happened to you in your childhood. As you move through time you will reinterpret them many times, focusing on different aspects, and seeing them in a different light. Likewise, the friendship that you used to see as a barometer of yourself may be later seen as not helping you at all at a stage of life. A devastating romantic termination may be seen later as the "best thing that ever happened to me." While many of us do not seek difficulties, most of us say, in retrospect, that it is what produced the learning so essential to the next stage of our life. I was once talking to a fellow on a flight from Helsinki, Finland, to Boston. He was in a long-distance relationship with a Finnish woman, and he lived in Boston, and here is what he said. "I did fatherhood and marriage, so I guess I'm doing this for awhile"—making retrospective sense of his relationship that was allowing him to collect considerable frequent flyer miles!

BUILDING COMMUNITY

Relationships, like life, are complex, and our attempts to categorize, synthesize, and "capture" them intellectually are, by definition, insufficient. Then what is the use? Since they all are impermanent, shouldn't we just "get the most" from others and then move on to the next relationship, looking for even more devious ways to satisfy our cravings? Shouldn't you default to your individual needs, show disregard for others, and do what you most need, regardless of the impact on another?

One way out of the conundrum of "what's the use" is to recognize the *transcendent function of relationships*. The "missing piece" is to "bring men and women back from their enclaves into the creative space called relationship" (Bergman, 1991, p. 11). Whether on the personal, family, group, or work level, the investment in others allows us both to change and to have a positive impact on others. In their survey of the impact of teamwork on the job, Larson and LaFasto (1989, pp. 76–77) note, "in that identification there is a relinquishment of the self—not a denial of the self, but a voluntary redefinition of the self to include membership in the team as an important aspect of the self."

It is our ability to *commit to productive* relationships that both builds a valuable "self" and gives the world something back. As Tannen notes (1990, p. 25), "Life, then, is a community, a struggle to preserve intimacy and avoid isolation." Our "practices of commitment" keep the community alive (Bellah et al., 1985), and, of course, nurture the self at the same time. It has been noted, for example that those who generate social support are also the ones who receive it (Conn & Peterson, 1989). Within the confines of our individualized mainstream culture in the United States, such transcendence of the self becomes a positive step in moving out of our narcissistic, constricted sense of self-against-others attitudes that often flourish. Commitment to community building necessarily means some changes from putting the self first—in spiritual terms, it means some sacrifice (Guggenbuhl-Craig, 1977). Or as Chodron (1990, p. 43), puts it, "instead of wondering 'how can this relationship fulfill my needs?' we'll think 'what can I give to the other?' " Paradoxically, the commitment to community through communication serves as a "source of power" for the individual (Tannen, 1990).

What is *community?* We most often associate community with a "sense of place," building relationships bounded by geography composed of neighbors and those physically close to you. We tend to think of times when people knew their neighbors and were close to their kin as when "community" really flourished. For example, if you grew up in a small town (there are still some of them today, by the way) and move to a city, you are often struck by the anonymity and lack of connectedness between people—whereas, at home, you knew your neighbor as well as your second cousin, in the city you don't even know the person in the apartment next to you. Similarly, if you travel in Nepal or Tibet, and get to know some locals, you will be struck by the overlapping relationships. Go on a trek or climb led by a Sherpa, then ask him, "Where is a good place to stay," and you will have a guest house recommendation of one of his many relatives. If you say, "What is your connection to the trekking company?" you will discover that the owner is married to his sister, and the cook on the trek is married to his other sister. In these cultures, business and kin relationships are totally intertwined. And, furthermore, the original connections come from growing up in small villages where they all know one another.

This is not to suggest we drop place and overlapping networks as the definition of community. For example, there is some evidence that couples who have few shared family connections report lower marital satisfaction (Stein et al., 1992). Rather, we need to expand our notions of community and examine function rather than only place. In mobile western societies, we have "increasing freedom to choose social relations," and this has not led to a lessening of social ties but a changing of them (Fisher & Steuve, 1977). In one study in Toronto, for instance, the Torontonians' connections with the outside were not, as in Third World countries, connected to economic and political survival. Rather, the connections were based on a domestic focus. Yet "private, personal communities continue to flourish and support a wide array of network members" (Wellman & Wellman, 1992, p. 404). The Torontonians range far and wide but operate their personal communities from their homes rather than from kinship groups or local hangouts. As the authors say, "People are no longer stuck with unwanted kin or neighbors; nor must they put up with disliked habitués of pubs and caves" (Wellman & Wellman, 1992, p. 404). Others suggest that our mobility is not greater than in the past, but that it just affects different people (Fisher & Steuve, 1977).

Whether the community is based on place or function, what the relational connections give us is a sense of location in a network, and social support. It is the social involvement with others that is the key (Gerson, Stueve & Fisher, 1977; Peck, 1987), and that can be supported in a variety of ways. Artificial neighborhoods, for example, constructing retirement communities, are attempts to create neighborhoods, albeit based on stage of life rather than economic or kinship ties. Many people are trying to construct communities based on professions and other avenues—finding a sense of connection based on something other than kinship or location.

Electronic mail is opening up new pathways for community development. People used to send letters, but now the almost-instant connections of e-mail provide a way to build relationships that sometimes feel like they are somewhere between letters and phone calls. Most e-mail messages are short, and each time you send one you are plugging into a community-in-formation. With e-mail, the community members are "bound by a sense of identity," share some values in common, yet exclude some others, and use a common language and other features that distinguish it (Goode, 1969). There is even some evidence that computer-aided group interaction can approach the level of face-to-face communications (Walther, 1993). When I changed my e-mail address and my old one didn't continue to work, I felt it necessary to contact a few folks and let them know that, if they sent messages, I "wouldn't be at home" to receive them. Just as when you think the neighbor might come calling and you leave a note on the door saying "be back at 2:30," I felt that they might "come calling" at anytime and I should let them know where to find me.

Electronic connections allow a form of community to develop based on shared interests, history and involvement with others even if you have never met face-to-face. As Reingold (1993) says, "I suspect that one of the explanations for this phenomenon is the hunger for community that grows in the breasts of people around the world as more and more informal public spaces disappear from our lives." (p. 6) Such community building can, of course, lead to interesting consequences. Reinhold tells this story about when some members of the WELL, an electronic network in the San Francisco area met for a party.

> I remember the first time I walked into a room full of people . . . who knew many intimate details of my history and whose own stories I knew very well. Three months after I joined, I went to my first WELL party at the home of one of the WELL's online moderators. I looked around at a room full of strangers when I walked in. It was one of the oddest sensations of my life. I had contended with these people, shot the invisible breeze around the electronic watercooler, shared alliances and formed bonds, fallen off my chair laughing with them, become livid with anger at some of them. But there wasn't a recognizable face in the house. (p. 2)

Community, then, has a unifying theme, "that of a cohesive group of people held together by different things which they share, for example, territory, ideas, work, skills" (Thorns, 1976). It is the connectedness of people that builds community, pulling us out of our selves and into interpersonal relatedness. We build community at lots of levels too, not just in our most intimate relationships. Our "weak ties" to others, whether via e-mail, chatting with the neighbor across the street, or seeing a fellow worker once a year at a meeting, are no less important to a sense of community than kin ties have been in the past (and sometimes still are). If you do a "constellation check," you will find, as suggested in Chapter 1, numerous people to whom you are connected. Most North Americans have over one thousand informal relationships that "give a sense of place, help, carry reputation" and perform other interpersonal functions (Milardo & Wellman, 1992, p. 340; Parks, 1982, p. 93; Adelman, Parks, & Albrecht, 1987a). These "weak ties," such as changing jobs and moving from one network into another, are "indispensable to individuals' opportunities and to their integration into communities" (Granovetter, 1973, p. 1378).

Drawing the Boundaries

But *which* communities can we invest in? An individual relationship such as family, friends, work associates, and romantic partners? A larger, less intimately connected group such as your skiing buddies, social group, or roommates you are not very close to? To the larger ethnic or other group with whom you identify? To the United States as a whole? To the whole world? To a spiritual path? The answer is *yes*. All relationships with others transcend the features of the self that block us from activating our positive potential.

Figure 6-2 is one way to see the interconnection of all the levels. In this figure the "self" is in community with all levels, and while you might invest yourself in a worldwide issue, the next person might put more emphasis on their friendships or family— but the transcendent effects are potentially the same.

Community building poses, of course, some questions for us all. If we want to have a sense of a unique and functioning self, it requires drawing some boundaries around the self. Similarly, if we want a close relationship, it requires a "boundary of privacy that isolates the relationship parties from the outside" (Baxter & Widenmann, 1993,

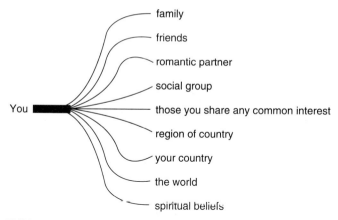

FIGURE 6-2.
Levels of Community.

p. 322). To fully function as an entity requires some boundary maintenance—you and your best friend share experiences and idioms that others don't. In marriage, we see them as a "collective entity" (Kamo, 1993). To effectively form with others, at whatever level, you have to join with them, forming and overcoming otherness in living unity (Arnett, 1986). You are probably a member of many communities, and they do not have to be mutually exclusive; as Pope John XXII said, "The fact that one is a citizen of a particular state does not detract in any way from his membership in the human family as a whole, nor from citizenship in the world community" (Christiansen, 1989, p. 54–55). You can define your loyalty in various terms—kin relations, romantic, social network, neighborhood, professional identity—but the process is the same: you can be a positive force for the betterment of the world. Here is how Oppenheim states it:

> Sages such as Moses, Buddha, Confucius and Jesus arose in various world cultures and religions. They pointed to a divine Spirit at work in the human world, one who could empower human selves to be transformed from self-centered alienation into genuine loyalty to the great community of humankind. (1989, p. 113)

Easy to say, hard to do: Real community building comes from a move to dialogic thinking and dialogic communication.

Doing Dialogue

Communication choices that build community and work for both self and other are transformative—they transform both the self and other, based on sharing and understanding (Stewart, 1978; Cahn, 1990b). They are mutual based on reciprocal actions where self and other coevolve and are seen as inseparably linked (Stewart, 1978). Verbally, they are *dialogic* (Stewart, 1978; Arnett, 1986).

Seeing yourself as a "community builder" goes beyond what is often emphasized in the United States. As Professor John Hammerback, a friend of mine, characterized the learnings many of us absorbed, "we aren't penalized for the pain we cause, we are rewarded for the gains we make." To transcend such one-sided views of communication, we begin to focus on a "we-ness," not only in our most intimate relations, but seeing the interdependence of all of us on one another (Derlega, 1989). And, as a side note, the real issue is not one of gender, with women doing dialogue and men doing monologue, for men and women are more alike than different (Hendrick & Hendrick, 1987). The real issue is staying focused on the quality of the communication occurring between two people.

There are two approaches to community building communication: (1) the overt, verbal, dialogic level; and (2) the implicit, nonverbal choices we make. On the overt, verbal level, communication as dialogue has been treated extensively (Stewart, 1978; Arnett, 1986). As Arnett (1986, p. 126) says, "When we cease to talk, we rupture our collective web and make it virtually impossible to learn from one another." A dialogic perspective sees communication as arising *between* persons, not within each of us, presuming that "we are inextricably interrelated" (Hanh, 1987, p. 38). It allows transcendence from the "self-boundary" (Hermans & Kempen, 1993). Here is the ending of a poem by Tubbs, that expresses the dialogic perspective well:

I must begin with myself, true;
But I must not end with myself:
The truth begins with two (Tubbs, 1976)

Dialogue is relationship-centered communication and uses a narrative that "bridges multiple self-perceptions" (Arnett, 1986). It causes each person to be preoccupied with the other (Buber, 1972).

You can tell when you are *not* in dialogue, by the presence of individual themes— talking as if your presence were the only important one. Sillars and Zietlow (1993) give examples of such individual-oriented talk in their research. Note the assumptions underlying this discourse from married couples:

"You have your friends and I have mine."
"Individual decisions are made individually."
"You bitch all the time."
"You're never home to discipline the kids."

Compare those to these statements, which assume a joint interest, develop communal themes, and promote dialogue:

"We enjoy the same things."
"We talk out disagreements, so we don't confuse the children."
"It's hard to be depressed when someone else is not."
"If you're irritable and I'm feeling irritable, that makes it worse."

One model for verbal dialogue, as applied to romantic relationships, comes from the co-commitment model from Hendricks and Hendricks. While this is developed only for romantic relationships, it does give us a clear picture of what dialogue might entail in such relationships.

1 I commit myself to full closeness and to clearing up anything that stands in the way.

2 I commit myself to my own complete development as an individual.

3 I commit to revealing myself fully in the relationship, not to concealing myself.

4 I commit myself to the full empowerment of people around me.

5 I commit myself to acting from the awareness that I am 100 percent the source of my reality.

6 I commit myself to having a good time in my close relationships. (Hendricks & Hendricks, 1990)

The second level to understand community-building communication is to look beyond dialogue. At the second level we tune into the implicit, symbolic forms of unspoken communication. Symbolic and indirect communication composed of the nonverbal elements always present accomplishes the same type of transformation that dialogue does. For example, as we noted earlier, many Japanese are "reluctant to express their ideas and feelings clearly because they subconsciously fear that, by doing so, they might damage the whole atmosphere of interpersonal harmony in the situation" (Klopf, 1991). Sitting quietly with a child with your arm around his shoulder, joining in ritualized family gatherings, partaking of any activity that can help build a sense of relationship with the other, and adapting to the other's cultural preferences for communication (Fontaine, 1990) all are forms of community-building communication. As you move north in the United States for instance, people are more touch avoidant (Andersen, Lustig, & Andersen, 1990), so adapting to that by not forcing touch on someone would be a community-building choice.

The dialogic approach would value all the participants, not overemphasizing the self or overemphasizing the other—it serves to value both people and factor their needs into the relationship equation. Most people writing about dialogue stress how you should incorporate the other into the communication event because of the frequent pattern of communication in the western world of being egocentric in our communication. Dialogue, however, presumes that *all* participants are to be valued, included, and given a voice in the communication event.

It is important to also remember that the dialogic approach can be seen in its usual verbal form and extended to the indirect forms of communication. When you adapt to, include, and show an active concern to the other, whether in verbal or indirect forms, it manifests a dialogic approach to communication. Understanding the dialogic approach is important, because our relationships are built from our communicative choices. And the type of communication we engage in creates a reality that not only affects all those in all our community connections, but also passes on down the line to subsequent generations. There is a "flow-through" on adjustment to the next generation (Homel et al., 1987). How you communicate not only affects the current person you are with but also builds a web of influence that extends far beyond the current encounter.

A RELATIONALLY BASED ETHIC

According to Confucian philosophy, "one's ability to achieve a harmonious relationship with others is the greatest spiritual accomplishment of one's life" (Chang & Holt, 1991, p. 255). This book has attempted to explore the issues surrounding a vision of a relationally based communication, demonstrating how one can unlink communication from the rampant individualism in current mainstream western culture. We can conceptualize and communicate, assuming that the self with other are "attached and continuous" (Bach, 1990, p. 3). Such a view would entail seeing the complexity of communication, knowing that the dialectic tensions will always exist, yet striving to move communication to a new level—honoring diversity, commitment, adaptability, and openness to others. We would both balance our own and others interests (Christiansen, 1989). We could practice compassion in our communication, using restraint against harming others, grounding ourselves in moral choices in all our relationships, whether the most intimate or the most fleeting casual encounters. We can commit acts of random kindness, knowing that our actions impact the world in ways we yet do not fully understand.

The relational view of communications presupposes that we are all connected to one another, and the splitting off of the self is a recent event in the world's history. If we open our view, we can see that relationship-based communication is occurring all around us, yet we often do not notice it. Make a list of all the kind things people do for you just in one day—take your phone messages, smile, recognize you, ask you how you are, give you assistance—and you can begin to see how relationally dependent we all are. When we begin to see our connectedness, it brings a heightened awareness of the importance of our communication choices. With such a perspective, we can develop our communication skills, not to gain personal advantage, but to contribute to our personal relationships and the wider social network a sense of connectedness that reverberates throughout our relationship constellations and the wider world as well.

It is not an easy task. Relationships are complex—there are as many types of them as there are grains of sands in the Ganges River. When we treat them as transformative connections, for both self and other, their importance takes on a new dimension.

Relationships are like a dance. Sometimes you dance without knowing your partner, sometimes you and the other do different steps, and sometimes the coordination between the two of you creates a beautiful flow. You may think you can "sit this one out." But, after all, the music *is* playing!

REFERENCES

Acitelli, L. K. (1988). When spouses talk to each other about their relationship. *Journal of Social and Personal Relationships, 5,* No. 2, 185–199.

Acitelli, L. K., Douvan, E., & Veroff, Joseph (1993). Perceptions of conflict in the first year of marriage: How important are similarity and understanding? *Journal of Social and Personal Relationships, 10,* 5–19.

Acker, M., & Davis, M. H. (1992). Intimacy, passion and commitment in adult romantic relationships: A test of the triangular theory of love. *Journal of Social and Personal Relationships, 9,* 21–50.

Adelman, M. B., Parks, M. R., & Albrecht, T. L. (1987a). Beyond close relationships: Support in weak ties. In Adelman, M.B., Parks, M.R., & Albrecht, T.L. (Eds.), *Communicating Social Support.* Newbury Park, CA: Sage, pp. 126–147.

Adelman, M. B., Parks, M. R., & Albrecht, T. L. (1987b). *Communicating Social Support.* Newbury Park, CA: Sage, pp. 105–125.

Adelman, M. B., & Siemon, M. (1986). Communicating the relational shift: Separation among adult twins. *American Journal of Psychotherapy, 15,* 96–106.

Alberts, J. K. (1988). An analysis of couples' conversational complaints. *Communication Monographs, 55,* 184–197.

Alberts, J. K. (1989). Perceived effectiveness of couples' conversational complaints. *Communication Studies, 40,* 280–291.

Alberts, J., & Driscoll, G. (1992). Containment versus escalation: The trajectory of couples' conversational complaints. *Western Journal of Communication, 56,* 394–412.

Albrecht, T. A., & Bach, B. W. (in press). *Organizational Communication: A Relational Approach.* New York: Harcourt, Brace & Jovanovich.

Althen, G. (1992). The Americans have to say everything. *Communication Quarterly, 40,* 413–421.

Altman, I. (1993). Dialectics, physical environments, and personal relationships. *Communication Monographs, 60,* 26–34.

Altman, I., & Taylor, D. A. (1973). *Social Penetration: The Development of Interpersonal Relationships.* New York: Holt, Rinehart & Winston.

Altman, I., Vinsel, A., & Brown, B. B. (1981). Dialectic conceptions in social psychology: An application to social penetration and privacy regulation. In Berkowitz, L. (Ed.),

Advances in Experimental Social Psychology, 14. New York: Academic Press, pp. 105–160.

Ambert, A. M. (1988). Relationship between ex-spouses: Individual and dyadic perspectives. *Journal of Social and Personal Relationships, 5,* No. 3, 327–346.

Andersen, Peter A. (1993). Cognitive schemata in personal relationships. In Duck, S. (Ed.), *Individuals in Relationships* (series on Understanding Relationship Processes), vol. 1. Newbury Park: Sage, pp. 1–29.

Andersen, P. A., Lustig, M. W., & Andersen, J. F. (1990). Changes in latitude, changes in attitude: The relationship between climate and interpersonal communication predispositions. *Communication Quarterly, 38,* 291–311.

Andrews, P. N. (1987). Gender differences in persuasive communication and attribution of success and failure. *Human Communication Research, 13,* 372–385.

Argyle, M., & Henderson, M. (1985). *The Anatomy of Relationships.* London: Heinemann.

Armstrong, S. L., Gleitman, H., & Gleitman, L. R. (1983). What some concepts might not be. *Cognition, 13,* 263–308.

Arnett, Ronald C. (1986). *Communication and Community: Implications of Martin Buber's Dialogue.* Carbondale: Southern Illinois University Press.

Aron, A., Aron, E. N., Tudor, M., & Nelson, G. (1991). Close relationships as including other in the self. *Journal of Personality and Social Psychology, 60,* 241–253.

Aron, A., Dutton, D. G., Aron, E. N., & Iverson, A. (1989). Experiences of falling in love. *Journal of Social and Personal Relationships, 6,* 243–257.

Bach, B. W. (1990). Making difference by doing differently: A response to Putnam. Paper presented to Arizona State Conference on Organizational Communication: Perspectives for the 90s, April 5–7, Tempe, AZ.

Barbee, A. P., Gulley, M. R., & Cunningham, M. R. (1990). Support seeking in personal relationships. *Journal of Social and Personal Relationships, 7,* 531–540.

Barnlund, D. (1989). *The Public and Private Self in Japan and the United States.* Tokyo: Simul.

Bateson, G. (1972). *Steps to an Ecology of Mind.* New York: Ballantine Books.

Bateson, G. (1979). *Mind and Nature: A Necessary Unity.* New York: Bantam Books.

Bavelas, J. B., Black, A., Chovil, N., & Mullett, J. (1990). *Equivocal Communication.* Newbury Park: Sage.

Baxter, L. A. (1979). Self-disclosure as a relationship disengagement strategy: An exploratory investigation. *Human Communication Research, 5,* 215–222.

Baxter, L. A. (1982). Strategies for ending relationships: Two studies. *Western Journal of Speech Communication, 46,* 223–241.

Baxter, L. A. (1983). Relationship disengagement: An examination of the reversal hypothesis. *Western Journal of Speech Communication, 47,* 85–98.

Baxter, L. A. (1984). Trajectories of relationship disengagement. *Journal of Social and Personal Relationships, 1,* 29–48.

Baxter, L. A. (1986). Gender differences in the heterosexual relationship rules embedded in break-up accounts. *Journal of Social and Personal Relationships, 3,* 289–306.

Baxter, L. A. (1987a). Self-disclosure and relationship development. In Derlega, V., & Berg, J. H. (Eds.), *Self-Disclosure: Theory, Research, and Therapy.* New York: Plenum.

Baxter, L. A. (1987b). Symbols of relationship identity in relationship cultures. *Journal of Social and Personal Relationships, 4,* 261–280.

Baxter, L. A. (1988). Cognition and communication in the relationship process. In Burnett, R., P. McGhee, & David Clarke (Eds.), *Accounting for Relationships.* New York: Methuen.

Baxter, L. A. (1990). Dialectical contradictions in relationship development. *Journal of Social and Personal Relationships, 7,* No. 1, 69–88.

Baxter, L. A. (1992a). Forms and functions of intimate play in personal relationships. *Human Communication Research, 18,* 336–363.

Baxter, L. A. (1992b). Root metaphors in accounts of developing romantic relationships. *Journal of Social and Personal Relationships, 9,* 253–275.

Baxter, L. A. (1993). Thinking dialogically about communication in personal relationships. In Conville, R. L. (Ed.), *Uses of Structure in Communication Studies.* Westport, CT: Praeger, pp. 23–37.

Baxter, L. A. (1994a). Thinking dialogically about communication in personal relationships. In Richard Conville (Ed.), *Uses of Structure in Communication Studies.* New York: Praeger, pp. 23–37.

Baxter, L. A. (1994b). Self-reported maintenance strategies and three external contradictions of relating. Paper presented to Interpersonal Communication Interest Group, Western States Communication Association, San Jose, CA.

Baxter, L. A. (1994c). A dialogic approach to relationship maintenance. In D. J. Canary, & L. Stafford (Eds.), *Communication and Relational Maintenance.* New York: Academic Press, pp. 233–254.

Baxter, L. A., & Bullis, C. (1986). Turning points in developing romantic relationships. *Human Communication Research, 12,* 469–494.

Baxter, L. A., & Dindia, K. (1990). Marital partners' perceptions of marital maintenance strategies. *Journal of Social and Personal Relationships, 7,* 187–208.

Baxter, L. A., & Philpott, J. (1982). Attribution-based strategies for initiating and terminating friendships. *Communication Quarterly, 30,* 217–224.

Baxter, L. A., & Simon, E. P. (1993). Relationship maintenance strategies and dialectical contradictions in personal relationships. *Journal of Social and Personal Relationships, 10,* 225–242.

Baxter, L. A., & Widenmann, S. (1993). Revealing and not revealing the status of romantic relationships to social networks. *Journal of Social and Personal Relationships, 10,* 321–337.

Baxter, L. A., & Wilmot, W. W. (1983). Communication characteristics of relationships with differential growth rates. *Communication Monographs, 50,* 264–272.

Baxter, L. A., and Wilmot, W. W. (1984). Secret tests: Social strategies for acquiring information about the state of the relationship. *Human Communication Research, 11,* 171–201.

Baxter, L. A., & Wilmot, W. W. (1985). Taboo topics in close relationships. *Journal of Social and Personal Relationships, 2,* 253–269.

Baxter, L. A., Wilmot, W. W., Simmons, C. A., & Swartz, A. (1993). Ways of doing conflict: A folk taxonomy of conflict events in personal relationships. In P. Kalbfleisch (Ed.), *Interpersonal Communication: Evolving Interpersonal Relationships.* Hillsdale, NJ: Lawrence Erlbaum Associates.

Beach, S.n R. H. (1991). Social cognition and the relationship repair process: Toward better outcome in marital therapy. In Fletcher, G. J. O., & Fincham, F. D., (Eds.), *Cognition in Close Relationships.* Hillsdale, NJ: Lawrence Erlbaum Associates, pp. 307–328.

Beach, W. A. (1990). On (not) observing behavior interactionally. *Western Journal of Speech Communication, 54,* 603–612.

Beatty, M. J., & Dobos, J. A. (1993). Adult males perceptions of confirmation and relational partner communication apprehension: Indirect effects of fathers on son's partners. *Communication Quarterly, 41,* 66–76.

Belenky, M. F., Clinchy, B. M., Goldberger, N. R., & Tarule, J. M. (1986). *Women's Ways of Knowing.* New York: Basic Books.

Bell, R. A., & Buerkel-Rothfuss, N. L. (1990). S(he) loves me, s(he) loves me not: Predictors of relational information-seeking in courtship and beyond. *Communication Quarterly, 38,* 64–82.

Bell, R. A., Buerkel-Rothfuss, N. L., & Gore, K. E. (1987). Did you bring the yarmulke for the Cabbage Patch Kid? The idiomatic communication of young lovers, *Human Communication Research, 14,* No. 1, Fall, 47–67.

Bell, R. A., & Healey, J. G. (1992). Idiomatic communication and interpersonal solidarity in friends' relational cultures. *Human Communication Research, 18,* 307–335.

Bell, R. A., & Roloff, M. E. (1991). Making a love connection: Loneliness and communication competence in the dating marketplace. *Communication Quarterly, 39,* 58–74.

Bellah, R. (1989). Afterword. In S. J. Gelpi (Ed.) *Beyond Individualism: Toward a Retrieval of Moral Discourse in America.* Notre Dame, IN: University of Notre Dame Press, pp. 219–225.

Bellah, R. N., Madsen, R., Sullivan, W., Swidler, A., & Tipton, S. (1985). *Habits of the Heart: Individualism and Commitment in American Life.* Berkeley, CA: University of California Press.

Belsky, J., Lang, M. E., & Rovine, M. (1985). Stability and change in marriage across the transition to parenthood: A second study. *Journal of Marriage and the Family, 47,* 855–865.

Benjamin, J. (1988). *The Bonds of Love: Psychoanalysis, Feminism and the Problem of Domination.* New York: Pantheon Books.

Benoit, W. L., & Benoit, P. J. (1988). Factors influencing the accuracy of verbal reports of conversational behavior. *Central States Speech Journal, 39,* 218–232.

Berardo, F. (1974). Marital invisibility and family privacy. In Margulis, S. (Ed.), *Privacy.* Stony Brook, NY: Environmental Design Research Association.

Berger, C. R. (1986). Uncertain outcome values in predicted relationships: Uncertainty Reduction theory then and now. *Human Communication Research, 13,* 34–38.

Berger, C. R., & Bell, R. A. (1988). Plans and the Initiation of Social Relationships, *Human Communication Research, 15,* No. 2, Winter, 217–235.

Berger, C. R., & Bradac, J. J. (1982). *Language and Social Knowledge: Uncertainty in Interpersonal Relations.* London: Edward Arnold.

Bergman, S. J. (1991). Men's psychological development: A relational perspective. *Work in Progress,* No. 48. Wellesley, MA: Stone Center.

Bernal, G., & Baker, J. (1979). Toward a metacommunicational framework of couple interactions. *Family Process, 18,* 293–302.

Berndt, T. J. (1981). Relations between social cognition, nonsocial cognition and social behavior: The case of friendship. In Flavell, J. H., & Ross, L. (Eds.), *Social Cognitive Development.* New York & London: Columbia University Press.

Bettini, L. M., & Norton, M. L. (1991). The pragmatics of intergenerational friendships. *Communication Reports, 4,* 64–72.

Blau, M. (1990). Co-dependency: No life to live. *American Health, 9,* 57–61.

Bochner, A. P. (1982). On the efficacy of openness in close relationships. In Burgoon, Michael (Ed.), *Communication Yearbook 5.* New Brunswick, NJ: International Communication Association/Transaction Books, pp. 109–124.

Booth-Butterfield, M. (1989). Perception of harassing communication as a function of locus of control, work force participation, and gender. *Communication Quarterly, 37,* 262–275.

Borgmann, A. (1992). *Crossing the Postmodern Divide.* Chicago: University of Chicago Press.

Bormann, E. G. (1972). Fantasy and rhetorical vision: The rhetorical criticism of social reality, *Quarterly Journal of Speech, 59,* 396–407.

Bowen, M. (1965). Family psychotherapy with schizophrenia in the hospital and in private practice. In Boszormenyi-Nagy, I., & Framo, J. L. (Eds.), *Intensive Family Therapy: Theoretical and Practical Aspects.* New York: Harper & Row, pp. 213–243.

Brand, S., & Hirsch, B. J. (1990). The contribution of social networks, work-shift schedules, and the family life cycle to women's well-being. In Duck, S. (Ed.), *Personal Relationships and Social Support.* London: Sage, pp. 150–172.

Brandstadter, J. (1990). Development as a personal and cultural construction. In Semin, G. R., & Gergen, K. J. (Eds.), *Everyday Understanding: Social and Scientific Implications.* London: Sage Publications, 83–129.

Bridge, K., & Baxter, L. A. (1992). Blended relationships: Friends as work associates. *Western Journal of Communication, 56,* 200–225.

Broome, B. J. (1991). Building shared meaning: Implications of a relational approach to empathy for teaching intercultural communication. *Communication Education, 40,* 235–249.

Buber, M. (1972). *Between Man and Man.* New York: Macmillan.

Buchanan, K., & Middleton, D. J. (1993). Discursively formulating the significance of reminiscence in later life. In Coupland, N., & Nussbaum, J. F. (Eds.), *Discourse and Lifespan Identity.* Newbury Park, CA: Sage, pp. 55–80.

Buehler, C., & Legg, B. H. (1993). Mothers' receipt of social support and their psychological well-being following marital separation. *Journal of Social and Personal Relationships, 10,* 21–38.

Bugental, J. F. T. (1978). *Psychotherapy and Process: The Fundamentals of an Existential-Humanistic Approach.* New York: Random House.

Bugental, J. F. T. (1987). *The Art of the Psychotherapist.* New York: Norton.

Burfeind, J. W., Dole, D. P., & Cooper, J. M. (1992). The University of Montana Sexual Victimization Survey. Unpublished Paper, Missoula, MT.

Burggraf, C. S., & Sillars, A. L. (1987). A critical examination of sex differences in marital communication. *Communication Monographs, 54,* 276–294.

Burgoon, J. K., & Hale, J. I. (1987). Validation and measurement of the fundamental themes of relational communication. *Communication Monographs, 54,* 19–41.

Burgoon, J. K., Coker, D. A., & Coker, R. A. (1986). Communicative effects of gaze behavior: A test of two contrasting explanations. *Human Communication Research, 12,* 495–524.

Burgoon, J. K., & Newton, D. A. (1991). Applying a social meaning model to relational message interpretations of conversational involvement: Comparing observer and participant perspectives. *The Southern Communication Journal, 56,* 96–113.

Burgoon, J. K., Parrott, R., Le Poire, B. A., Kelley, D. L., Walther, J. B., & Perry, D. (1989). Maintaining and restoring privacy through communication in different types of relationships. *Journal of Social and Personal Relationships, 6,* 131–158.

Burleson, B. R. (1990). Comforting as social support: Relational consequences of supportive behaviors, in Duck, S. (Ed.), *Personal Relationships and Social Support.* London: Sage, pp. 66–82.

Burleson, B. R., & Samter, W. (1994). A social skills approach to relationship maintenance. In Canary, D. J., & Stafford, L. (Eds.), *Communication and Relational Maintenance.* New York: Academic Press, pp. 61–90.

Burleson, B. R., Samter, W., & Lucchetti, A. E. (1992). Similarity in communication values as a predictor of friendship choices: Studies of friends and best friends. *The Southern Communication Journal, 57,* 260–276.

Cahn, D. D. (Ed.) (1990a). *Intimates in Conflict: A Communication Perspective.* Hillsdale, NJ: Lawrence Erlbaum.

Cahn, D. D. (1990b). Perceived understanding and interpersonal relationships. *Journal of Social and Personal Relationships, 7,* 231–244.

Camden, C. T., & Kennedy, C. W. (1986). Manager communicative style and nurse morale. *Human Communication Research, 12,* No. 4, Summer, 551–563.

Campbell, S. M. (1980). *The Couple's Journey: Intimacy as a Path to Wholeness.* San Luis Obispo, CA: Impact Publishers.

Canary, D. J., & Cupach, W. R. (1988). Relational and episodic characteristics associated with conflict tactics. *Journal of Social and Personal Relationships, 5,* No. 3, 305–325.

Canary, D. J., & Hause, K. S. (1993). Is there any reason to research sex differences in communication? *Communication Quarterly, 41,* 129–144.

Canary, D. J., & Spitzberg, B. H. (1987). Appropriateness and effectiveness perceptions of conflict strategies. *Human Communication Research, 14,* No. 1, Fall, 93–118.

Canary, D. J., & Stafford, L. (1992). Relational maintenance strategies and equity in marriage. *Communication Monographs, 59,* 243–267.

Canary, D. J., & Stafford, L. (1994). Maintaining relationships through strategic and routine interaction. In D. J. Canary, & L. Stafford (Eds). *Communication and Relational Maintenance.* New York: Academic Press, pp. 3–22.

Cantor, Nancy, & Malley, Janet. (1991). Life tasks, personal needs, and close relationships. In Fletcher, G. J. O., & Fincham, F. D. (Eds.), *Cognition in Close Relationships.* Hillsdale, NJ: Lawrence Erlbaum Associates, pp. 101–125.

Capella, J. N. (1984). The relevance of the microstructure of interaction to relationship change. *Journal of Social and Personal Relationships, 1,* 239–264.

Capra, F. (1983). *The Tao of Physics* (2d ed.), New York: Bantam Books.

Carbaugh, D. (1990a). Communication rules in Donahue discourse. In Carbaugh, D. (Ed.), *Cultural Communication.* Hillsdale, NJ: Lawrence Erlbaum Associates, pp. 119–149.

Carbaugh, D. (Ed.) (1990b). *Cultural Communication.* Hillsdale, NJ: Lawrence Erlbaum Associates.

Carnelley, K. B., & Janoff-Bulman, R. (1992). Optimism about love relationships: General vs. specific lessons from one's personal experiences. *Journal of Social and Personal Relationships, 9,* 5–20.

Cegala, D. J., & Waldron, V. R. (1992). A study of the relationship between communicative performance and conversation participants' thoughts. *Communication Studies, 43,* 105–123.

Cermak, T. L. (1987). *Diagnosing and Treating Co-dependence: A Guide for Professionals who Work with Chemical Dependents, Their Spouses, and Children.* Minneapolis, MN: Johnson Institute Books.

Cermak, T. L. (1988). *A Time to Heal: The Road to Recovery for Adult Children of Alcoholics.* Los Angeles: Jeremy P. Tarcher, Inc.

Chang, H-C., & Holt, G. R. (1991). More than relationship: Chinese interaction and the principle of Kuan-Hsi. *Communication Quarterly, 39,* 251–271.

Chodron, T. (1990). *Open Heart, Clear Mind.* Ithaca, NY: Snow Lion Publications.

Christiansen, D. S. J. (1989). The common good and the politics of self-interest: A Catholic contribution to the practice of citizenship. In Gelpi, S. J. (Ed.), *Beyond Individualism: Toward a Retrieval of Moral Discourse in America.* Notre Dame, IN: University of Notre Dame Press, pp. 54–86.

Christopher, F. S., Owens, L. A., & Stecker, H. L. (1993). An examination of single men's and women's sexual aggressiveness in dating relationships. *Journal of Social and Personal Relationships, 10,* 511–527.

Cissna, K. N., & Anderson, B. (1990). The contributions of Carl R. Rogers to a philosophical praxis of dialogue. *Western Journal of Speech Communication, 54,* 125–147.

Cissna, K. N., Cox, D. E., & Bochner, A. P. (1990). The dialectic of marital and parental relationships within the stepfamily. *Communication Monographs, 57,* 44–61.

Cline, R. J. W. (1989). The politics of intimacy: Costs and benefits determining disclosure intimacy in male-female dyads. *Journal of Social and Personal Relationships, 6,* 5–20.

Cloven, D. H., & Roloff, M. E. (1991). Sense-making activities and interpersonal conflict: Communicative cures for the mulling blues. *Western Journal of Speech Communication, 55,* 134–158.

Coker, D. A., & Burgoon, J. K. (1987). The nature of conversational involvement and nonverbal encoding patterns. *Human Communication Research, 13,* 463–494.

Conn, M. K., & Peterson, C. (1989). Social support: Seek and ye shall find. *Journal of Social and Personal Relationships, 6,* No. 3, 345–358.

Connidis, I. A. (1992). Life transitions and the adult sibling tie: A qualitative study. *Journal of Marriage and the Family, 54,* 972–982.

Contarello, A., & Volpato, C. (1991). Images of friendship: Literary depictions through the ages. *Journal of Social and Personal Relationships, 8,* 49–75.

Conville, R. L. (1988). Relational transitions: An inquiry into their structure and function. *Journal of Social and Personal Relationships, 5,* No. 4, 423–437.

Cooney, T. M. (1994). Young adults' relations with parents: The influence of recent parental divorce. *Journal of Marriage and the Family, 56,* 45–56.

Courtright, J. A., Millar, R. E., Rogers, E., & Bagarozzi, D. (1990). Interaction dynamics of relational negotiation: Reconciliation versus termination of distressed relationships. *Western Journal of Speech Communication, 54,* 429–453.

Craig, R. T., Tracy, K., & Spisak, F. (1986). The discourse of requests: Assessment of a politeness approach, *Human Communication Research, 12,* 437–468.

Craik, F. I. M. (1979). Human memory. *Annual Review of Psychology, 30,* 63–102.

Crawford, L. (1988). The stillpoint: Taoist quietism, human relationships and living peacefully. Paper presented to the Speech Communication Association, Peace Communication Commission. New Orleans, LA (ERIC document reproduction service No. ED 299 627).

Crohan, S. E. (1992). Marital happiness and spousal consensus on beliefs about marital conflict: A longitudinal investigation. *Journal of Social and Personal Relationships, 9,* 89–102.

Cupach, W. R., & Comstock, J. (1990). Satisfaction with sexual communication in marriage: Links to sexual satisfaction and dyadic adjustment. *Journal of Social and Personal Relationships, 7,* 179–186.

Cupach, W. R., & Metts, S. (1986). Accounts of relational dissolution: A comparison of marital and non-marital relationships. *Communication Monographs, 53,* 311–334.

Dainton, M., & Stafford, L. (1993). The dark side of "normal" family interaction. Paper presented to the Western States Communication Association, Albuquerque, NM, February.

Dainton, M., & Stafford, L. (1993). Routine maintenance behaviors: A comparison of relationship time, partner similarity and sex differences. *Journal of Social and Personal Relationships, 10,* 255–271.

Dalai Lama, H. H., Benson, H., Thruman, R. A. F., Gardner, H. E., & Goleman, D. (1991). *Mind Science: An East-West Dialogue.* Boston, MA: Wisdom Publications.

Daly, J. A., Bell, R. A., Glenn, P. J., & Lawrence, S. (1985). Conceptualizing Conversational Complexity. *Human Communication Research, 12,* 30–53.

Daly, J. A., Vangelisti, A. L., & Daughton, S. M. (1987). The nature and correlates of conversational sensitivity. *Human Communication Research, 14,* 167–202.

Davis, K. E., & Latty-Mann, H. (1987). Love styles and relationship quality: Contributions to validation. *Journal of Social and Personal Relationships, 4,* 409–428.

Davis, K. E., & Todd, J. M. (1985). Assessing friendship: Prototypes, paradigm cases and relationship description. In Duck, S. W., & Perlman, D. (Eds.), *Understanding Personal Relationships: An Interdisciplinary Approach* London: Sage, pp. 17–38.

Davis, M. S. (1973). *Intimate Relations.* New York: Free Press.

Deal, J. E., & Wampler, K. S. (1986). Dating violence: The primacy of previous experience. *Journal of Social and Personal Relationships, 3,* 457–471.

Dell, P. F., & Goolishian, H. A. (1981). Order through fluctuation: An evolutionary epistemology for human systems. *Australian Journal of Family Therapy, 2,* 175–184.

DeMaris, A., & Rao, K. V. (1992). Premarital cohabitation and subsequent marital stability in the United States: A reassessment. *Journal of Marriage and the Family, 54,* 178–190.

Derlega, V. J. (1989). Self-Disclosure: Inside or outside the mainstream of social psychological research? In Leary, Mark (Ed.), *The State of Social Psychology: Issues, Themes, and Controversies.* Newbury Park, CA: Sage, pp. 27–44.

Dick, S. (1990). Relationships as unfinished business: Out of the frying pan and into the 1990s. *Journal of Social and Personal Relationships, 7,* No. 1, 5–28.

Dickson-Markman, F. (1986). Self-disclosure with friends across the life-cycles. *Journal of Social and Personal Relationships, 259–264.*

Dillard, J. P. (1987). Close relationships at work: Perceptions of the motives and performance of relational participants. *Journal of Social and Personal Relationships, 4,* 179–193.

Dillard, J. P., & Witteman, H. (1985). Romantic relationships at work: Organizational and personal influences. *Human Communication Research, 12,* 99–116.

Dindia, Kathryn (1987). The effects of sex of subject and sex of partner on interruptions. *Human Communication Research, 13,* 345–371.

Dindia, K., & Allen, M. (1992). Sex differences in self-disclosure: A meta-analysis. *Psychological Bulletin, 112,* 106–124.

Dindia, K., & Baxter, L. A. (1987). Strategies for maintaining and repairing marital relationships. *Journal of Social and Personal Relationships, 4,* No. 2, 143–158.

Dindia, K., & Canary, D. J. (1993). Definitions and theoretical perspectives on maintaining relationships. *Journal of Social and Personal Relationships, 10,* 163–173.

Doi, T. (1973). *The Anatomy of Dependence.* Tokyo: Kodansha International Ltd.

Dosser, D., Balswick, J. O., & Halverson, C. F., Jr. (1986). Male inexpressiveness and relationships. *Journal of Social and Personal Relationships, 3,* 241–258.

Downs, V. C., Javidi, M., & Nussbaum, J. F. (1988). A comparative analysis of the relationship between communication apprehension and loneliness for elderly nursing home and non-nursing home residents. *Western Journal of Speech Communication, 52,* 308–320.

Droge, D. (1991). Person-construction: A dramatistic view of the self in interpersonal communication. Paper presented to the Western Speech Communication Association, February, Phoenix, AZ.

Duck, S. W. (1982). A topology of relationship disengagement and dissolution. In Duck, S. W. (Ed.), *Personal relationships, Vol. IV: Dissolving personal relationships.* New York: Academic Press, pp. 1–30.

Duck, S. (1988). *Relating to Others.* Chicago, IL: The Dorsey Press.

Duck, S. (1991). New lamps for old: A new theory of relationships and a fresh look at some old research. Paper presented to the Third Conference of the International Network on Personal Relationships, Normal/Bloomington IL, May.

Duck, S. W., & Miell, D. E. (1986). Charting the development of personal relationships. In Gilmour, R. and Duck, S. W. (Eds.), *Emerging field of personal relationships.* Hillsdale, NJ: LEA, pp. 133–144.

Duck, S., & Pond, K. (1991). On public display of private intimacy: An analysis of valentine's day messages. Paper presented to third conference of the International Network on Personal Relationships, Normal/Bloomington, IL, May.

Duck, S., Rutt, D. J., Hurst, M. H., & Strejc, H. (1991). Some evident truths about conversations in everyday relationships: All communications are not created equal. *Human Communication Research, 18,* 209–227.

Duran, R. L. (1992). Communicative adaptability: A review of conceptualization and measurement. *Communication Quarterly, 40,* 253–268.

Duran, R. L., & Kelly, L. (1989). The cycle of shyness: A study of self-perceptions of communication performance. *Communication Reports, 2,* 30–38.

Dykstra, P. A. (1993). The differential availability of relationships and the provision and effectiveness of support to older adults. *Journal of Social and Personal Relationships, 10,* 355–370.

Edwards, R. (1990). Sensitivity to feedback and the development of self. *Communication Quarterly, 38,* 101–111.

EEO/Affirmative Action Office (1989). Sexual Harassment: Remaining Silent Won't Make it Stop. Missoula, MT: University of Montana.

Eggert, L. (1987). Support in family ties: Stress, coping, and adaptation. *Communicating Social Support.* Newbury Park, CA: Sage, pp. 80–104.

Eidelson, R. J., & Epstein, N. (1982). Cognition and relationship maladjustment: Development of a measure of dysfunctional relationship beliefs. *Journal of Consulting and Clinical Psychology, 50,* 715–720.

Einstein, A. (1954) Dialogues with scientists and sages. In Weber (Ed.), Sonja Bargmann (trans.), *Ideas and Opinions.* New York: Crown Publishers, p. 203.

Elgin, S. H. (1993). *Genderspeak: Men, Women, and the Gentle Art of Verbal Self-Defense.* New York: Wiley.

Epstein, S., & Feist, G. J. (1988). Relation between self-and other-acceptance and its moderation by identification. *Journal of Personality and Social Psychology, 54,* 309–315.

Farrell, T. B. (1984). Narrative in natural discourse: On communication and rhetoric. *The Journal of Communication, 34,* 109–127.

Fehr, B. (1993). How do I love thee? Let me consult my prototype. In Duck, S. (Ed.), *Individuals in Relationships* (series on Understanding Relationship Processes). Newbury Park: CA, vol. 1, pp. 87–120.

Fehr, B., & Russell, J. A. (1991). The concept of love viewed from a prototype perspective. *Journal of Personality and Social Psychology, 60,* 425–438.

Fincham, F. D., & Bradbury, T. N. (1989). The impact of attributions in marriage: An individual difference analysis. *Journal of Social and Personal Relationships, 6,* No. 1, 69–85.

Fischer, C. S. (1982). What do we mean by "Friend"? An inductive study. *Social Network, 3,* 287–306.

Fisher, B. A., & Drecksel, G. L. (1983). A cyclical model of developing relationships: A study of relational control interaction. *Communication Monographs, 50,* 66–78.

Fisher, C. S., & Stueve, C. A. (1977). "Authentic community": The role of place in modern life. In C. S. Fisher et al., (Eds.), *Networks and Places: Social Relations in the Urban Setting.* New York: The Free Press.

Fisher, W. R. (1973). Reaffirmation and subversion of the American dream. *Quarterly Journal of Speech, 59,* 160–167.

Fisher, W. R. (1987). *Human Communication as Narration: Toward a Philosophy of Reason, Value, and Action.* Columbia, SC: University of South Carolina Press.

Fitzpatrick, M. A., & Indvik, J. (1982). Implicit theories in enduring relationships: Psychological gender differences in perceptions of one's mate. *Western Journal of Speech Communication, 46,* 311–325.

Fletcher, G. J. O., & Fincham, F. D. (Eds.) (1991a). *Cognition in Close Relationships.* Hillsdale, NJ: Lawrence Erlbaum Associates.

Fletcher, G. J. O., & Fincham, F. D. (1991b). Attribution processes in close relationships. In Fletcher, G. J. O., & Fincham, F. D. (Eds.), *Cognition in Close Relationships.* Hillsdale, NJ: Lawrence Erlbaum Associates, p. 7–35.

Fontaine, G. (1990). Cultural diversity in intimate intercultural relationships. In D. Cahn (Ed.), *Intimates in Conflict: A Communication Perspective,* pp. 209–224.

Frazier, P. A., & Cook, S. W. (1993). Correlates of distress following heterosexual relationship dissolution. *Journal of Social and Personal Relationships, 10,* 55–67.

Frentz, T. S. (1993). Reconstructing a rhetoric of the interior. *Communication Monographs, 60,* 83–89.

Gardner, H. (1983). *Frames of Mind.* New York: Basic Books.

Geertz, C. (1979). From the native's point of view: On the nature of anthropological understanding. In Rabinow, P., & Sullivan, W. M. (Eds.), *Interpretive Social Science.* Berkeley: University of California Press, pp. 225–241.

Gelles, R. J., & Cornell, P. C. (1990). *Intimate Violence in Families,* 2d ed., Newbury Park, CA: Sage Publications.

Gelpi, S. J. (1989). Conversion: Beyond the impasses of individualism. In Gelpi, S. J. (Ed.), *Beyond Individualism: Toward a Retrieval of Moral Discourse in America.* Notre Dame, IN: University of Notre Dame Press, pp. 1–30.

Gergen, K. J. (1991). *The Saturated Self: Dilemmas of Identity in Contemporary Life.* New York: Basic Books.

Gergen, K. J., & Semin, Gun R. (1990) Everyday understanding in science and daily life. In Semin, Gun R., & Gergen, K. J. (Eds.), *Everyday Understanding: Social and Scientific Explanations.* London: Sage Publications, pp. 1–18.

Gerson, K., Stueve, C. A., & Fischer, C. S. (1977). Attachment to place. In Fisher, C. S., et al., (Eds.), *Networks and Places: Social Relations in the Urban Setting.* New York: The Free Press.

Gerstein, Lawrence H., & Tesser, Abraham (1987) Antecedents and responses associated with loneliness. *Journal of Social and Personal Relationships, 4,* 329–363.

Gilligan, G. (1986). Love and the individual: Romantic rightness and platonic aspiration. In Heller, T. C., Sosna, M., & Wellbery, D. E. (Eds.), *Reconstructing Individualism: Autonomy, Individuality, and the Self in Western Thought.* Stanford CA: Stanford University Press, pp. 237–252.

Gilligan, C. (1982). *In a Different Voice.* Cambridge, MA: Harvard University Press.

Gitlin, T. (1989). Postmodernism: Roots and politics. *Dissent,* Winter, 100–108.

Glenn, N. D., & Weaver, C. N. (1988). The changing relationship of marital status to reported happiness. *Journal of Marriage and the Family, 50,* 317–324.

Goffman, E. (1959). *The Presentation of Self in Everyday Life.* Garden City, NY: Doubleday, Anchor Books.

Goldsmith, D. (1990). A dialectic perspective on expression of autonomy and connection in romantic relationships. *Western Journal of Speech Communication, 54,* 537–556.

Goldsmith, D., & Parks, M. R. (1990). Communicative strategies for managing the risks of seeking social support. In S. Duck (Ed.), *Personal Relationships and Social Support.* London: Sage, pp. 104–122.

Goleman, D. (1991). Tibetan and western models of mental health. In H. H. Dalai Lama, et al. (Eds.), *Mind Science,* pp. 91–102.

Goode, W. J. (1969). Community within community: The Professions. In D. W. Minar, & S. Greer (Eds.), *The Concept of Community.* Chicago: Aldine Publishing, pp. 152–162.

Goodwin, M. H. (1990). *He-Said-She-Said: Talk as Social Organization Among Black Children.* Bloomington: Indiana University Press.

Goodwin, R. (1990a). Dating agency members: Are they "different"? *Journal of Social and Personal Relationships, 7,* 423–430.

Goodwin, R. (1990b) Taboo topics among close friends: A factor-analytic investigation. *The Journal of Social Psychology, 130,* (5), 691–692.

Gotcher, J. M. (1993). The effects of family communication on psychosocial adjustment of cancer patients. *Journal of Applied Communication, 21,* 176–188.

Gottman, J. M. (1979). *Marital Interaction: Experimental Investigations.* New York: Academic Press.

Gottman, J. M. (1982). Temporal form: Toward a new language for describing relationships. *Journal of Marriage and the Family, 44,* No. 4, 943–962.

Graham, E. E., Papa, M. J., & Brooks, G. P. (1992). Functions of humor in conversation: Conceptualization and measurement. *Western Journal of Communication, 56,* 161–183.

Granovetter, M. S. (1973). The strength of weak ties. *American Journal of Sociology, 78,* 1360–1380.

Griffin, E., & Sparks, G. G. (1990). Friends forever: A longitudinal exploration of intimacy in same-sex friends and platonic pairs. *Journal of Social and Personal Relationships, 7,* No. 1, 29–46.

Grigg, F., Fletcher, G. J. O., & Fitness, J. (1989). Spontaneous attributions in happy and unhappy dating relationships. *Journal of Social and Personal Relationships, 6,* No. 1, 61–68.

Gryl, F. E., Stith, S. M., & Bird, G. W. (1991). Close dating relationships among college students: Differences by use of violence and by gender. *Journal of Social and Personal Relationships, 8,* 243–264.

Gudykunst, W. B., & Nishida, T. (1986a). Attributional confidence in low-and high-context cultures. *Human Communication Research, 12,* 525–550.

Gudykunst, W. B., & Nashida, T. (1986b). The influence of cultural variability on perceptions of communication behavior associated with relationship terms. *Human Communication Research, 13,* 147–166.

Gudykunst, W. B., Nishida, T., & Chua, E. (1987). Perceptions of social penetration in Japanese-North American dyads. *International Journal of Intercultural Relations, 11,* 171–189.

Gudykunst, W. B., & Ting-Toomey, S. (1988). *Culture and Interpersonal Communication.* Newbury Park, CA: Sage Publishers.

Gudykunst, W. B., & Tsukasa, N. (1986). Attributional confidence in low- and high-context cultures. *Human Communication Research, 12,* 525–549.

Guerrero, L. K., & Andersen, P. A. (1991). The waxing and waning of relational intimacy: Touch as a function of relational stage, gender and touch avoidance. *Journal of Social and Personal Relationships, 8,* 147–166.

Guggenbuhl-Craig, A. (1977). *Marriage Dead or Alive.* Murray Stein (trans.). Dallas, TX: Spring Publications.

Guinan, P. J., & Scudder, J. N. (1989). Client-oriented interactional behaviors for professional-client settings. *Human Communication Research, 15,* 444–462.

Guisinger, S., & Blatt, S. J. (in press). Dialectics of individuality and interpersonal relatedness: An evolutionary perspective. *The American Psychologist.*

Guisinger, S., Cowan, P. A., & Schuldberg, D. (1989). Changing parent and spouse relations in the first years of remarriage of divorced fathers. *Journal of Marriage and the Family, 51,* 445–456.

Haas, A., & Sherman, M. A. (1982). Reported topics of conversation among same-sex adults. *Communication Quarterly, 30,* 332–342.

Haley, J. (1988). *Problem Solving Therapy.* (2d ed.), San Francisco: Jossey-Bass.

Hall, E. T. (1959). *The Silent Language.* Garden City, NJ: Doubleday.

Hanh, T. N. (1987). *Being Peace.* Edited by Arnold Kotner. Berkeley, CA: Parallax Press.

Hahn, T. N. (1988). *The Heart of Understanding: Commentaries on the Prajnaparamita Heart Sutra.* Edited by Peter Levitt. Berkeley, CA: Parallax Press.

Hanh, T. N. (1992). Peaceful heart, peaceful politics. *Lotus, 1,* No. 3, Spring, 28–31.

Hansson, R. O., Jones, W. H., & Fletcher, W. L. (1990). Troubled relationships in later life: Implications for support. *Journal of Social and Personal Relationships, 7,* 451–463.

Harré, R. (1989). Language games and texts of identity. In Shotter, J., & Gergen, K. J. (Eds.), *Texts of Identity.* London: Sage, pp. 20–35.

Harris, L. M., & Sadeghi, A. R. (1987). Realizing: How facts are created in human interaction. *Journal of Social and Personal Relationships, 4,* 481–495.

Harvey, J. H., Flanary, R., & Morgan, M. (1986). Vivid memories of vivid loves gone by. *Journal of Personal and Social Relationships, 3,* 359–373.

Hatfield, E. (1982). Passionate love, companionate love, and intimacy. In Fisher, M., & Stricker, G. (Eds.), *Intimacy.* New York: Plenum, pp. 267–292.

Hatfield, E., & Traupmann, J. (1981). Intimate Relationships: A perspective from equity theory. In S. Duck, & R. Gilmour (Eds.), *Personal Relationships,* vol. 1. New York: Academic Press, pp. 165–178.

Hawken, L., Duran, R. L., & Kelly, L. (1991). The relationship of interpersonal communication variables to academic success and persistence in college. *Communication Quarterly, 39,* 297–308.

Hays, R. B. (1989). The day-to-day functioning of close versus casual friendships. *Journal of Social and Personal Relationships, 6,* No. 1, 21–37.

Hecht, Michael L. (1984). Satisfying communication and relationship labels: Intimacy and length of relationship as perceptual frames of naturalistic conversations, *Western Journal of Communication, 48,* 201–216.

Hecht, M. L. (1993). 2002—A research odyssey: Toward the development of a communication theory of identity. *Communication Monographs, 60,* 76–82.

Hecht, M. L., Collier, J. J., & Ribeau, S. A. (1993). *African American Communication: Ethnic Identity and Cultural Interpretation.* vol. 2 in Language and Language Behaviors. Newbury Park, CA: Sage.

Hecht, M. L., Ribeau, S., & Alberts, J. K. (1989). An Afro-America perspective on interethnic communication. *Communication Monographs, 56,* 383–410.

Hendrick, S. (1988). A generic measure of relationship satisfaction. *Journal of Marriage and the Family, 50,* 93–98.

Hendrick, S S., & Hendrick, C. (1987). Love and sexual attitudes, self-disclosure and sensation seeking. *Journal of Social and Personal Relationships, 4,* No. 3, 281–297.

Hendricks, G., & Hendricks, K. (1990). *Conscious Loving: The Journey to Co-commitment.* New York: Bantam Books, 1990.

Hendrick, S. S., & Hendrick, C. (1993). Lovers as friends. *Journal of Social and Personal Relationships, 10,* 459–466.

Hendrick, S. S., Hendrick, C., & Adler, N. L. (1988). Romantic relationships: Love, satisfaction, and staying together. *Journal of Personality and Social Psychology, 54,* No. 6, 980–988.

Heritage, J. (1984). *Garfinkel and Ethnomethodology.* Cambridge: Polity Press.

Hermans, H. J. M., & Kempen, H. J. G. (1993). *The Dialogical Self.* New York: Academic Press.

Hermans, H. J. M., Kempen, H. J. G., & van Loon, R. J. P. (1992). The dialogic self: Beyond individualism and rationalism. *American Psychologist, 47,* 23–33.

Hinde, R. A., (1979). *Towards Understanding Relationships.* London: Academic Press.

Hocker, J. L., & Wilmot, W. W. (1989). *Interpersonal Conflict* (3d ed.). Dubuque, IA: Wm. C. Brown, Publishers.

Hocker, J. L., & Wilmot, W. W. (1994). *Interpersonal Conflict,* (4th ed.). Dubuque, IA: Wm. C. Brown, Publishers.

Hofstede, G. (1980). *Culture's Consequences.* Beverly Hills: Sage.

Hollihan, T. A., & Riley, P. (1987). The rhetorical power of a compelling story: A critique of a 'toughlove' parental support group. *Communication Quarterly, 35,* 13–25.

Homel, R., Burns, A., & Goodnow, J. (1987). Parental social networks and child development. *Journal of Social and Personal Relationships, 4,* 159–177.

Honeycutt, J. M. (1993). Memory structures for the rise and fall of personal relationships. In Duck, S. (Ed.), *Individuals in Relationships* (series on Understanding Relationship Processes), vol. 1. Newbury Park, CA: Sage, pp. 60–86.

Honeycutt, J. M., & Cantrill, J. G. (1991). Using expectations of relational actions to predict number of intimate relationships: Don Juan and Romeo unmasked. *Communication Reports, 4,* 14–21.

Honeycutt, J. M., Cantrill, J. G., & Greene, R. W. (1989). Memory structures for relational escalation: A cognitive test of the sequencing of relational actions and stages, *Human Communication Research, 16,* 62–90.

Hopper, R. (1989a). Sequential ambiguity in telephone openings: "What are you doin?" *Communication Monographs, 56,* 240–252.

Hopper, R. (1989b). Speech in telephone openings: Emergent interaction v. routines. *Western Journal of Speech Communication, 53,* 178–194.

Hopper, R., & Drummond, K. (1992). Accomplishing interpersonal relationship: The telephone openings of strangers and intimates. *Western Journal of Speech Communication, 56,* 185–199.

Hopper, R., Knapp, M. L., & Scott, L. (1981). Couples' personal idioms: Exploring intimate talk. *Journal of Communication, 31,* 23–33.

Hortacsu, N. (1989). Current and dissolved relationships: Descriptive and attributional dimensions of predictors of involvement. *Journal of Social and Personal Relationships, 6,* No. 3, 373–383.

House, J. S., Landis, K. R., & Umberson, D. (1988). Social relationships and health. *Science, 241,* 540–545.

Humphreys, C. (1951). *Buddhism.* Harmondsworth, England: Penguin Books.

Huston, T. L., McHale, S., & Crouter, A. (1986). When the honeymoon's over: Changes in the marriage relationship over the first year. In Gilmour, R., & Duck, S. (Eds.). *The Emerging Field of Personal Relationships* Hillsdale, NJ: Lawrence Erlbaum, pp. 109–132).

Imahori, T. T., & Lanigan, M. L. (1989). Relational model of intercultural communication competence. *International Journal of Intercultural Relations, 13,* 269–286.

Imai, M. (1981). *16 Ways to Avoid Saying No: Invitation to Experience Japanese Management From the Inside.* Tokyo: Nihon Keizai Shimbun.

Infante, D. A., & Gordon, W. I. (1985). Superiors' argumentativeness and verbal aggressiveness as predictors of subordinates' satisfaction. *Human Communication Research, 12,* 117–125.

Infante, D. A., & Wigley, C. J. III. (1986). Verbal aggressiveness: An interpersonal model and measure. *Communication Monographs, 53,* 61–69.

Infante, D. A., Chandler, T. A., & Rudd, J. E. (1989). Test of an argumentative skill deficiency model of interspousal violence. *Communication Monographs, 56,* 163–177.

Jackson, D. D. (1959). Family interaction, family homeostasis and some implications for conjoint family psychotherapy. In J. H. Masserman (Ed.), *Individual and Familial Dynamics.* New York: Grune and Stratton, 1959.

Jacobson, N. S. (1984). A component analysis of behavioral marital therapy: The relative effectiveness of behavior change and communication/problem-solving training. *Journal of Consulting and Clinical Psychology, 52,* 295–305.

Jessop, D. J. (1981). Family relationships as viewed by parents and adolescents: A specification. *Journal of Marriage and the Family, 43,* No. 1, 95–107.

Jones, D. C. (1991). Friendship satisfaction and gender: An examination of sex differences in contributions to friendship satisfaction. *Journal of Social and Personal Relationships, 8,* 167–185.

Jones, D. C. (1992). Parental divorce, family conflict and friendship networks. *Journal of Social and Personal Relationships, 9,* 219–235.

Jordan, Judith (1992). Relational Resilience. Paper No. 57, The Stone Center, Wellesley College, Wellesley, MA.

Kamo, Y. (1993). Determinants of marital satisfaction: A comparison of the United States and Japan. *Journal of Social and Personal Relationships, 10,* 551–568.

Kayser, E., Schwinger, T., & Cohen, R. L. (1984). Layperson's conceptions of social relationships: A test of contract theory. *Journal of Social and Personal Relationships, 1,* 433–458.

Kellermann, K. (1986). Anticipation of future interaction and information exchange in initial interaction. *Human Communication Research,* 41–75.

Kellermann, K. (1989). The negativity effect in interaction: It's all in your point of view. *Human Communication Research, 16,* 147–183.

Kellermann, K. (1991). The conversation MOP II. Progression through scenes in discourse. *Human Communication Research, 17,* 385–414.

Kelley, H. H. (1983). Love and commitment. In Kelley, H. H., Berscheid, E., Christensen, A., et al., (Eds.), *Close Relationships.* New York: W. H. Freeman.

Kelly, C., Huston, T. L., & Cate, R. M. (1985). Premarital relationship correlates the erosion of satisfaction in marriage. *Journal of Social and Personal Relationships, 2,* 167–178.

Kenny, D. A. (1988). Interpersonal perception: A social relations analysis. *Journal of Social and Personal Relationships, 5,* No. 2, 247–261.

Kharash, A. U. (1986). The other and its function in the development of the self. *Soviet Psychology and Sciences Press, 29,* (1), 31–46.

King, L. A. (1993). Emotional expression, ambivalence over expression, and marital satisfaction. *Journal of Social and Personal Relationships, 10,* 601–607.

King, S. W., & K. K. Sereno (1984). Conversational appropriateness as a conversational imperative. *Quarterly Journal of Speech, 70,* 264–273.

Kingsbury, N. M., & Minda, R. B. (1988). An analysis of three expected intimate relationship states: Commitment, maintenance and termination. *Journal of Social and Personal Relationships, 5*, No. 4, 405–422.

Kirchler, E. (1988). Marital happiness and interaction in everyday surroundings: A time-sample diary approach for couples. *Journal of Social and Personal Relationships, 5*, No. 3, 375–382.

Kitzinger, C. (1989). Liberal humanism as an ideology of social control: The regulation of lesbian identities. In Shotter, J., & Gergen, K. J. (Eds.), *Texts of Identity*. London: Sage, pp. 82–98.

Klopf, D. W. (1991). Japanese communication practices: Recent comparative research. *Communication Quarterly, 39*, 130–143.

Knapp, M. L. (1984). *Interpersonal Communication and Human Relationships*. Boston: Allyn & Bacon.

Knapp, M. L., & Vangelisti, A. (1992). *Interpersonal Communication and Human Relationships*. Boston: Allyn & Bacon.

Knapp, M. L., Ellis, D. G., & Williams, B. A. (1980). Perceptions of communication behavior associated with relationship terms. *Communication Monographs, 47*, 262–278.

Knapp, M. L., Hart, R. P., Friedrich, G. W., & Shulman, G. M. (1973). The rhetoric of goodbye: Verbal and nonverbal correlates of leave taking. *Speech Monographs, 40*, 182–198.

Kovacs, L. (1983). A conceptualization of marital development. *Family Therapy, X*, 183–210.

Krokoff, L. J., Gottman, J. M., & Roy, A. K. (1988). Blue-collar and white-collar marital interaction and communication orientation. *Journal of Social and Personal Relationships, 5*, No. 2, 201–221.

Krueger, D. L. (1983). Pragmatics of dyadic decision making: A sequential analysis of communication patterns. *Western Journal of Speech Communication, 47*, 99–117.

Kurdek, L. A. (1989). Relationship quality in gay and lesbian cohabiting couples: A 1-year follow-up study. *Journal of Social and Personal Relationships, 6*, No. 1, 39–59.

Kurdek, L. A. (1991). Marital stability and changes in marital quality in newly wed couples: A test of the contextual model. *Journal of Social and Personal Relationships, 8*, 27–48.

Kurdek, L. A. (1992). Relationship stability and relationship satisfaction in cohabitating gay and lesbian couples: A prospective longitudinal test of the contextual and interdependence models. *Journal of Social and Personal Relationships, 9*, 125–142.

Ladd, G. W. (1991). Introduction: Family-peer relations during childhood: Pathways to competence and pathology? *Journal of Social and Personal Relationships, 8*, 307–314.

LaGaipa, J. J. (1981). Children's friendships. In Duck, S., & Gilmour, R. (Eds.), *Personal Relationships, 1*. New York: Academic Press, pp. 161–185.

LaGaipa, J. J. (1990). The negative effects of informal support systems. In S. Duck (Ed.), *Personal Relationships and Social Support*. London: Sage, pp. 122–139.

Laing, R. D., Phillipson, H., & Lee, A. R. (1966). *Interpersonal Perception*. Baltimore: Perennial Library.

Lannaman, J. W. (1989). Communication theory applied to relational change: A case study in Milan systemic family therapy. *Journal of Applied Communication Research, 17*, 71–91.

Lannaman, J. W. (1991). Interpersonal communication research as ideological practice. *Communication Theory, 1*, 179–203.

Larson, C. E., & LaFasto, F. M. (1989). *Teamwork: What Must Go Right/What Can Go Wrong*. Newbury Park, CA: Sage.

Lasch, C. (1978). *The Culture of Narcissism: American Life in an Age of Diminishing Expectations.* New York: W. W. Norton.

Lea, M. (1989). Factors underlying friendship: An analysis of responses on the acquaintance description form in relation to Wright's friendship model. *Journal of Social and Personal Relationships, 6,* No. 3, 275–292.

Leary, Mark R. (Ed) (1989). The State of Social Psychology: Issues, Themes and Controversies. Newbury Park, CA: Sage.

Leary, T. (1955). The theory and measurement methodology of interpersonal communication. *Psychiatry, 18,* 147–161.

Leatham, G., & Duck, S. (1990). Conversations with friends and the dynamics of social support. In S. Duck (Ed.), *Personal Relationships and Social Support.* London: Sage, pp. 1–29.

Leigh, L. A. (1989). Stress in the dual-income couple: Do social relationships help or hinder? *Journal of Social and Personal Relationships, 6,* 451–461.

Leslie, L. A. (1989). Stress in the dual-income couple: Do social relationships help or hinder? *Journal of Social and Personal Relationships, 6,* 451–462.

Levinger, G., & Shoek, J. D. (1978). Attraction in relationships: A new look at interpersonal attraction. In Levinger, G., & Shoek, J. D. *Attraction in Relationships.* Morristown, NJ: General Learning Press.

Lewis, R. A., & Spanier, G. G. (1979). Theorizing about the quality and stability of marriage. In Burr, W. R., Hill, B., Nye, F. I., & Reiss, I. L. (Eds.), *Contemporary Theories About the Family: Research Based Theories,* vol. I. New York: Basic Books.

Liberman, K. (1990). Intercultural communication in central Australia. In Carbaugh, D. (Ed.), *Cultural Communication.* Hillsdale, NJ: Lawrence Erlbaum Associates, pp. 177–183.

Lieberman, D. A., Rigo, T. G., & Campain, R. F. (1988). Age-related differences in nonverbal decoding ability. *Communication Quarterly, 36,* 290–297.

Lifton, R. J. (1993). *The Protean Self: Human Resilience in an Age of Fragmentation.* New York: Basic Books.

Liska, J. (1993). Bee dances, bird songs, monkey calls, and cetacean sonar: Is speech unique? *Western Journal of Communication, 57,* 1–26.

Livingston, J. (1982). Responses to sexual harassment on the job: Legal, organizational, and individual actions. *Journal of Social Issues, 38,* 5–22.

Lloyd, S. A., & Cate, R. M. (1985). The developmental course of conflict in dissolution of premarital relationships. *Journal of Social and Personal Relationships, 2,* 179–194.

Logan, R. D. (1991). Reflections on changes in self-apprehension and construction of the other in western history. *Psychohistory Review, 19,* 295–326.

Ma, R. (1992). The role of unofficial intermediaries in interpersonal conflicts in the Chinese culture. *Communication Quarterly, 40,* 269–278.

Mace, David R. (1985). The coming revolution in human relationships. *Journal of Social and Personal Relationships, 2,* 81–94.

Maltz, D. N., & Borker, R. A. (1982). A cultural approach to male-female miscommunication. In Gumpertz, J. J. (Ed.), *Language and Social Identity.* Cambridge, England: Cambridge University Press.

Mandelbaum, J. (1989). Interpersonal activities in conversational storytelling. *Western Journal of Speech Communication, 53,* 114–126.

Markman, H. J. (1979). Application of a behavioral model of marriage in predicting relationship satisfaction of couples planning marriage. *Journal of Consulting and Clinical Psychology, 47,* 743–749.

Marshall, L. L., & Rose, Patricia (1987). Gender, stress and violence in the adult relationships of a sample of college students. *Journal of Social and Personal Relationships, 4,* 299–316.

Marston, P. J., Hecht, M. L., & Robers, T. (1987). "True love ways": The subjective experience and communication of romantic love. *Journal of Social and Personal Relationships, 4,* 387–407.

Masheter, C. (1991). Postdivorce relationships between ex-spouses: The roles of attachment and interpersonal conflict. *Journal of Marriage and the Family, 53,* 103–110.

Masheter, C. (1994). Dialogues between ex-spouses: Evidence of dialectic relationship development. In Conville, Richard (Ed.), *Uses of Structure in Communication Studies.* New York: Praeger, pp. 83–101.

Masheter, C., & Harris, L. (1986). From divorce to friendship: A study of dialectic relationship development. *Journal of Social and Personal Relationships, 3,* 177–189.

Matsumoto, D. (1991). Cultural influences on facial expressions of emotion. *The Southern Communication Journal, 56,* 128–137.

McAdams, D. P., & Losoff, M. (1984). Friendship motivation in fourth and sixth graders: A thematic analysis. *Journal of Social and Personal Relationships, 1,* 11–27.

McCall, G. (1988). The organizational life cycle of relationships. In Duck, S. W. (Ed.), *Handbook of Personal Relationships.* New York: Wiley, pp. 467–486.

McClintock, E. (1983). Interaction, in close relationships. In Kelley, H. H., et al. (Eds.), *Close Relationships.* New York: W. H. Freeman, pp. 68–109.

McCornack, S. A., & Parks, M. R. (1990). What women know that men don't: Sex differences in determining the truth behind deceptive messages. *Journal of Social and Personal Relationships, 7,* No. 1, 107–118.

McCroskey, J. C. (1977). Oral communication apprehension: A summary of recent theory and research. *Human Communication Research, 4,* No. 1 (Fall): 78–96.

McCroskey, J. C. (1992). Reliability and validity of the willingness to communicate scale. *Communication Quarterly, 40,* 16–25.

McCroskey, J. C., Booth-Butterfield, S., & Payne, S. K. (1989). The impact of communication apprehension on college student retention and success. *Communication Quarterly, 37,* 100–107.

McCroskey, J. C., & Richmond, V. P. (1990). Willingness to communicate: Differing cultural perspectives. *The Southern Communication Journal, 56,* 72–77.

McFarland, C., & Miller, D. T. (1990). Judgments of self-other similarity: Just like other people, only more so. *Personality and Social Psychology Bulletin, 16,* 475–484.

McGonagle, K. A., Kessler, R. C., & Gotlib, I. H. (1993). The effects of marital disagreement style, frequency, and outcome on marital disruption. *Journal of Social and Personal Relationships, 10,* 385–404.

McKay, V. C. (1993). Making connections: Narrative as the expression of continuity between generations of grandparents and grandchildren. In Coupland, N., & Nussbaum J. F. (Eds.), *Discourse and Lifespan Identity.* Newbury Park, CA: Sage, pp. 173–185.

Medin, D. L. (1989). Concepts and conceptual structure. *American Psychologist, 44,* 1469–1481.

Mellor, S. (1989). Gender differences in identity formation as a function of self-other relationships. *Journal of Youth and Adolescence, 18,* No. 4, 361–375.

Metts, S. (1989). An exploratory investigation of deception in close relationships. *Journal of Social and Personal Relationships, 6,* No. 2, 159–179.

Metts, S. (1993). Relational transgressions. Paper presented at the Western States Communication Convention, Albuquerque, NM, February.

Metts, S., & Cupach, W. R. (1990). The influence of relationships beliefs and problem-solving responses on satisfaction in romantic relationships. *Human Communication Research, 17,* 170–185.

Metts, S., Cupach, W. R., & Bejlovec, R. A. (1989). "I love you too much to ever start liking you": Redefining romantic relationships. *Journal of Social and Personal Relationships, 6,* No. 3, 259–274.

Metts, S., Cupach, W. R., & Imahori, T. T. (1992). Perceptions of sexual compliance-resisting messages in three types of cross-sex relationships. *Western Journal of Communication, 56,* 1–17.

Michaels, J. W., Acock, A. C., & Edwards, J. N. (1986). Social exchange and equity determinants of relationship commitment. *Journal of Social and Personal Relationships, 3,* 161–175.

Milardo, R. M., & Wellman, B. (1992). The personal is social. *Journal of Social and Personal Relationships, 9,* 339–342.

Miller, A. (1986). *Thou Shalt Not Be Aware: Society's Betrayal of the Child.* New York: Meridian Books.

Miller, A. (1992). Facing the truth about child abuse. *Lotus: The Journal of Inner Peace, Mindfulness and Compassionate Living, 1,* 28–31.

Miller, J. B. (1976). *Toward a New Psychology of Women.* Boston: Beacon Press.

Miller, J. B. (1991). The development of women's sense of self. In Jordan, J. V., Kaplan, A. G., Miller, J. B., Stiver, I. P., & Surrey, J. (Eds.), *Women's Growth in Connection: Writings from the Stone Center,* New York: Guilford Press, pp. 1–26.

Miller, L. C., & Read, S. J. (1991a). On the coherence of mental models of persons and relationships: A knowledge structure approach. In Fletcher, G. J. O., & Fincham, F. D. (Eds.), *Cognition in Close Relationships.* Hillsdale, NJ: Lawrence Erlbaum Associates, pp. 69–99.

Miller, L. C., & Read, S. J. (1991b). Inter-personalism: Understanding persons in relationships. In Jones, W. H., & Perlman, D. (Eds.), *Advances in Personal Relationships,* vol 2. London: Jessica Kingsley, pp. 233–267.

Minuchin, S. (1974). *Families and Family Therapy.* Cambridge, MA: Harvard University Press.

Montgomery, B. M. (1993). Relationship maintenance versus relationship change: A dialectical dilemma. *Journal of Social and Personal Relationships, 10,* 205–223.

Montgomery, B. M., & Duck, S. (Eds.) (1991). *Studying Interpersonal Interaction.* New York: Guilford Press.

Morgan, D. L., & March, S. J. (1993). The impact of life events on networks of personal relationships: A comparison of widowhood and caring for a spouse with Alzheimer's disease. *Journal of Social and Personal Relationships, 9,* 563–584.

Morton, T. L., & Douglas, M. A. (1981). Growth of relationship. In Duck, S., & Gilmour, R. (Eds.), *Personal Relationships,* vol. 11. New York: Academic Press, pp. 3–26.

Motely, M. T. (1990a). On whether one can(not) not communicate: An examination via traditional communication postulates. *Western Journal of Speech Communication, 54,* 1–20.

Motley, M. T. (1990b). Communication as interaction: A reply to Beach and Bavelas. *Western Journal of Speech Communication, 54,* 613–623.

Mulac, A., Studley, L. B. Wiemann, J. M., & Bradac, J. J. (1987). Male/female gaze in same-sex and mixed-sex dyads: Gender-linked differences and mutual influence. *Human Communication Research, 13,* 323–343.

Murdock, M. (1990). *The Heroine's Journey.* Boston, MA: Shambhala Publications.

Mutan, E. (1987). Family, social ties and self-meaning in old age: The development of an affective identity. *Journal of Social and Personal Relationships, 4,* 463–480.

Nakanishi, M. (1986). Perceptions of self-disclosure in initial interaction. *Human Communication Research, 13,* 167–190.

Neimeyer, G. J., & Neimeyer, R. A. (1985). Relational trajectories: A personal construct contribution. *Journal of Social and Personal Relationships, 2,* 325–349.

Neisser, U. (1987). *Concepts and Conceptual Development: Ecological and Intellectual Factors in Categorization.* Cambridge, England: Cambridge University Press.

Neulip, J. W., & Hazleton, V., Jr. (1986). Enhanced conversational recall and reduced conversational interference as a function of cognitive complexity. *Human Communication Research, 13,* 211–224.

Newman, H. M. (1984). Talk about a past relationship partner: Metacommunicative implications. Unpublished paper, Department of Communications, New York: Hunter College.

Newman, H. M., & Ellen J. Langer, (1981). Post-divorce adaptation and the attribution of responsibility. *Sex Roles, 7,* 223–232.

Newton, D. A., & Burgoon, J. K. (1990). The use and consequences of verbal influence strategies during interpersonal disagreements. *Human Communication Research, 16,* 477–518.

Nofsinger, R. (1989). Collaborating on context: Invoking alluded-to shared knowledge. *Western Journal of Speech Communication, 53,* 227–241.

Noller, P. (1993). Gender and emotional communication in marriage: Different cultures or differential social power? *Journal of Language and Social Psychology, 12,* 132–152.

Noller, P., & Hiscock, H. (1989). Fitzpatrick's typology: An Australian replication. *Journal of Social and Personal Relationships, 6,* No. 1, 87–91.

Noller, P., & Ruzzene, M. (1991). Communication in marriage: The influence of affect and cognition. In Fletcher, G. J. O., & F. D. Fincham, (Eds.), *Cognition in Close Relationships.* Hillsdale, NJ: Lawrence Erlbaum Associates, pp. 203–233.

Noller, P., & Vanardos, C. (1986). Communication awareness in married couples. *Journal of Social and Personal Relationships, 3,* 31–42.

Nordbook, J. L. (1987). *Scandinavian Humor & Other Myths.* New York: Perennial Library.

Notarius, C. I., & Vanzetti, N. A. (1983). The marital agendas protocol. In Filsinger, Erik E. (Ed.), *Marriage and Family Assessment.* Newbury Park, CA: Sage, pp. 209–227.

Nussbaum, Jon F. (Ed.) (1989). *Life-Span Communication: Normative Processes.* Hillsdale, NJ: Lawrence Erlbaum Associates.

O'Neill, N., & O'Neill, G. (1972). *Open Marriage.* New York: M. Evans.

Ogilvie, D. M., & Ashmore, R. D. (1991). Self-with-other representation as a unit of analysis in self-concept research. In Curtis, R. C. (Ed.), *The Relational Self.* New York: Guilford Press, pp. 282–314.

Olson, D. H., & McCubbin, H. I. (1983). *Families: What Makes Them Work.* Beverly Hills, CA: Sage Publications.

Oppenheim, F. M., Jr. (1989). A Roycean response to the challenge of individualism. In Gelpi, S. J. (Ed.), *Beyond Individualism: Toward a Retrieval of Moral Discourse in America.* Notre Dame, IN: University of Notre Dame Press, pp. 87–119.

Osherson, D. N., & Smith, E. E. (1981). On the adequacy of prototype theory as a theory of concepts. *Cognition, 9,* 35–58.

Owen, W. F. (1984a). Interpretive themes in relational communication. *Quarterly Journal of Speech, 70,* 274–287.

Owen, W. F. (1984b). The verbal expression of love as metacommunication in personal relationships. Unpublished manuscript.

Owen, W. F. (1987). The verbal expression of love by women and men as a critical communication event in personal relationships. *Women's Studies in Communication, 10,* Spring, 15–24.

Owen, W. F. (1990). Delimiting relational metaphors. *Communication Studies, 41,* 35–53.

Palisi, B. J., & Ransford, H. E. (1987). Friendship as a voluntary relationship: Evidence from national surveys. *Journal of Social and Personal Relationships, 4,* No. 3, 243–259.

Palmer, M. T. (1989). Controlling conversations: Turns, topics and interpersonal control. *Communication Monographs, 56,* 1–18.

Park, M-s., & Kim, M-s. (1992). Communication practices in Korea. *Communication Quarterly, 40,* 398–404.

Parks, M. R. (1977). Anomia and close friendship communication networks. *Human Communication Research, 4,* No. I (Fall):48–57.

Parks, M. R. (1980). A test of the cross-situational consistency of communication apprehension. *Contribution Monographs, 47,* No. 3 (August):220–232.

Parks, M. R. (1982). Ideology in interpersonal communication: Off the couch and into the world. In Burgoon, M. (Ed.), *Communication Yearbook 5.* New Brunswick, N.J.: International Communication Association/Transaction Books, pp. 79–107.

Parks, M. R., & Eggert, L. L. (1991). The role of social context in the dynamics of personal relationships. In Jones, W. H., & Perlman, D. (Eds.), *Advances in Personal Relationships,* vol 2. London: Jessica Kingsley, pp. 1–34.

Patterson, B. R., Bettini, L., & Nussbaum, J. F. (1993). The meaning of friendship across the life-span: Two studies. *Communication Quarterly, 41,* 145–160.

Pavitt, C. (1990). The ideal communicator as the basis for competence judgments of self and friend. *Communication Reports, 3,* 9–14.

Pearce, W. B., Cronen, V. E., Johnson, K., Jones, G., & Raymond, R. (1980). The structure of communication rules and form of conversation: An experimental simulation. *Western Journal of Speech Communication, 44,* 20–34.

Peck, M. S. (1987). *The Different Drum.* New York: Simon and Schuster.

Peters, T. J., & Waterman, B. H., Jr. (1982). *In Search of Excellence: Lessons From America's Best Run Companies.* New York: Harper & Row.

Petronio, S. (1991). Communication boundary management: A theoretical model of managing disclosure of private information between marital couples. *Communication Theory, 1,* No. 4, 311–335.

Petronio, S., & Bradford, L. (1993). Issues interfering with the use of written communication as a means of relational bonding between absentee, divorced fathers and their children. *Journal of Applied Communication Research, 21,* 163–175.

Petronio, S., Olson, C., & Dollar N. (1988). Relational embarrassment: impact on relational quality and communication satisfaction. Paper presented to the Western States Communication Association meeting, 1988.

Pettit, G. S., Harrist, A. W., Bates, J. E., & Dodge, K. A. (1991). Family interaction, social cognition and children's subsequent relations with peers at kindergarten. *Journal of Social and Personal Relationships, 8,* 383–402.

Phillips, G. M. (1977). Rhetoritherapy versus the medical model: Dealing with reticence. *Communication Education, 26,* 34–43.

Pilkington, C. J., & Richardson, D. R. (1988). Perceptions of risk in intimacy. *Journal of Social and Personal Relationships, 5,* No. 4, 503–508.

Pingleton, J. P. (1984). An integrated model of relational maturity. *Journal of Psychology and Christianity, 3,* 57–68.

Planalp, S. (1985). Relational schemata: A test of alternative forms of relational knowledge as guides to communication. *Human Communication Research, 12,* No. 1, Fall, 3–29.

Planalp, S. (1993). Friends and acquaintances' conversations II: Coded differences. *Journal of Social and Personal Relationships, 10,* 339–354.

Planalp, S., & Benson, A. (1992). Friends' and acquaintances' conversations I: Perceived differences. *Journal of Social and Personal Relationships, 9,* 483–506.

Polanyi, L. (1985). Conversational storytelling. In T. A. van Kijk (Ed.), *Handbook of Discourse Analysis,* vol. 3. New York: Academic Press, pp. 183–201.

Prager, K. J. (1989). Intimacy status and couple communication. *Journal of Social and Personal Relationships, 6,* 435–449.

Prentice, D. A. (1990). Familiarity and differences in self-and other-representations. *Journal of Personality and Social Psychology, 59,* 369–383.

Price, S., & McHenry, P. (1988). *Divorce.* Newbury Park, CA: Sage.

Prins, K. S., Buunk, B. P., & VanYperen, N. W. (1993). Equity, normative disapproval and extramarital relationships. *Journal of Social and Personal Relationships, 10,* 39–53.

Prusank, D. T., Kuran, R. L., & DeLillo, D. A. (1993). Interpersonal relationships in women's magazines: Dating and relating in the 1970s and 1980s. *Journal of Social and Personal Relationships, 10,* 307–320.

Putnam, L., & Cheney, G. (1985). Organizational communication: Historical developments and future directions. In Benson, T. W. (Ed.), *Speech Communication in the 20th Century.* Carbondale, IL: Southern Illinois University Press, pp. 130–156.

Ragan, S. (1989). Communication between the sexes: A consideration of differences in adult communication. In Nussbaum, J. F. (Ed.), *Life-Span Communication: Normative Processes.* Hillsdale, NJ: Lawrence Erlbaum. pp. 179–193.

Rawlins, W. K. (1983). Openness as problematic in ongoing friendships: Two conversational dilemmas. *Communication Monographs, 50,* 1–13.

Rawlins, W. K. (1992). *Friendship Matters: Communication, Dialectics, and the Life Course.* Hawthorne, NY: Aldine De Gruyter.

Rawlins, W. K. (1994). Being there and growing apart. In Canary, D. J., & Stafford, L. (Eds.), *Communication and Relational Maintenance.* New York: Academic Press, pp. 275–294.

Rawlins, W. K., & Holl, M. R. (1988). Adolescents' interaction with parents and friends: Dialectics of temporal perspective and evaluation. *Journal of Social and Personal Relationships, 5,* 27–46.

Register, L. M., & Henley, R. B. (1993). The phenomenology of intimacy. *Journal of Social and Personal Relationships, 9,* 467–482.

Reingold, H. (1993). *The Virtual Community.* Reading, MA: Addison-Wesley.

Reissman, C., Aron, A., & Bergen, M. R. (1993). Shared activities and marital satisfaction—causal direction and self-expansion versus bondage. *Journal of Social and Personal Relationships, 10,* 243–254.

Revenson, T. A., & Majerovitz, S. D. (1990). Shared activites and marital satisfaction-causal direction and self-expansion versus bondage. *Journal of Social and Personal Relationships, 7,* 575–586.

Roberts, J. (1988). Setting the frame: Definition, functions, and typology of rituals. In Imber-Black, E., Roberts, J., & Whiting, R. (Eds.), *Rituals in Families and Family Therapy.* New York: W. W. Norton, pp. 3–46.

Roberts, J. M. (1987). *History of the World.* London: Penguin Books.

Roland, A. (1991). The self in cross-civilizational perspective: An Indian-Japanese-American comparison. In Curtis, R. C. (Ed.), *The Relational Self.* New York: Guilford Press, pp. 160–180.

Roloff, M. E. (1981). *Interpersonal Communication: A Social Exchange Approach.* Beverly Hills, CA: Sage Publications.

Roloff, M. E., Janiszewski, C. A., McGrath, M. A., Burns, C. S., & Manrai, L. A. (1988). Acquiring resources from intimates: When obligation substitutes for persuasion. *Human Communication Research, 14,* 364–396.

Roscoe, B., Cavanaugh, E., & Kennedy, D. R. (1988). Dating infidelity: Behaviors, reasons and consequences. *Adolescence, 23,* 35–43.

Rose, S., & Serafica, F. C. (1986). Keeping and ending casual, close and best friendships. *Journal of Social and Personal Relationships, 3,* 275–288.

Rosenfeld, L. B., & Bowen, G. L. (1991). Marital disclosure and marital satisfaction: Direct-effect versus interaction-effects models. *Western Journal of Communication, 55,* 69–84.

Ross, M., & Holmberg, D. (1993). Are wives' memories for events in relationships more vivid than their husbands' memories? *Journal of Social and Personal Relationships, 9,* 585–604.

Rossi, A. S., & Rossi, P. H. (1990). *Of Human Bonding: Parent-Child Relations Across the Life Course.* New York: Aldine de Gruyter.

Rubin, L. (1983). *Intimate Strangers: Men and Women Together.* New York: Harper and Row.

Rubin, L., & Borgers, S. (1990). Sexual harassment in universities during the 1980's. *Sex Roles, 23,* 397–411.

Rubin, R. B., Perse, E. M., & Barbato, C. A. (1988). Conceptualization and measurement of interpersonal communication motives. *Human Communication Research, 14,* 602–628.

Rusbult, C. (1987). Responses to dissatisfaction in romantic involvements: The exit-voice-loyalty-neglect model. In Perlman, D., & Duck, S. W. (Eds.) *Intimate Relationships: Development, Dynamics and Deterioration.* Newbury Park, CA: Sage, pp. 209–237.

Rusbult, C. E., Drigotas, S. M., & Veritte, J. (1994). An interdependence analysis of commitment processes and relationship maintenance phenomena. In Canary, D. J., & Stafford, L. (Eds.), *Communication and Relational Maintenance.* New York: Academic Press, pp. 115–139.

Rushing, J. H., (1976). Impression management as communicative action: A nonverbal strategy in interpersonal encounters. Paper presented to the Western Speech Communication Association Convention, San Francisco.

Rushing, J. H. (1983). The rhetoric of the American western myth. *Communication Monographs, 50,* 14–32.

Rushing, J. H., & Frentz, T. S. (1978). The rhetoric of "Rocky": A social value model of criticism. *Western Journal of Speech Communication, 42,* 63–72.

Russo, N. F., Kelly, R. M., & Deacon, M. (1991). Gender and success-related attributions: Beyond individualistic conceptions of achievement. *Sex Roles, 25,* 331–350.

Salzinger, L. L. (1982). The ties that bind: The effect of clustering on dyadic relationships. *Social Networks, 4,* 117–145.

Sampson, E. E. (1989). The deconstruction of the self. In Shotter, J., & Gergen, K. J. (Eds.), *Texts of Identity.* London: Sage Publications, pp. 1–19.

Sapadin, L. A. (1988). Friendship and gender: Perspectives of professional men and women. *Journal of Social and Personal Relationships, 5,* No. 4, 387–403.

Satir, V. (1967). *Conjoint Family Therapy*. rev. ed. Palo Alto, CA: Science and Behavior Books.

Schofield, M. J., & Kafer, N. F. (1985). Children's understanding of friendship issues: Development by stage or sequence? *Journal of Social and Personal Relationships, 2,* 151–166.

Segrin, C., & Fitzpatrick, M. A. (1992). Depression and verbal aggressiveness in different marital types. *Communication Studies, 43,* 79–91.

Selman, R. L., & Selman, A. P. (1979). Children's ideas about friendship: A new theory. *Psychology Today* (October), 71–80.

Senn, D. J. (1989). Myopic social psychology: An overemphasis on individualistic explanations of social behavior. In Leary, M. R. (Ed.), *The State of Social Psychology: Issues, Themes and Controversies*. Newbury Park, CA: Sage, pp. 45–52.

Sered, S. S. (1989). The religion of relating: Kinship and spirituality among middle eastern Jewish women in Jerusalem. *Journal of Social and Personal Relationships, 6,* No. 3, 309–325.

Shimanoff, S. B. (1987). Types of emotional disclosures and request compliance between spouses. *Communication Monographs, 54,* 85–100.

Shimanoff, S. B. (1988). Degree of emotional expressiveness as a function of face-needs, gender, and interpersonal relationship. *Communication Reports, 1,* 1–8.

Shine, J. (1993). Lessons in the land of Edo. *Sky,* December, 22–26.

Shulman, N. (1975). Life-cycle variations in patterns of close relationships. *Journal of Marriage and the Family, 4,* 813–821.

Sillars, A. L., & Scott, M. D. (1983). Interpersonal perception between intimates: An integrative review. *Human Communication Research, 10,* 153–176.

Sillars, A. L., Pike, G. R., Jones, T. S., & Murphy, M. A. (1984). Communication and understanding in marriage. *Human Communication Research, 10,* 317–350.

Sillars, A. L., Weisberg, Judith, Burggraf, Cynthia S., & Wilson, Elizabeth A. (1987). Content themes in marital conversations. *Human Communication Research, 13,* No. 4, Summer, 495–528.

Sillars, A. L., & Wilmot, W. W. (1989). Marital communication across the life-span. In Nussbaum, J. (Ed.), *Life-Span Communication: Normative Processes*. Hillsdale, NJ: Lawrence Erlbaum Associates, pp. 225–253.

Sillars, A. L., & Zeitlow, P. H. (1993). Investigations of marital communication and life-span development. In Coupland, N., & Nussbaum, J. F. (Eds.), *Discourse and Lifespan Identity*. Newbury Park, CA: Sage, pp. 237–261.

Simon, E. P., & Baxter, L. A. (1993). Attachment-style differences in relationship maintenance strategies. *Western Journal of Communication, 57,* 416–430.

Slugoski, B. R., & Ginsburg, G. P. (1989). Ego identity and explanatory speech. In Shotter, J., & Gergen, K. J. (Eds.), *Texts of Identity*. London: Sage Publications, pp. 36–55.

Smith, C. R., & Arntson, P. H. (1991). Identification in interpersonal relationships: One foundation of creativity. *The Southern Communication Journal, 57,* 61–72.

Smith, D. R., & Williamson, L. K. (1977). *Interpersonal Communication: Roles, Rules, Strategies, and Games*. Dubuque, IA: Wm. C. Brown.

Spanier, G. B., & Margolis, R. L. (1983). Marital separation and extramarital sexual behavior. *Journal of Sex Research, 19,* 23–48.

Spanier, G. B., & Thompson, L. (1984). *Parting: The Aftermath of Separation and Divorce*. Beverly Hills: Sage.

Spitzberg, B. H. (1993a). The dialectics of (in)competence. *Journal of Social and Personal Relationships, 10,* 137–158.

Spitzberg, B. H. (1993b). The dark side of (in)competence. Paper presented to the Western States Communication Association, Albuquerque, NM: February.

Spitzberg, B. H., & Canary, D. J. (1985). Loneliness and relationally competent communication. *Journal of Social and Personal Relationships, 2,* 387–402.

Sprecher, S. (1987). The effects of self-disclosure given and received on affection for an intimate partner and stability of the relationship. *Journal of Social and Personal Relationships, 4,* 115–127.

Sprecher, S., & Felmlee, D. (1992). The influence of parents and friends on the quality and stability of romantic relationships: A three-wave longitudinal investigation. *Journal of Marriage and the Family, 54,* 888–900.

Stacks, D. W., & Murphy, M. A. (1993). Conversational sensitivity: Further validation and extension. *Communication Reports, 6,* 18–24.

Stafford, L., & Bayer, Cherie L. (1993). *Interaction Between Parents and Children.* Newbury Park, CA: Sage Publications.

Stafford, L., Burggraf, C. S., & Sharkey, W. F. (1987). Conversational memory: The effects of time, recall, mode, and memory expectancies on remembrances of natural conversations. *Human Communication Research, 14,* 203–229.

Stafford, L., & Canary, D. J. (1991). Maintenance strategies and romantic relationship type, gender and relational characteristics. *Journal of Social and Personal Relationships, 8,* 217–242.

Stafford, L., & Dainton, M. (1994). The dark side of normal family interaction. In Cupach, W., & Spitzberg, B. (Eds.), *The Dark Side of Interpersonal Communication.* Hillsdale, NJ: Lawrence Erlbaum Associates, pp. 259–280.

Stafford, L., Waldron, V. R., & Infield, L. L. (1989). Actor-observer differences in conversational memory. *Human Communication Research, 15,* 590–611.

Stamp, G. H., Vangelisti, A. L., & Daly, J. A. (1992). The creation of defensiveness in social interaction. *Communication Quarterly, 40,* 177–190.

Stein, C. H. (1993). Ties that bind: Three studies of obligation in adult relationships with family. *Journal of Social and Personal Relationships, 9,* 525–548.

Stein, C. H., Bush, E. G., Ross, R. R., & Ward, M. (1992). Mine, yours and ours: A configural analysis of the networks of married couples in relation to marital satisfaction and individual well-being. *Journal of Social and Personal Relationships, 9,* 365–383.

Stephen, T. (1986). Communication and interdependence in geographically separated relationships. *Human Communication Research, 13,* 191–210.

Stephen, T. (1987). Attribution and adjustment to relationship termination. *Journal of Social and Personal Relationships, 4,* 47–61.

Stets, J. E., & Pirog-Good, M. A. (1990). Interpersonal control and courtship aggression. *Journal of Social and Personal Relationships, 7,* 371–394.

Stevens, A. (1990). *On Jung.* London: Routledge.

Stewart, J. (1978). Foundations of dialogic communication. *Quarterly Journal of Speech, 64,* 183–201.

Stewart, J. (1990). *Bridges Not Walls: A Book About Interpersonal Communication.* New York: McGraw-Hill.

Stewart, J. (1991). A postmodern look at traditional communication postulates. *Western Journal of Communication, 55,* 354–379.

Stiff, J. B., & Miller, Gerald R. (1986). Come to think of it . . . interrogative probes, deceptive communication, and deception detection. *Human Communication Research, 12,* No. 3, Spring, 339–357.

Street, Richard L., Jr., Mulac, Anthony, & Wiemann, J. M. (1988). Speech evaluation differences as a function of perspective (participant versus observer) and presentational medium. *Human Communication Research, 14,* No. 3, Spring, 333–363.

Suitor, J. Jill. (1987). Friendship networks in transitions: Married mothers return to school. *Journal of Social and Personal Relationships, 4,* 445–461.

Suitor, J. J., & Pellemer, K. (1993). Status transitions and marital satisfaction: The case of adult children caring for elderly parents suffering from dementia. *Journal of Social and Personal Relationships, 9,* 549–562.

Sunnafrank, M. (1986). Predicted outcome value during initial interactions: A reformulation of uncertainty reduction theory. *Human Communication Research, 13,* 3–33.

Sunnafrank, M. (1990). Predicted outcome values and uncertainty reduction theories: A test of competing perspectives. *Human Communication Research, 17,* 76–103.

Surra, C. A. (1987). Reasons for changes in commitment: Variations by courtship type. *Journal of Social and Personal Relationships, 4,* 17–33.

Surra, C. A. (1990). Research and theory on mate selection and premarital relationships in the 1980s. *Journal of Marriage and the Family, 52,* 844–865.

Surra, C. A., & Bohman, T. (1991). The development of close relationships: A cognitive perspective. In Fletcher, G. J. O., & Fincham, F. D. (Eds.) *Cognition in Close Relationships.* Hillsdale, NJ: Lawrence Erlbaum Associates.

Surra, C. A., & Ridley, C. A. (1991). Multiple perspectives on interaction: Participants, peers, and observers. In Montgomery, B. M., & Duck, S. (Eds.), *Studying Interpersonal Interaction.* New York: Guilford Press. pp. 35–55.

Surrey, J. L. (1987). Relationship and empowerment. *Work in Progress,* No. 30. Wellesley, MA: Stone Center.

Surrey, J. L. (1991). The relational self in women: Clinical implications. In Jordan, V., Kaplan, A. G., Miller, J. B., Stiver, I. P., & Surrey, J. (Eds.), *Women's Growth in Connection: Writings From the Stone Center,* New York: Guilford Press, pp. 35–43.

Swensen, C. H., Eskew, R. W., & Kohlhepp, K. A. (1981). Stage of family life cycle, ego development, and the marriage relationship. *Journal of Marriage and the Family, 43,* No. 4, 841–853.

Tannen, D. (1990). *You Just Don't Understand: Women and Men in Conversation.* New York: William Morrow and Company.

Tavris, Carol (1992). *The Mismeasure of Woman.* New York: Simon and Schuster

Thomson, E., & Colella, U. (1992). Cohabitation and marital stability: Quality or commitment? *Journal of Marriage and the Family, 54,* 259–267.

Thorns, D. C. (1976). *The Quest for Community.* New York: Wiley.

Tolhuizen, J. H. (1989). Communication strategies for intensifying dating relationships: Identification, use and structure. *Journal of Social and Personal Relationships, 6,* 413–434.

Tschann, J. M. (1988). Self-disclosure in adult friendship: Gender and marital status differences. *Journal of Social and Personal Relationships, 5,* No. 1, 65–81.

Tubbs, W. (1976). Beyond perls. *Journal of Humanistic Psychology, 16,* (Spring), p. 5.

Vallaume, W. A. (1988). Identity and similarity chains in the conversation of high-involved and low-involved speakers: Evidence of integrated discourse strategies. *Western Journal of Speech Communication, 52,* 185–202.

Van Kijk, T. A. (Ed.) (1985). *Handbook of Discourse Analysis.* New York: Academic Press.

van Tilburg, T. (1992). Support networks before and after retirement. *Journal of Social and Personal Relationships, 9,* 433–445.

Vangelisti, A. L. (1993). Communication in the family: The influence of time, relational prototypes and irrationality. *Communication Monographs, 60,* 42–54.

Vangelisti, A. L., Daly, J. A., & Rudnick, J. R. (1991). Making people feel guilt in conversations: Techniques and correlates. *Human Communication Research, 18,* 3–39.

Vangelisti, A. L., & Huston, T. L. (1994). Maintaining marital satisfaction and love. In Canary, D. J., & Stafford, L. (Eds.), *Communication and Relational Maintenance.* New York: Academic Press, pp. 165–186.

VanLear, C. A., Jr. (1987). The formation of social relationships: A longitudinal study of social penetration, *Human Communication Research, 13,* 299–322.

VanLear, C. A. (1992). Marital communication across the generations: Learning and rebellion, continuity and change. *Journal of Social and Personal Relationships, 9,* 103–123.

Vaughan, D. (1990). *Uncoupling: Turning Points in Intimate Relationships.* New York: Vintage Books.

Veroff, J., Sutherland, L., Chadiha, L., & Ortega, R. M. (1993). Newlyweds tell their stories: A narrative method for assessing marital experiences. *Journal of Social and Personal Relationships, 10,* 437–457.

Walther, J. B. (1993). Impression development in computer-mediated interaction. *Western Journal of Communication, 57,* 381–398.

Watson, A. K., Monroe, E. E., & Atterstrom, H. (1989). Comparison of communication apprehension across cultures: American and Swedish children. *Communication Quarterly, 37,* 67–76.

Watts, A. W. (1951). *The Wisdom of Insecurity.* New York: Vintage Books.

Watzlawick, P. (1978). *The Language of Change.* New York: Basic Books.

Watzlawick, P., Beavin, J., & Jackson, D. D. (1967). *The Pragmatics of Human Communication.* New York: W. W. Norton.

Weber, D. J., & Vangelisti, A. L. (1991). Because I love you . . . : The tactical use of attributional expressions in conversation. *Human Communication Research, 17,* 606–624.

Weick, K. E. (1979). *The Social Psychology of Organizing.* (2d ed.). Reading, MA: Addison-Wesley.

Weinberg, H. (1994). Marital reconciliation in the United States: Which couples are successful? *Journal of Marriage and the Family, 56,* 80–88.

Weiss, R. S. (1969). The fund of sociability. *Trans-Action, 6,* (July/August), 36–43.

Weiss, R. S. (1975). *Marital Separation.* New York: Basic Books.

Wellman, B., & Wellman, B. (1992). Domestic affairs and network relations. *Journal of Social and Personal Relationships, 9,* 385–409.

Welwood, J. (1993). Relationship as a spiritual path. *Lotus, 2,* Summer, 70–74.

Werner, C. M., & Baxter, L. A. (1994). Temporal qualities of relationships: Organismic, transactional, and dialectical views. In M. L. Knapp, & G. R. Miller (Eds.), *Handbook of Interpersonal Communication,* (2d ed.), Thousand Oaks, CA: Sage Publications, pp. 323–379.

Werner, C. M., Brown, B. B., Altman, I., & Staples, B. (1992). Close relationships in their physical and social contexts: A transactional perspective. *Journal of Social and Personal Relationships, 9,* 411–431.

Wheeler, L., Reis, H., & Nezlek, J. (1983). Loneliness, social interaction, and sex roles. *Journal of Personality and Social Psychology, 45,* 943–953.

Whiffen, V. E., & Gotlib, I. H. (1989). Stress and coping in maritally distressed and nondistressed couples. *Journal of Social and Personal Relationships, 6,* No. 3, 327–344.

White, L. K., & Riedmann, A. (1992). When the Brady Bunch grows up: Step/half- and fullsibling-relationships in adulthood. *Journal of Marriage and the Family, 54,* 197–208.

Wiemann, J. M. (1977). A description of competent and incompetent communication behavior. Paper presented to the Speech Communication Association Convention, Washington, DC.

Wilber, K. (1983). *Up From Eden: A Transpersonal View of Human Evolution.* Boulder, Co: Shambhala Press.

Wilden, A. (1980). *System and Structure: Essays on Communication and Exchange.* (2d ed.), London: Tavistock Publication.

Wilder, C. (1979). The Palo Alto Group: Difficulties and directions of the interactional view. *Human Communication Research, 5,* 171–186.

Wilmot, W. W. (1980). Metacommunication: A Re-examination and extension. In Nimmo, D. (Ed.), *Communication Yearbook 4.* New Brunswick, NJ: Transaction Books, pp. 61–69.

Wilmot, W. W. (1987). *Dyadic Communication.* New York: Random House.

Wilmot, W. W. (1994). Relationship rejuvenation. In Canary, D. J., & Stafford, L. (Eds.), *Communication and Relational Maintenance.* New York: Academic Press, pp. 255–273.

Wilmot, W. W., & Baxter, L. A. (1983). Reciprocal framing of relationship definitions and episodic interaction. *Western Journal of Speech Communication, 47,* 205–217.

Wilmot, W. W., & Baxter, L. A. (1984). Defining relationships: The interplay of cognitive schemata and communication. Paper presented to the Western Speech Communication Association Convention, Seattle, WA.

Wilmot, W. W., & Baxter, L. A. (1989). The relationship schemata model: On linking relationships and communication. Paper presented to Western Speech Communication Association Convention, Spokane, WA.

Wilmot, W. W., & Carbaugh, D. A. (1986). Long distance lovers: Predicting the dissolution of their relationships. *Journal of the Northwest Communication Association, 14,* 43–59.

Wilmot, W. W., Carbaugh, D. A., & Baxter, L. A. (1985). Communicative strategies used to terminate romantic relationships. *The Western Journal of Speech Communication, 49,* 204–216.

Wilmot, W. W., & Hocker, J. L. (1993). Couples and change. Intervention through discourse and images. In Coupland, N., & Nussbaum, J. F. (Eds.), *Discourse and Lifespan Development.* Hillsdale, NJ: Lawrence Erlbaum Associates, pp. 262–283.

Wilmot, W. W, & Shellen, W. N. (1990). Language in friendships. In Giles, H., & Robinson, W. P. (Eds.), *Handbook of Language and Social Psychology.* New York: Wiley, pp. 413–431.

Wilmot, W. W., & Sillars, A. L. (1989). Developmental issues in personal relationships. In J. Nussbaum (Ed.), *Life-Span Communication: Normative Processes.* Hillsdale, NJ: Lawrence Erlbaum Associates, pp. 119–135.

Wilmot, W. W., & Stevens, D. C. (1994). Relationship rejuvenation: Arresting decline in personal relationships. In Conville, R. (Ed.), *Communication and Structure.* Ablex Publishing, pp. 103–124.

Wolin, S. J., & Bennett, L. A. (1984). Family rituals. *Family Process, 23,* 401–420.

Wood, J. T. (1992). Telling our stories: Narratives as a basis for theorizing sexual harassment. *Journal of Applied Communication Research, 20,* 349–362.

Wood, J. T., & Inman, C. C. (1993). In a different mode: Masculine styles of communicating closeness. *Journal of Applied Communication Research,* (August), 279–295.

Xiaohe, X., & Whyte, M. K. (1990). Love matches and arranged marriages: A Chinese replication. *Journal of Marriage and the Family, 52,* 709–722.

Xing, L. (1993). Han Fei Tzu's theory of persuasion and its impact on Chinese superior/inferior interpersonal communication. Presented to Western States Communication Association, Albuquerque, NM.

Yum, J. O. (1988). The impact of Confucianism on interpersonal relationships and communication patterns in east Asia. *Communication Monographs, 55,* 374–388.

Zablocki, B. (1971). *The Joyful Community.* Baltimore, MD: Penguin Books.

Zakahi, W. R., & Duran, R. L. (1982). All the lonely people: The relationship among loneliness, communicative competence, and communication anxiety. *Communication Quarterly, 30,* No. 3 (Summer):203–209.

Zakahi, W. R., & Duran, R. L. (1985). Loneliness, communicative competence, and communication apprehension: Extension and replication. *Communication Quarterly, 33,* No. I (Winter):50–60.

Zakahi, W. R., & McCroskey, J. C. (1989). Willingness to communicate: A potential confounding variable in communication research. *Communication Reports, 2,* 96–104.

Zietlow, P. H., & Sillars, A. L. (1988). Life-stage differences in communication during marital conflicts. *Journal of Social and Personal Relationships, 5,* No. 2, 223–245.

Ziller, R. C. (1973). *The Social Self.* New York: Pergamon Press.

Zimbardo, P. (1977). *Shyness.* Reading, MA: Addison-Wesley.

Zimmer, T. (1986). Premarital anxieties. *Journal of Personal and Social Relationships, 3,* 149–159.

AUTHOR INDEX

SUBJECT INDEX